Paul Schalow
February 2, 1996
Rutgers University

MALE COLORS

MALE COLORS

The Construction of Homosexuality in Tokugawa Japan

GARY P. LEUPP

UNIVERSITY OF CALIFORNIA PRESS
BERKELEY   LOS ANGELES   LONDON

The costs of publishing this book have been defrayed in part by the 1994 Hiromi Arisawa Memorial Award from the Books on Japan Fund with respect to *Encounters with Aging: Mythologies of Menopause in Japan and North America*, published by the University of California Press. The Fund is financed by The Japan Foundation from generous donations contributed by Japanese individuals and companies.

University of California Press
Berkeley and Los Angeles, California

University of California Press, Ltd.
London, England

Library of Congress Cataloging-in-Publication Data
Leupp, Gary P.
    Male colors: the construction of homosexuality in
Tokugawa Japan / Gary P. Leupp.
        p. cm.
    Includes bibliographical references (p.   ) and index.
    ISBN 0-520-08627-9 (alk. paper)
    1. Homosexuality, Male—Japan—History.   2. Japan—
History—Tokugawa period, 1600–1868.   3. Japan—Social
life and customs.
    I. Title.
    HQ76.3.J3L48   1995
    306.76′6′0952—dc20   94-40395
                                                  CIP
                                                   r95

Printed in the United States of America
9 8 7 6 5 4 3 2 1

The paper used in this publication meets the minimum requirements of American National Standard for Information Sciences—Permanence of Paper for Printed Library Materials, ANSI Z39.48–1984.

Contents

Illustrations

Introduction

It is no secret to any careful student of Japanese society in the Tokugawa period (1603–1868) that during these two and a half centuries male homosexual behavior was extremely common, at least in towns and cities. Sex between males was not only widely tolerated among the articulate classes but positively celebrated in popular art and literature. Homosexual behavior was formally organized in such institutions as samurai mansions, Buddhist monasteries, and male brothels linked to the kabuki theater. It was, indeed, a salient feature of mainstream culture.

The generous vocabulary of terms relating to male–male sex in early modern Japanese reflects a society at ease with the phenomenon. Anyone perusing the abundant primary and secondary sources will encounter numerous allusions to the "male eros" (*nanshoku*); "the way of youths" (*wakashūdō*, often abbreviated as *jakudō* or *shudō*);[a] the "way of men" (*nandō*); "the beautiful way" (*bidō*); and the "secret way" (*hidō*). All these are euphemisms for male-male sex, conforming to certain specific conventions.

Such references occur not only in places one would most expect to find them—works on the "history of sex life,"[b] the "history of manners,"[c] and the history of prostitution, as well as in com-

---

a. This term may also be pronounced *shūdō*.
b. *sei seikatsu shi*
c. *fūzoku shi*

1

pilations of erotic prints—but also in local histories, works of art
history, studies of the popular theater, biographies, diaries, law
codes, personal testaments, medical treatises, popular fiction,
travelogues, humorous anecdotes, and satirical poetry. The ubiq-
uity of such allusions confirms that homosexuality was more than a
marginal phenomenon in Tokugawa Japan; rather, it was a highly
conspicuous, central, institutionalized element of social life.

Thus, just as one cannot understand the aesthetics, erotics, po-
etics, morals, even politics of ancient Greece without discussing
the nature of Greek homosexuality, one cannot grasp many aspects of Tokugawa society and culture without understanding the
specific construction of male-male sexual relationships during this
era.[1] Even so, although an increasing number of scholars have addressed questions of gender and sexuality in Japanese history, few
have seriously studied the homosexual tradition.[2]

The hesitation to do so is understandable. The topic of same-
sex relations remains controversial, both in Japan and in the
West, despite the advent of the "Queer Studies" field in recent
years. Scholars who are not gay, nor inclined to identify with
much of the Queer Studies scholarship, may have avoided it, fear-
ing that even to broach the subject might lead to assumptions
about their own sexuality within a still rather homophobic aca-
deme.[3] This consideration aside, the Japanese sources are often
difficult. Addressing the subject properly, moreover, inevitably
means dealing with a formidably substantial, evolving discourse
on sexuality elsewhere in world history—particularly in Western
classical antiquity. Debates within the field of the history of sexuality are often intense; one who casually begins a paper on some
aspect of this history may, in soliciting colleagues' feedback, come
to regret having strayed into a minefield.

I myself have not entered this minefield without some hesitation. My training as a social historian specializing in Tokugawa
Japan has allowed me to study the sources and draw some con-
clusions about the nature of Tokugawa sexuality. It has not, however, obliged me to engage the huge literature on homosexuality
produced by historians of other eras and societies, to say nothing

of works by scholars in such fields as psychology, anthropology, sociology, and literature. In connection with the present work—the first in-depth examination of male homosexuality in the Tokugawa period in any language—I have familiarized myself with some of this material. But I write primarily as an historian addressing students of Japanese history, not as an authority on the world history of sex.

The idea for this study took shape while I researched a doctoral dissertation on the topic of servants, shophands, and casual laborers in Tokugawa cities.[4] At that time my problematic had more to do with incipient capitalism than with issues of sexuality. But in studying class relations—specifically employer-employee relationships in Tokugawa urban households—I encountered numerous references to sexual involvements between masters and their manservants, especially in samurai mansions, and was struck by various data that cropped up in my reading.[5] I learned, for example, that at least fourteen wards[d] in the metropolis of Edo (modern Tokyo) in the mid-eighteenth century specialized in "male sex teahouses,"[e] that nearly six hundred extant literary works of the period dealt with homoerotic topics, and that at least seven of the fifteen Tokugawa shoguns (military rulers) had well-documented, sometimes very conspicuous, homosexual involvements.[6]

The more I read, the more I became persuaded that homosexual behavior was not merely common in Tokugawa society—at least urban society—but *normative*: the sources express the prevalent assumption that at least urban males were, *in general*, inclined toward sexual involvements with other males and that such involvements met with widespread tolerance. In particular, the literature candidly acknowledges men's passion for boys or female-role actors. This is not to say that most men in Tokugawa society lacked sexual interest in women; rather, the sources suggest that heterosexual relationships, including marriage, were widely viewed as compatible, even complementary, with male-

d. *machi* or *chō*
e. *nanshoku jaya*

male sexual activity. There is some evidence for exclusive homosexuality in Tokugawa society, but male bisexuality appears to
have been the rule.

Such hypotheses were not entirely new, but they seemed dramatic enough to warrant a major study.[7] This book is the result.
My discussion is limited, for the most part, to male homosexuality. Nevertheless, this question itself cannot be separated from
broader questions of the social construction of gender nor, therefore, from the gamut of female sexual experience. I will thus also
have occasion to touch upon Tokugawa lesbianism, though I con-
cede that this topic deserves separate treatment.

In Chapter 1 I review the ancient Chinese homosexual tradition
that influenced Japanese ideas and institutions, examine some of
the earliest references to homosexuality in Japan, and describe
the emergence of monastic and samurai homosexual traditions in
the ancient and medieval periods. I observe that these traditions
are to be explained largely by the absence of women in priestly
and martial society. In Chapter 2 I discuss how the profound
social changes accompanying the establishment of the Tokugawa
order facilitated the emergence of a new, uniquely *bourgeois* homosexual culture centering around male teahouses and the kabuki
theater. This homosexuality also resulted in part from a lack of
women in early Tokugawa cities, but the tradition remained
strong even as the urban sex ratio became more balanced.

In Chapter 3 I discuss the nature of homosexual life and suggest that, though there is some evidence for exclusively homosexual men, bisexuality was far more common. I also examine the
role of class, status, and age in the construction of male-male relationships. In Chapter 4 I examine popular attitudes toward homosexuality, noting how an overall climate of social tolerance did
not preclude the expression of ambivalent feelings toward it.
Here I also examine ruling-class views as reflected in law and the
writings of shogunate officials. The relationships between the homosexual tradition, the status of women, the Tokugawa fascination with androgyny, and heterosexual romance are examined in
Chapter 5, where I also make some comparisons between the Jap-

anese and other homosexual traditions. In my afterword I summarize my argument and discuss the decline of the homosexual tradition following Japan's modern opening to the West.

In writing a study of this kind, one is constantly reminded of the inadequacy of traditional English vocabulary to discuss the history of sexuality. The term "homosexuality" itself, which has been with us barely a century, initially referred to a posited psychological condition in which the sexual instinct becomes focused primarily upon members of one's own sex.[8] But in various historical situations, men who preferred or enjoyed heterosexual intercourse also engaged in sex with other males—for ritualistic reasons (such as the male cult prostitution of the ancient Near East), for reasons of deprivation (as among the Caribbean pirates of the seventeenth century), or (particularly in cultures lacking a homophobic tradition) simply because male-male sex was a physically possible and potentially pleasurable option.[9] The same motivations exist today.

No single form of sexual desire necessarily underlies the "homosexuality" of such situations. In some societies, a male's wish to engage in a particular act (such as oral or anal sex) or to have sex with a partner of a particular age, ethnicity, or body type may be as important as the issue of the partner's gender. Historians must therefore initially apprehend homosexuality not as an ahistorical psychological condition but as *behavior*—a range of acts that may, in different contexts, signify significantly different constructions of sexual desire.

Sigmund Freud regarded the "sexual impulse" or instinct as a force independent of any given sexual object. Though he attempted to explain modern forms of homosexuality ("inversion") in culturally specific terms (a childhood fixation of the male upon his mother, followed by self-identification with the mother and narcissism), he also noted that "all men are capable of homosexual object selection."[10] He observed that male-male sex "was an institution endowed with important functions" in classical (European) cultures and hinted that, if the topic were studied *in histor-ical context*, "the pathological features" might be "separated from the anthropological."[11] This amounts to a suggestion that what is pathological (i.e., relating to disease or abnormality) in some cultures might in others represent no such abnormality but indeed might be produced and encouraged by the dominant culture. Even so, rather than invoking the posited classical, non-pathological homosexuality in support of a value-neutral "anthropological" approach to modern "inversion," Freud and some of his disciples assumed that the latter was a psychological condition to be treated and, if possible, cured.[12]

Even neo-Freudians such as Jacques Lacan, who would not regard homosexual desire as pathological, nevertheless explain it through reference to the Oedipus complex, conceptualized as a universal stage in the development of the individual. However, as French anti-psychiatry-movement theorists Gilles Deleuze and Felix Guattari emphasize, this complex itself is unique to modern *capitalist* society and the patriarchal family system underlying it.[13] We have learned a great deal since Freud's day about homosexual behavior in both past and present societies, and we now more clearly understand that the sexual impulse evolves according to different rules in these different societies. As Maurice Godelier wrote, "It is not sexuality which haunts society, but society which haunts the body's sexuality."[14]

One might add, with Karl Marx and Friedrich Engels, that "life is not determined by consciousness, but consciousness by life." Study of the "real life-process" of human beings allows us to "demonstrate the development of the ideological reflexes and echoes of this life-process."[15] Social structures such as family, class, and state shape sexual feelings, and in any class society the ruling elite determine what attitudes toward, and analyses of, sexual feelings and behavior will be widely articulated and promoted. Thus, in studying male-male sex in any historical context, we must examine how class-bound social structures, as well as ruling-class ideology, encourage particular forms of sexual desire and influence sexual behavior.[16] We must attempt to explain the meaning of the specific construction of homosexual behavior in given past societies and contribute to the emergence of what David Halperin calls a "radical, historical sociology of psychology."[17]

Rejecting, then, any depiction of homosexuality as a specific, ahistorical psychological condition, I nevertheless find it difficult to abandon the term "homosexuality" itself. There are no particularly attractive substitutes, although I will also use the recently popular if inelegant term "male-male sex." In this work, both words should be understood to refer to some kind of sexual attraction or sexual intercourse between males. And, because I am writing in English and wish to avoid monotony, I find myself obliged to employ some other terms that, although somewhat tendentious, would be difficult to avoid without constructing a forbiddingly technical new lexicon. Rather than overusing such unwieldy expressions as "transgenerational homosexuality," I employ words such as "pederasty" and "catamite" when they seem applicable. I use "sodomy" only when quoting hostile (e.g., Jesuit) sources or when translating the similarly derogatory Sino-Japanese term *keikan*.

I will frequently use the Japanese term *nanshoku* to refer to the specifically constructed homosexuality of premodern Japan. Of the terms for male-male sex cited earlier, this one was probably used most widely in the Tokugawa period. It is written with the characters for "male" and "color." Since ancient times in China, possibly as a result of the association between women's cosmetics and eroticism, the latter character has been understood as a euphemism for sex. (Mishima Yukio exploited this association in entitling his novel about modern gay life in Japan *Forbidden Colors* [*Kinjiki*]).[18] Chinese and Japanese dictionaries include "sensual pleasure" as one of the definitions of the character, and so, although I have chosen to entitle this study *Male Colors*, I acknowledge that this may in fact be a rather misleading, too literal translation of *nanshoku*.

The difficulty in rendering Japanese terms for male-male sex into English is illustrated by the definitions for *nanshoku* found in standard Japanese-English dictionaries. *Kenkyusha's New Japanese-English Dictionary* defines it as follows:

n. sodomy; pederasty; buggery; a crime against nature; an unnatural act. ———*ka*: a sodomite; a pederast; a bugger; (vulgar) a homo; (vulgar) a fairy. ———*o okonau*: practice sodomy; go after strange flesh.[19]

Nelson's authoritative *Japanese-English Character Dictionary*, meanwhile, renders *nanshoku* simply as "sodomy."[20]

One is struck by the fact that *homosexuality* does not appear as an equivalent for *nanshoku* in these reference works, perhaps to convey the archaic quality of the Japanese word. In any case, the definitions given above do more than indicate the dictionary editors' homophobia; they suggest the problems of political consciousness, accuracy, and style that accompany any effort to describe *nanshoku* in English.

Of the terms given in the Kenkyusha dictionary, "sodomy" is inappropriate, partly because its very derivation associates male-male sex with damnation and death. Reflecting a generally homophobic Judeo-Christian tradition, it is offensive to many people, and it would in any case be an inaccurate substitute for *nanshoku*. Although, unlike "homosexuality," it refers only to physical actions and in the context of an historical discussion may conjure up fewer anachronistic images than "homosexuality," "sodomy" can also refer to bestiality or to certain heterosexual acts.

"Pederasty," meanwhile, is at least *etymologically* inoffensive and is a roughly apt description of many *nanshoku* relationships.[21] It can serve as an equivalent for other Japanese terms, such as *shudō*.[22] But since *nanshoku* relationships between adult males separated by only a few years were not uncommon, pederasty is not an accurate translation of *nanshoku*. Although nearly all references to male-male sex in Japan involve anal intercourse, the term "buggery" is also unsuitable as an equivalent for *nanshoku*, not only because many find the word offensive but also because it refers only to a physical act.[23] Japanese terms such as *nanshoku*, by contrast, sometimes connote an emotional condition, or an etiquette, and stress the refinement and dignity of male-male sex. One need say nothing about the other dictionary definitions.

There simply is no ideal English rendering of *nanshoku*, and so in this work I will often use the Japanese term and its various synonyms without attempting to translate them. I hope the reader will garner some sense of their nuances through the contexts in which they occur.

Aside from the problems posed by terms for "homosexuality" in the broadest sense, there are problems in conceptualizing and describing specific sexual acts. Although I recognize that some dispute the accuracy of reference to "passive" and "active" roles in homosexual (or heterosexual) intercourse, I find them as appropriate to *nanshoku* as the more precise dichotomies "inserter" and "insertee" or "penetrator" and "penetrated." I therefore use all these sets of terms. The latter may be more suitable than "passive" and "active" in describing oral sex, but in Tokugawa Japan the only homosexual act commonly referred to is role-structured anal sex.

For such terms as *onnagata*, *oyama*, *kagema*, and *kage-ko*, I use "cross-dressing actor" or "cross-dressing male prostitute" but also such phrases as "female-role actor-prostitute."

Historians traditionally justify their calling by arguing that study of the past helps us to understand and improve the present world. In studying the history of sexuality, we may come to understand how contingent our sexual practices and prejudices are upon transient social institutions. Such an understanding may help, at least in some small way, to dissolve biases and phobias rooted in religious myth and encourage fair-minded people to tolerate sexual diversity in the contemporary world. I have in any case written this book in that hope.

This study has benefited enormously from comments, suggestions, leads, criticisms and shared research from many friends and colleagues, including Sandra Buckley, Margaret Childs, David Greenberg, Bret Hinsch, Earl Jackson, Jr., William Johnston, Neil Miller, Stephen O. Murray, Greg Pflugfelder, Paul Schalow, Laurence Senelick, Howard Solomon, John Solt, Taira Masayuki, Tao Demin, Tōno Haruyuki, and Walter Williams. I alone, of course, am responsible for the contents.

I would also like to express my thanks to Sheila Levine, Laura Driussi, Scott Norton, and all at University of California Press, who have been wonderfully supportive throughout this project; to Christine Cavalier, for her expert photographic work; and to the students who have studied in my various Japanese history courses at Tufts University, especially my seminar on gender and sexuality in Japanese history. Their broad minds, hard work, and enthusiasm are a constant inspiration. Most of all, I thank my wife Mari for her encouragement and Sophie and Erik just for being themselves. May they inherit a more tolerant and rational world.

Chapter One

The Pre-Tokugawa Homosexual Tradition

[Japanese Buddhist priests] are drawn to sins against nature and don't deny it, they acknowledge it openly. This evil, moreover, is so public, so clear to all, men and women, young and old, and they are so used to seeing it, that they are neither depressed nor horrified.

Francis Xavier, 1549

The Continental Traditions: China and Korea

One must assume that male homosexual behavior, however specifically constructed, occurs to some extent in every society, in every era. But the historical record concerning its occurrence, forms, and conventions in early Japan is rather obscure. Although the unified Japanese state emerged in the mid-fourth century, Japan's historical record is, at least by East Asian standards, rather short. The first extant mytho-historical text, the *Kojiki* (Record of ancient matters) was completed as late as A.D. 712, and our first clear references to sex between males appear only in the late tenth century.

In China, by contrast, tales of courtly homosexuality date back to the sixth century B.C. Thus, it is not surprising that the Japanese, who from the sixth century A.D. borrowed much of their higher civilization from their continental neighbor, should have adopted various elements of the Chinese homosexual tradition. Even the term *nanshoku* itself is simply the Japanese reading of the Chinese *nanse,* which bears the same meaning.[1]

Long before the Tokugawa period, the Japanese had come to believe that they had "learned" *nanshoku* from the Middle Kingdom. The attribution, questionable though it may be, is of great importance in understanding the evolution of the homosexual tradition. Many societies have regarded the male-male sexuality in their own midst as a foreign import, and their view of homosexuality has been influenced by the nature of their relations with the foreign country concerned. The ancient Hebrews associated homosexuality with the pagan Egyptian and Canaanite cultures;[2] the ancient Greeks believed they had "learned" pederasty from the Persians;[3] medieval Europeans regarded "sodomy" as an Arab peccadillo introduced into their culture by returning Crusaders.[4] Many English of the Renaissance were convinced that the "unmentionable vice" had reached their islands from abroad; depending upon the state of their international relations, they blamed Castile, Italy, Turkey, or France.[5]

In all of these cases, homosexuality was linked with rival or enemy cultures. Such associations did not necessarily lead to a negative view of male-male sexuality itself; the Greeks, for example, accepted *paiderastia* despite its putative origins in an enemy land. Still, Greek men regarded the insertee role in anal sex as far more suitable for Persians than for themselves. In Athens, male citizens were forbidden to prostitute themselves; the city's male brothels were largely peopled by foreign boys.[6]

The Japanese, unlike these other peoples, associated *nanshoku* with a neighboring empire only rarely seen as threatening—and one acknowledged, moreover, to have provided the models for much of Japan's high culture. The degree of Japanese respect for China varied through time, but the grandeur of this historical legacy was seldom questioned.[7] *Nanshoku*, viewed as a component of this heritage, was a refined thing, a *teaching* or "way."[a] Even during periods of tension with the Chinese empire, the Japanese

a. *dō*, as in *shudō*, Ch. *dao*

never seem to have abandoned their tolerant attitude toward *nan-shoku*. And regardless of the state of Sino-Japanese relations, the Japanese *nanshoku* tradition drew heavily upon that of the Chinese. Tokugawa works on the topic repeatedly allude to famous homosexual relationships in the Chinese past, to continental homoerotic literature, and to Daoist and *yin-yang* theories of sexuality. Thus, a brief survey of the Chinese homosexual tradition seems appropriate at the outset of this study.[8]

Most of the earliest references to homosexuality in China refer to relationships between emperors or other rulers and their favorites.[b] The latter were sometimes eunuchs, "ravishing boys,"[c] or studymates of about the same age as the royal patron; many were appointed to official posts or came to wield political power indirectly. The *Han Fei Zi*, written before 233 B.C., refers to a sexual relationship between Duke Ling of Wei (534–493 B.C.) and his minister Mizi Zia.[9] Other late Zhou works record such loves as that of Prince Zhongxian of Chu for the young scholar Pan Zhang. Falling in love "at first sight," these two "were as affectionate as husband and wife, sharing the same coverlet and pillow with unbounded intimacy for one another."[10] The fourth-century relationship between Prince Ai of Wei and his minister Lung Yang resulted in the term *lungyang* as a synonym for male-male sexuality.[11]

All of the adult Former Han (206 B.C.–A.D. 8) emperors had male favorites: Gao (r. 206–195 B.C.), according to the *Historical Records*,[d] was "won by the charms of a boy named Ji," and Hui (r. 194–188 B.C.) "had a boy favorite named Hong." Neither partner, notes the work, "had any particular talent or ability; both won prominence simply by their looks and graces."[12] Emperor Wen (r. 179–157 B.C.) developed a passion for a boatman named Deng Tong, and a castrated actor shared the bed of Emperor Wu (r. 140–87 B.C.). The most celebrated imperial homosexual relationship was that between Emperor Ai (r. 6 B.C.–A.D. 1) and the boy

b. *bi*
c. *luantong*
d. *Shiji* (before 85 B.C.)

Dong Xian. According to *History of the Han*,[e] the emperor, called to a meeting while lying with his lover, cut off his sleeve rather than stir the boy from his sleep. Subsequently the term *duanxiu* ("cut sleeve") became synonymous with homosexuality throughout East Asia.[13]

Such relationships became so prevalent as to warrant a special section in the *Shiji* and other historical works. The *Shiji* chapter begins with the observation, "It is not women alone who can use their looks to attract the eye of the ruler; courtiers and eunuchs can play at that game as well. Many were the men of ancient times who gained favor in this way."[14] Here and elsewhere one finds no condemnation of homosexual activity as such, although the author implicitly criticizes rulers for favoring base or unsuitable partners.

Evidence of homosexual relationships among the literati as well as the nobility dates from at least the third century A.D. An early anecdote describes how the philosopher Xi Kang (223–262) and the poet Yuan Ji (210–263) were observed having sex at the home of a mutual friend by the friend's inquisitive wife. "Their talents are much greater than yours," the wife is supposed to have told her husband. "They must have befriended you for your knowledge."[15] This reference, though humorous, suggests a tolerant and matter-of-fact attitude toward homosexuality among this class.

There seems to be evidence for homosexual relationships involving such poets and scholars as Li Bo (d. 762), Bo Juyi (772–846), Su Dongpo (1036–1102), and others in the Tang (618–907) and Northern Song (960–1126) periods.[16] By the Qing period (1644–1912) the term *Hanlin feng* ("tendency of the academicians," literally "tendency of the Hanlin [Academy]") had been added to the long list of synonyms for male-male sexuality.[17]

Meanwhile, one finds increasing evidence of homosexuality among ordinary people. From the Tang period on, men of the southern coastal provinces acquired a reputation for homosexual interests; Fujian, with a tradition of maritime homosexuality, pro-

e. *Han shi* (before A.D. 92)

duced many eunuchs for the court, and homosexual marriage became common there. An older partner known as the *qidi*
("promised elder brother") acquired a boy-bride called a *qixiong*
("promised younger brother") in an arrangement approved and
celebrated by the latter's family. When the boy reached adulthood, his "brother" would arrange his marriage to a woman and
pay the expenses. Apparently, involvement in such a relationship
did not adversely affect one's prospects for heterosexual marriage.[18]

The spread of male prostitution provides additional evidence
for male-male sex among the common people. A work written
early in the Northern Song period describes a "honeycomb maze
of alleys" in a quarter of the capital Kaifeng, where "customers go
to ... men who sell their bodies." There were also restaurants
where male prostitutes plied this trade.[19] In the Zhonghe era
(1111–1117), however, for reasons that remain unclear, such
prostitution was forbidden. Henceforth, according to the law,
male prostitutes were to be punished with one hundred strokes
of a bamboo rod and a hefty fine.[20]

The law seems to have been observed in the breach, however,
and in the Southern Song period (1127–1279) male prostitution
flourished more than ever. Outside the new capital of Hangzhou,
a homosexual red-light district employed youths from Zhejiang,
Fujian, and Guandong.[21] The fact that cross-dressing male prostitutes were allowed to form their own guild, with their own patron
god, suggests that they met with general tolerance.[22] Ming (1368–
1644) sources compare the homosexual pleasure quarters of contemporary Beijing with those of Song-period Hangzhou and note
how boy-singers, doubling as prostitutes, had become a must at
literati parties.[23]

This tradition of male prostitution continued in Beijing well
into the Qing period (1644–1912). For most of this era, high-
class female prostitution was effectively suppressed, yet male
prostitution was allowed to flourish in such districts as the lanes
off Qianmen Street in the capital's Outer City.[24] Court officials
patronized elegant brothels staffed by youths brought from
Jiangsu, Zhejiang, Anhui, and Hubei. In preparation for their

work, the boys' bodies were depilated and softened with medicines, their anuses were dilated, and their faces were treated with meat juice. All these processes were designed to make them as "feminine" as possible.[25]

At times government attitudes hardened against male prostitution and homosexuality in general. Not only sex for hire but even "sodomy"[f] between any consenting adults was banned after 1679.[26] The Kangxi emperor (r. 1661–1722) seems to have been particularly determined to halt the sale of boys for sexual purposes, but the laws against male prostitution, renewed in 1740, 1819, and 1852, had little effect. In Tianjin in 1860 thirty-five brothels employed eight hundred boy-prostitutes, and in Beijing such houses, along with barber stalls, bathhouses, inns, and canal pleasure boats, paired clients with painted youths until well into this century.[27]

From ancient times rulers had retained actors for sexual purposes, and by the Ming period actor-prostitutes had become a conspicuous feature of urban life.[28] Matteo Ricci, writing in Beijing in 1610, described boys who "play music, sing and dance," wear rouge like women, and practice the "terrible vice." Boy-actors, he declared, were the "vilest and most vicious people in this whole country."[29] In the Qing period the performers of the Beijing opera typically doubled as prostitutes. Female impersonators (*dan*) were in greatest demand, the most attractive becoming the objects of universal worship. "The whole country went mad about" a certain Wei Zhangsheng, who was forbidden to perform in 1782 because of his allegedly damaging effect upon public morals.[30] Wei was a true talent, but many "actors," facetiously referred to as *xianggong* ("chief ministers"), were merely boy-prostitutes. Lodged in the homes of wealthy actors[g] and theoretically undergoing an apprenticeship in the opera, they were visited by wealthy patrons.[31] The association between male-male sexuality and the theater was so immediate that when a character in the

---

f. *jijian* (Jp. *keikan*), a word of complicated etymology, with negative overtones

g. *xianggong tangji*

eighteenth-century novel *Rulin waishi* (An unauthorized history of the scholars) confides to a friend that he despises women but pines for a male lover, his confidant replies, "You should look for a friend among the actors."[32]

Aside from the abundant evidence of male prostitution, there are literary works from the Ming and Qing periods that depict noncommercial sexual relations between men.[33] The anonymous seventeenth-century work *Duanxiu pian* (Records of the cut sleeve) documents fifty male-male relationships, with commentary.[34] One thus finds much evidence for homosexual behavior in Chinese history. One does not, however, find much of a range of sexual acts; there is little reference to anything other than anal intercourse.[35] Generally, homosexual relationships were class-structured and transgenerational; the "active" partner was the social superior or, at least, the older partner. In the case of the *dan* actor, they were also transgenderal, the "passive" partner dressing and behaving as a female. However, there is also some evidence for egalitarian relationships between men of masculine gender identity, equal status, and comparable ages.[36]

The Korean homosexual tradition may also be relevant to a study of *nanshoku*. Until the eighth century, Japan's contacts with the Korean kingdoms were at least as significant as its ties to China, and the Korean tradition seems to have been modeled upon that of the Middle Kingdom. In Korea, too, homosexuality was at times common in courtly society. Eunuchs were employed by the Korean kings, as they were by the Chinese rulers, and probably served as sexual partners. Moreover, the Koreans established the unique institution of the *hwarang* ("flower boys"). During the Silla dynasty (57 B.C.?–A.D. 935), probably in the sixth century, the court established a corps of young warriors of this name. These aristocratic youths were chosen for their beauty, education, and martial prowess; aside from soldiering, they performed ritual dances and recited prayers for the welfare of the state. The Japanese scholar Ayukai Fusanoshin has suggested that they served as courtiers' sexual partners from the time of King Chinhung (r. 540–

576), when, he asserts, male-male sexuality was prevalent at the Silla court.[37]

This claim has been challenged, but sections of the *Lives of Eminent Korean Monks*[h] (1215) by the Buddhist cleric Kakhun support Ayukai's interpretation.[38] A chapter on Chinhung is included in this work because late in life he took holy orders. Here he is credited with founding a group of "handsome youths" who "powdered their faces, wore ornamented dresses," and excelled as both performers and generals. Kakhun cites earlier sources on the *hwarang*, all of them quite ambiguous but stressing the youths' beauty and public service. He concludes the section by paraphrasing Ban Gu's *Shiji*:

> After [King] Chinhung first worshiped Buddhism and initiated the way of the *hwarang*, people gladly followed him and imitated his example. Their excitement was as great as when visiting a treasure house or when going to the spring terrace. The [king's] aim was to make the people progress toward goodness and justice and to lead them to the Great Way. Emperor Ai of the [Former] Han loved only lust. Pan Ku therefore remarked, "The tenderness which seduces man belongs not only to woman, but to man as well." This indeed cannot be compared with our story [of the *hwarang*].[39]

Kakhun alludes to the *Shiji* in order to draw a contrast between the male favorites of the Chinese rulers, who were wont to create scandals, and the morally upright Korean youth. But had the *hwarang* not been associated with homosexuality, the very comparison with the Chinese case would seem inappropriate.

Historical records refer to pederastic relationships involving several kings of the Koryō dynasty (918–1392); King Kongmin (r. 1352–1374) appointed at least five youths as "little-brother attendants"[i] and used them as sexual partners.[40] The use of the term *longyang*[j] in this period and the subsequent employment of other Chinese terms, including *nanse*,[k] testify to the Chinese in-

h. *Haedong kosūng chōn*
i. *chajewi*
j. Kor. *yongyang*
k. Kor. *namsaek*; the characters used are the same as in Ch. *nanse* and Jp. *nanshoku*

fluence upon the Korean homosexual tradition. In later periods of Korean history, the term *hwarang* came to be applied to itinerant performers, often clubbed in "male temple-troupes."[l] By the late Yi period (1392–1910), if not earlier, these entertainers had acquired a clear reputation for homosexual prostitution, much as had their counterparts in China. They were also associated with shamanistic practices, although their relationship to the "transvestite" shamanism common in Korea from ancient times is a bit obscure.

Meanwhile, references to "beautiful boys"[m] in puppet plays and collections of humor from the seventeenth century suggest that many men in the gentry (*yangban*) class retained boys for sexual purposes. Homosexuality seems to have been especially associated with provincial gentlemen. Some of these men (like the literati of Fujian in China) even kept boy-wives whose status was publicly acknowledged in the village. Upon reaching adulthood, such boys would normally enter into a heterosexual marriage.[41]

There is also some evidence for widespread monastic homosexuality in Korea.[42] But the Korean homosexual tradition may have been less developed than that in the neighboring archipelago; a Korean ambassador to Japan during the rule of the shogun Yoshimune (1716–1745) observed that among the nobles and wealthy merchants "there is no one who does not keep" beautiful young men "like flowers" and declared, "I have never seen such a thing in other countries!"[43]

One could expand this survey of the homosexual tradition in continental East Asia to include, for example, Vietnam.[44] But Japan's profoundest and most sustained contacts have been with China and Korea, and its own homosexual tradition has been most influenced by the Chinese. Before turning to Japan, let us consider the relevance to Japanese *nanshoku* of the general ideological heritage common to the East Asian cultures. This heritage includes

l. *namsangdang*
m. *midong*

Confucian thought, Daoism, and *yin-yang* concepts, all of which are of Chinese origin; and Buddhism, an Indian faith colored throughout East Asia by Chinese adaptations.

Confucian philosophy, of course, has much to say on the topic of proper male-female relations, but thinkers of this school in China and elsewhere have not been notably concerned about the topic of homosexuality. Indeed, as noted above, the term "persuasion of the academicians" was used in China to refer to male-male sexuality, and such intellectuals were generally committed to Confucianism. This school of thought emphasizes filial piety and the duties of marriage and procreation. One reason that Confucians have typically held Buddhism in contempt is that most Buddhist schools demand a celibate clergy. Similarly, Confucians could be expected to oppose exclusive homosexuality, but the bisexual behavior more common until recent times seems to have produced little objection. Richard Rutt suggests that in Korea "during the Yi dynasty homosexual practices were regarded by disgust by the Confucian gentry," but he seems to contradict himself by noting that provincial *yangban*, who were typically Confucian scholars, had a reputation for pederasty.[45]

Yin-yang[n] thought, unlike Confucian morals, deals directly and specifically with sexuality. Overlapping Confucian and Daoist thought, it was perhaps developed most thoroughly by the latter school. According to *yin-yang* theory, the universe consists of two fundamental principles or forces, *yin* (which represents the female, among other things) and *yang* (which represents the male, among other things). The interaction of these two forces produces all phenomena. Both principles exist within people and indeed within all things. To properly adapt to the world, one must attain a balance of these forces within oneself.

Sex is one activity that contributes to this balance. Indulgence in heterosexual intercourse is absolutely necessary for a person's health; a man must exchange some of his *yang* energy for the female's *yin*. If a man abstains, he will suffer from boils, ulcers, and other ailments. However, too much heterosexual activity saps a

n. Jp. *in-yō*

man's strength and leads to early death. This is because the female *yin* essence, modeled after water, can quench the male *yang* essence, which is modeled after fire. Homosexual intercourse, by contrast, results in no net loss of vital *yang* force for either male.[46] Some Chinese Daoist thinkers, indeed, may have advocated homosexual practices for precisely this reason.[47]

However, most Buddhist sects generally viewed sexual pleasure in negative terms.[48] Sex and reproduction do not fit in well with the religious goals of conquering desire and obtaining release from the cycle of rebirth. One scripture suggests that, when offered a (female) prostitute, the historical Buddha responded, "Why try to tempt me with that thing? It is a bag full of shit and piss. I wouldn't touch it with my foot."[49] Those joining the Buddhist order as monks were forbidden any form of sexual activity.

Homosexual activity, however, may have been viewed as a lesser offense than heterosexual involvements.[50] The scriptures thought to be of greatest antiquity treat it lightly; in one of the many *Vinaya* (monastic regulations supposed to have been established by the historical Buddha), the following anecdote appears:[51]

> At that time the venerable Upananda, of the Sakya tribe, had two novices, Kandaka and Makhaka; these committed sodomy with each other. The Bhikkhus were annoyed . . . : "How can novices abandon themselves to such bad conduct?"
>
> They told this to the Blessed One . . . [who declared] "Let no one, O Bhikkhus, ordain two novices. He who does is guilty of a *dukkata* offence."[52]

The novices referred to are boys, perhaps less than sixteen years of age, undergoing religious training under the supervision of a monk (*bhikku*). Here their sexual involvement is seen as the result of their environment; perhaps they share a cell with the monk who ordained them. Although their behavior is plainly regarded as "bad conduct," they are apparently not punished for it. Rather, the monk responsible for them is censured.

At some point, however, attitudes seem to have hardened. Some Indian and Chinese sutras clearly condemn homosexual acts. A Theravada text included in the Chinese canon, *The Sutra of the Remembrance of the True Law* (*Saddharma-smrti-upas-*

thana), refers to a "Hell of Many Rains" where "those who commit homosexual acts are attracted ... to a man of flame who burns them with his embrace." Even those men who have had oral or anal sex with women are punished by having molten copper poured into their mouths.[53]

Nevertheless, monastic life itself probably encourages homosexual behavior; in the late medieval Christian West, "sodomy" was regarded largely as a clerical vice, and it has been common in this century in Buddhist monasteries in various parts of Asia.[54] Jokes and stories from China's Song period and Korea's Yi period tell of Buddhist clerics seducing their acolytes or other boys.[55] Korean monasteries even occasionally raised funds through the performances of entertainers who also served as male prostitutes.[o][56] On the continent, however, Buddhist clerics seem in general to have taken the proscription of homosexual behavior more seriously than did their Japanese counterparts.[57]

Earliest Japanese References: Male-Male Sex at Court

The record of courtly *nanshoku* in Japan is much less substantial than the corresponding Chinese record and, naturally, of far less antiquity. The first truly unequivocal reference to male-male sex in Japan dates from as late as 985.

There may be earlier references, but they are somewhat obscure. For example, Iwata Jun'ichi confidently proclaimed an intriguing passage in the second oldest surviving Japanese text, *Nihongi* (Chronicles of Japan, A.D. 720), to be "the first description of homosexuality in all the Japanese chronicles."[58] His discussion is unconvincing, however. The passage in question describes a visit by the Empress Jingū (traditional reign dates A.D. 201–269) through a part of Kii province that had been cast into perpetual darkness as a result of what the text refers to as *azunai no tsumi*.[59]

Iwata rendered the latter phrase "the sin[p] of homosexuality,"

o. *namch'ang*; corresponds to Jp. *nanchō*
p. *tsumi*; in the ancient period this term connoted a taboo rather than a moral violation

but this is a very problematic interpretation.[60] The meaning of *azunai* (pronounced *adunafi* in the ancient language) is unclear.[61] In the *Nihongi*, local people explain that the sun no longer shines in the region because a certain Shinto priest, following the death of a beloved friend in the same profession, committed suicide and was interred with him in a joint grave. The empress orders the bodies disinterred and buried separately, and light returns to Kii province.

Perhaps there is some allusion to male homosexuality here, but it seems equally likely that this passage refers to a taboo against suicide or against retainers' practice, enduring in Japan and elsewhere in East Asia despite growing Buddhist influence, of following their lords to the next world.[62] There is at any rate no reference to *azunai*, nor anything resembling a taboo against male-male sex, in the *Kojiki* or *Nihongi*.

Another possible allusion to male homosexuality in early literature occurs in the *Shoku Nihongi* (Chronicles of Japan, continued), completed in 869. An entry for the year 757 describes how a Crown Prince Funado no Ō is disgraced and exiled as a result of his misbehavior following the death of his grandfather: "Funado no Ō had already been appointed [Crown Prince], but he did not respect the imperial teachings. Rather he pursued whatever lewd thought[q] he had.... Even before the official mourning period [for the ex-emperor] was finished, even before the grass upon his tomb had dried up, [Funado no Ō] secretly had sexual relations with boy-attendants[r] and was disrespectful to the former emperor."[63]

I have rendered the Japanese term *jidō* as "boy-attendants"; this became its meaning, at least, in later periods. The problem is that it may also have referred to maidservants at the time this text was written.[64] Even if this tale does refer to homosexuality, Prince Funado's offense seems not to be homosexual behavior as such but rather sexual indulgence of any sort during a time of official mourning.

q. *ishi*
r. *hisoka ni jidō ni tsūjite*

The first great Japanese poetic compilation, the *Manyōshū*
(Treasury of myriad leaves, ca. 750), contains no explicit references
to male-male sex, but some of its poems may have stemmed from
homosexual feelings. For example, the courtier Ōtomo Yakamochi
(d. 785), "upon parting from a friend," wrote the following verses:

> It must be because
> you listen to others' slander
> that, although I wait for you, my Lord,
>   intensely,
> you do not come.
>   If rather our friendship ended,
> would I now be yearning like this,
> making you the thread
>   of my vital breath?
>   I who long for him
> though he does not think of me;
> with all my heart consumed,
> with each tiny fiber exhausted.[65]

The *Ise monogatari* (Tales of Ise), written nearly two centuries
later (951), contains the following:

Once a man had a friend to whom he was very much attached. The
two were always together and always on the best of terms. But then
the friend was obliged to go to the provinces, and they parted with
many laments. After some time a letter came: "How long it has been
since our last meeting! I am terribly afraid that you will have forgotten me. It is after all only human to forget someone who is never
around." The man composed this poem and sent it to him:

> *Mekaru to mo*
> *Omōenaku ni*
> *Narinureba*
> *Toki shi nakereba*
> *Omokage ni tatsu.*
>
> I cannot believe that you
> Are far away,
> For I can never forget
> you,
> And thus your face
> Is always before me.[66]

This work heads Iwata's bibliography of homosexual references in Japanese literature, but, like the *Manyōshū* poetry (or the flowery declarations of male affection one finds in Elizabethan correspondence), it is too subtle to be regarded as a definite reference to male homosexuality. One scholar notes, "direct literary expressions of affection for friends of the same sex was conventional ... and not of any unusual [sic] significance."[67] One also finds rather ambiguous passages in prose literature. The authoress of the *Kagerō nikki* (Gossamer diary, 954–975) records what might be an instance of homosexual banter between her husband, Fujiwara Kaneie, and the Minister of War, but again the text is quite obscure.[68] Some courtly fiction of the Heian period (794–1185), meanwhile, seems to hint at homosexual relations.[69] The *Genji monogatari* (Tale of Genji, ca. 1010), massive work that it is, contains only one possible allusion. The hero, Genji, rejected by a certain lady, consoles himself by sleeping with her younger brother.

> "Well, you at least must not abandon me." Genji pulled the boy down beside him.
>
> The boy was delighted, such were Genji's youthful charms. Genji, for his part, or so one is informed, found the boy more attractive than his chilly sister.[70]

But obviously the passage is enigmatic.

The best evidence for homosexual relationships at court in the Heian period comes from diaries. Fujiwara Sukefusa (eleventh century), Ōe Tadafusa (1040–1111), Fujiwara Yorinaga (1120–1156), and Fujiwara Kanezane (1147–1207) all make fairly clear allusions.[71] Yorinaga, for example, mentions sexual encounters with various partners, ranging from manservants to aristocrats.[72]

The first of these occurs in 1142, when the young Yorinaga summons a dancer[s] to his home at midnight. Twice in 1147 he mentions going to bed with such entertainers, and in on the fifth day of the first month of 1148 he writes, "Tonight I took Yoshimasa to bed and really went wild;[t] it was especially satisfying. He

s. *maibito*
t. *burei ni oyonda*

had been ill for awhile and resting, so tonight was the first time [in awhile]." Three months later he visits Tennōji Temple in Naniwa (Osaka), where he is smitten with another dancer. A dream, however, warns him that he should enter the temple hall for devotions the next day rather than allow himself to be rendered impure by sexual contact of any sort before completing his pilgrimage.[73]

The first references I have found to emperors or abdicated emperors involved in homosexual relationships occur in the diaries of Fujiwara Yorinaga and Fujiwara Kanezane. Both mention handsome boys retained for sexual purposes by Emperors Shirakawa (r. 1073–1087) and Toba (r. 1107–1123).[74] Emperor Go-Shirakawa (r. 1156–1158) slept with Fujiwara Nobuyori (1133–1159), expressing his affection by appointing the youth to high posts. The latter, however, rebelled against his patron in the Heiji Rebellion (1159) and as a result lost his head.[75] The ambitious Go-Daigo (1288–1339), who attempted to restore the imperial house to actual political power and bring down the Kamakura shogunate, apparently received the favors of a Kumawaka (Hino Kunimitsu), the son of his loyal retainer Hino Suketomo (d. 1332).[76]

Throughout Heian literature one finds evidence that this courtly culture was well-acquainted with problems of gender identity. In *Genji* and other major works, men are very often described as so moved by other men's beauty that they say to themselves, "If only he were a woman!"[77] In the twelfth-century work *Torikaebaya* (The changelings), a youth falls in love with his best friend's sister, not realizing that she is in fact a cross-dressing male. The youth is also attracted to his friend and in the culminating scene seems on the point of raping him, only to discover that the friend is actually a cross-dressing girl.[78]

The psychological insight of the work is extraordinary; the authors of the *Princeton Companion to Classical Japanese Literature* declare that it "suggests that there must have been men and women of the time who wondered what it was like to be of the other sex, and perhaps even some who would have liked a try at change. The work goes no small distance in showing how society defines maleness or femaleness on bases termed sexual but actually social."[79]

But all in all, the evidence for male-male sexual behavior at the imperial court during the Heian period seems sparse, particularly by comparison with the references for such behavior at the Chinese court and the courts of samurai lords. The Japanese ruling class does not appear to have produced an ongoing homosexual culture distinguishable from the monastic or samurai traditions; Go-Daigo's relationship with Kumawaka probably had little to do with earlier Heian precedents. By the fourteenth century, however, the palaces of Japan's military rulers were becoming centers of homosexual activity; the shoguns of the Muromachi period (1333–1573) were as apt to retain male lovers as the Former Han emperors had been. Their relationships reflect a new tradition of martial homosexuality that developed among the samurai rather than an ancient imperial tradition.

The lack of evidence for homosexual behavior involving Japan's rulers prior to the late eleventh century lends some credence to one scholar's claim that homosexuality "absolutely did not exist" in antiquity.[80] Even given Japan's late acquisition of written language, one might expect to find some references to male-male sexuality in the taboo lists and myths produced by preliterate Yamato society. No such references seem to exist. And whereas ancient Hebrew, Persian, and Hindu laws against sex between men have been preserved, the Japanese prayer-chants first set down in the ninth century contain no similar prohibition.[81] Here, among bans on parent-child incest, bestiality, and defecation in the wrong places, references to male-male (or female-female) sex are conspicuous by their absence.[82] Such an omission might connote approval; if so, however, it is strange that the cheerfully scatological Shintō mythology, which sheds light upon behavior and attitudes long predating the historical period, offers no analogues to the divine homosexuality found in Egyptian, Mesopotamian, Greco-Roman, Scandinavian, Hindu, and Aztec myths.[83]

Monastic Homosexuality

Monasteries, rather than imperial courts, produced the first substantial, documented homosexual tradition in Japan. One of the

most striking features about premodern Japanese homosexuality is
the degree to which it was associated with the Buddhist religious
establishment. This connection seems to have been far stronger
here than in neighboring Buddhist countries, perhaps reflecting a
relatively larger monastic population in Japan.

Evidence from the ninth century indicates that many males entered monastic life to escape harsh corvée labor obligations.[84]
One Japanese authority estimates that there may have been
90,000 Buddhist establishments during the medieval period
(1185–1572), with much of the growth occurring in the sixteenth
century. Most monasteries were small, but not a few housed more
than 1,000 men and boys.[85] The Mount Hiei complex of the Tendai sect was the home of up to 3,000 men and boys, many of
whom were obliged to remain on the mountain for twelve
years.[86] At some point before or during the thirteenth century,
the homosexuality prevalent in such centers came to be openly
and positively acknowledged in the art and literature of the articulate classes.

The popular association of monks and *nanshoku* is reflected in a
folk explanation of the origins of homosexuality in Japan. Like the
ancient Greeks, who traced the origins of *paiderastia* to the myth-
ical Theban hero Laios, the Japanese were inclined to regard
male-male sex as the innovation of an individual.[87] It was said
that none other than Kūkai (or Kōbō Daishi, 774–835), the
founder of the Shingon Buddhist sect in Japan and one of the
great religious figures in the country's history, introduced *nanshoku* into Japan after returning from Tang China in 806 (Figure
1).[88] A spurious text now in the hands of a private collector supposedly contains Kūkai's "secret teachings"[u] on this topic.[89] One
tradition has it that male-male sex first occurred in Japan in Kūkai's Mount Kōya monastic community, established in 816.

A humorous tale in the collection *Uji shūi monogatari* (Tales
gleaned from Uji, 1212–1221) may refer to homosexuality among
monks. It refers to the act of *kawatsurumi*. A monk, having committed this offense, wonders whether he has become ritually de-

u. *hiden*

Fig. 1. According to legend, the priest Kūkai (Kōbō Daishi) introduced homosexuality into Japan in A.D. 806. From a medieval painting. Source: E. Papinot, *Historical and Geographical Dictionary of Japan* (Tokyo and Rutland, Vt.: Tuttle, 1972), p. 321.

filed, as he would have become had he engaged in sex with a woman. Fujitani Mitsue (1768–1823), a Kyoto poet and scholar, wrote in his *Kitabe zuihitsu* (Kitabe's miscellany) that this term meant *nanshoku*. It was derived, he suggested, from the words *kawaya* ("toilet"—an allusion to the "active" partner's contact

with feces) and *tsurumu* ("copulation" among animals—a reference to the supposed similarities between homosexual and animal coitus).[90] But this etymology seems highly speculative, and
other sources identify the offense as masturbation.[91]

In any case, by the Tokugawa period, the connection in the
popular consciousness between *nanshoku*, Buddhism, and Kūkai
was so close that Chikamatsu Monzaemon, the renowned play-
wright, could introduce an act of a drama set on the sacred mountain with the following words:

> On Kōya the mountain
> Where women are hated[v]
> Why does the maiden-pine grow? Yet even if the maiden-pines
> Were all rooted out,
> Would not the stars of love
> Still shoot through the night?[92]

The absence of women in this monastic environment does not,
in other words, entail abstention from sex. As though it were necessary to elaborate, Chikamatsu adds: "More fitting than pine, the
plum or willow is the minion cherry, the temple page,[w] for his is
the way of Monju the Minion[x] spread by the Great Teacher, the
love of fair youths respected even by the laity:[y] this is the home
of the secrets of pederasty."[z] (The "Great Teacher" here refers
to Kūkai.)[93]

The link is, to be sure, mere legend; because Kūkai, universally
recognized as a genius, was credited with inventing the Japanese
syllabary, among other innovations, it is not surprising that he
should have become associated with the introduction of *nanshoku* as well. Of course, it is conceivable that Japanese monks
did indeed develop homosexual interests while studying in
China. An Arab account suggests that homosexuality was widespread in "shrines" in the Middle Kingdom when Kūkai made his
visit during the ninth century, and in Fujian province, where Kū-

v. *onna kirayaru Kōya no yama ni*
w. *otera koshō no chigo zakura*
x. *chigo Monju*
y. *zoku mo tatsutomu wakashū no nasake*
z. *shudō himitsu no oyama to ka ya*

kai spent some weeks before traveling to the Tang capital of Changan, it met with particularly widespread acceptance.[94] It was also common in Zhejiang province, where Kūkai's contemporary Saichō (Dengyō Daishi) studied the Tiantai (Tendai) doctrine from 802 to 805.[95] Kūkai's experience would have been limited largely to monastic life, however, and there exists little evidence of homosexuality in Chinese cloisters during this period.[96] The Tendai monk Ennin, in China from 838 to 847, makes no mention of it in his famous travel diary, and the best Western sources on Chinese homosexuality say very little about its occurrence in monastic life.[97]

The first unambiguous reference to monastic homosexuality in Japan does not treat it as a "teaching" introduced from China by a revered religious figure. The *Ōjōyōshū* (Teachings essential for rebirth, 985) by the Tendai priest Genshin (942–1017) was the most popular religious work of its day, going through several printed editions and even receiving Chinese acclaim. It condemns to the Buddhist hell the man "who has accosted another's acolyte and wickedly violated him"[aa] and he "who commits the wickedness of loving and violating [another] man."[98][bb] Although the passage clearly refers to homosexual intercourse, it is somewhat obscure; the first part probably applies only to the sexual harassment or rape of a boy residing in the cloister. The phrase *"tanin no chigo,"* could mean "another acolyte," "another's acolyte," or perhaps simply "someone's child." There might be an allusion here to *another monk's* young bed partner, which would imply that formal sexual relationships between specific monks and their acolyte partners were accepted. But this is unlikely, as the second expression employed seems to condemn homosexual acts as such. It is certain that Genshin was drawing upon Sanskrit and Chinese scriptures (such as the *Saddharma-smrti-upasthana,* cited previously) that emphasize the sinfulness of male-male sexual contact.[99]

However, Genshin's work does not treat this as a particularly

aa. *tanin no chigo o shiisemete jakō o okoshite*
bb. *otoko ga otoko ni aijo shite jakō o okoshitaru mono*

heinous offense; the damned languish in the third highest of eight
hells alongside (for example) rice-wine merchants who dilute their
product with water. But the image is highly antipathetic, and it
seems probable that the Kūkai–Mount Kōya legend was developed by monks or laymen long after the holy man's death simply
to legitimatize *nanshoku* in the face of earlier Buddhist condemnation. The legend seems to date no further back than the Muromachi period; the oldest reference I have found is in a poem by
the celebrated Zen monk and poet Ikkyū (1394–1481).[100]

How, given the strong anti-homosexual biases of continental
Buddhist texts and of Genshin's work based upon them, do we
explain the emergence of a conspicuous monastic homosexual culture? Japan's distance from other centers of Buddhist culture and
the court's decision early in the ninth century to discontinue routine contact with China may have reduced the influence of texts
that condemned male-male sex.[101] Surely these factors allowed
Japanese Buddhism to produce ideas about sexuality and gender
that were at variance with continental views.[102]

If the traditional Buddhist hostility to male-male sex could thus
be neutralized in Japan, other religious and philosophical schools
could pose no more challenge there than in China or Korea. Had
these traditions been hostile to *nanshoku*, they would probably
have encouraged Buddhist opposition to the phenomenon, as Buddhism in Japan developed a close symbiotic relationship with the
native Shintō cult and served as the vehicle for Confucian and
other continental learning. But such hostility did not exist. The
native cult, as noted, had virtually nothing to say on the subject;
it simply regarded "sexual love [as] an unconditional good."[103]
Heterosexual sex, celebrated in the cult of roadside phallic deities (*Dōsojin*), was not closely monitored in ancient society.[104]
Peasant society (which embraced well over 95 percent of the population) placed little value on virginity and approved of premarital
sexual experimentation. Marriages seem to have been contracted
freely and informally and could be readily dissolved.[105]

The very tolerance toward various forms of sexual behavior

found in the Shintō tradition allowed Ihara Saikaku, the Tokugawa-period writer, to argue with tongue in cheek that the gods
favored male-male sex. Saikaku pointed out that the first three
generations of deities, described in the eighth-century *Nihongi*
chronicle, included no females: "This," he declared, "represents
the historical origin of *shudō*."[106] In the Tokugawa period, some
Shintō gods—among them Tenjin, Hachiman, Myōshin, and
Shinmei—came to be seen as guardian deities of *nanshoku*.[107]
Irreverent, satirical Tokugawa art even occasionally depicts gods
engaging in homosexual intercourse (Figure 2).

Japanese Confucian scholars were also largely unconcerned
with the issue of homosexuality. The monk Gen'e (1269–1352),
who expounded upon Confucian classics to Emperor Go-Daigo,
was himself sexually attracted to boys, and Tokugawa literature
even depicts professional Confucian scholars[cc] patronizing male
prostitutes.[108] The most influential Confucian scholar of the early
Tokugawa period, Hayashi Razan (1583–1657), pointed out in one
of his works the homoerotic content of a passage from classical
literature simply because he found it "interesting."[109]

Confucian writers such as Ogyū Sorai (1666–1728) and Arai
Hakuseki (1657–1725) seem to have taken *nanshoku* itself for
granted; they only raised objections when the fashions of men of
status began to emulate the costume of male prostitutes, when
sexual propositioning in public began to create violent incidents,
or when shoguns excessively rewarded their minions with land
and offices.[110] It is significant that Arai, a major thinker and ad-
viser to Shogun Ienobu (1709–12), praised Ienobu's chamberlain, Manabe Akifusa, as an honest and able politician. He did
not lend his voice to the ex–noh actor's critics, who alleged that
Ienobu "would lead his attendant, Manabe Akifusa, and other
pages ... to the rear quarters where he disported with them as if
they were maids."[111]

As elsewhere in East Asia, *yin-yang* thought influenced Japanese views about sex.[112] The Ming version of the *Jianjin Yao-
fang*, a treatise written by the seventh-century Daoist physician

cc. *jusha*

Fig. 2. The god of healing buggers the god of thunder, perhaps to punish him
for bringing famine or floods. Artist and date unknown. Source: Fukuda
Kazuhiko, *Nikuhitsu fūzoku emaki* (Tokyo: Kawade shobō, 1988), p. 137.

Sun Simo and expressing *yin-yang* concepts of sex, was reprinted
in Tokugawa Japan.[113] The Nativist scholar Miyahiro Sadao (1797–
1858), who had much to say about sexuality, seems to have been
much influenced by this intellectual tradition.[114] And the Confucian thinker Ōta Kinjō (1765–1825), repeating the water-fire

theory, referred to passion for males as "higher lust"[dd] and that for females as "lower lust."[ee][115]

Given the lack of moral sanction against *nanshoku* in these various religious and philosophical systems, many in the Buddhist clergy felt justified indulging in such behavior, regardless of their vows of chastity. Although sixteenth-century Jesuits reported that Buddhist priests denied that *nanshoku* was a sin, it seems clear that male-male sex was often viewed with some ambivalence, even by those who engaged in it. In Nanboku Tsuruya's drama *Sakura hime azuma bunshō* (Eastern documents of the cherry-blossom princess, 1817), a priest and acolyte attempt double suicide because their trysts have distracted the priest from his religious devotions; they find it hard "to go on living, wondering how the temple [monks] are criticizing [us]."[ff][116] Others felt fewer qualms. In one of Saikaku's tales, the monk Gengobei reflects: "When I abandoned the world [for the religious life], I vowed to Buddha that I would give up all thought of sex with women. However, I couldn't stop thinking about the 'beautiful way,'[gg] or about boys. From that time on, I've apologized to the buddhas, saying, 'Permit me, please, this single [pleasure],' so up to now no one has condemned me."[117]

The idea that homosexuality (the "beautiful way") serves as a reasonable and forgivable compromise between heterosexual involvements and complete sexual abstinence is also found in Kitamura Kigin's preface to *Iwatsutsuji* (Rock Azaleas), a collection of *nanshoku*-themed erotica authored around 1673 and published in 1713: "[T]he Buddha preached that Mt. Imose [a euphemism for male-female sex] was a place to be avoided and thus priests of the law first entered this way as an outlet for their feelings, since their hearts were, after all, made of neither stone nor wood."[118]

The effort to justify male-male sexuality in Buddhist terms reached its height during the Tokugawa period, when writers as-

dd. *jōin*
ee. *kain*
ff. *jimon no soshiri nanya ka ya omoimawaseba ikite orarenu*
gg. *bidō*

Fig. 3. Hōtei, one of the Seven Gods of Happiness, relaxes with a young female-role actor. Okumura Masanobu print, ca. 1710. Source: Robert Vergez, *Early Ukiyo-e Master: Okumura Masanobu* (Tokyo, New York, and San Francisco: Kodansha International, Ltd., 1983), p. 42.

sociated homosexuality with the boddhisattvas Monjushiri and Jizō.[119] Even the historical Buddha himself was depicted as regarding it with guarded approval.[120] Hotei, a boddhisattva regarded in Japan as one of the Seven Gods of Happiness, was often shown dallying with fair youths in Tokugawa paintings (Figure 3). And for unclear reasons, the name "Daruma" (Bodhidharma, the Indian Zen patriarch, who became a major figure in Japanese folklore) came to be applied to male and female prostitutes (Figure 4).[121]

In Buddhist Japan, as in Christian Europe from the later medieval period, clerics were in theory denied all sexual outlets. But whereas in the West homosexuality was reckoned even worse

Fig. 4. Courtesan with Zen patriarch Daruma (Bodhidharma), depicted in drag. Woodblock print by Takeda Harunobu (Tokugawa Period). Los Angeles County Museum of Art. Source: H. Neill MacFarland, *Daruma: The Founder of Zen in Japanese Art and Popular Culture* (Tokyo and New York: Kodansha, 1987), p. 24.

than heterosexual activity—a crime against nature as well as against monastic laws—in Japan it was seen only as a regrettable lapse in discipline. As noted previously, the Buddhist faith is traditionally anti-female, and though the misogyny was in some ways mitigated in Japan, particularly in the early centuries after the introduction of the religion, by the medieval period Japanese Buddhism insisted upon women's inherently evil and defiling nature.

This increasingly negative view of women may simply have represented the traditional Buddhist strategy of discouraging monks from seeking sexual contact with the opposite sex. But it may also have reflected institutional changes following the removal of the capital from Nara to Kyoto in 794. Thereafter the court was particularly careful to keep the Buddhist establishment, which had earlier intervened with near-disastrous effects in politics, at arm's length.[122] The newly introduced sects of Tendai and Shingon were usually obliged to locate their temples on mountains or hills, often in remote areas. Women were banned from these sacred mountains. Monks of earlier periods had often resided in close proximity to lay folk, including women, but they now had fewer opportunities for (the forbidden) heterosexual contact. Thus, they may have found it easier to vilify the sex to which they enjoyed so little exposure.[123]

But if sexual contact with women was regarded as debasing, sex with boys, if not a positive good, was regarded (to use Kitamura's term) as a tolerable "outlet for [monks'] feelings." It came to be accepted that monasteries maintained boy-acolytes (chigo) who, aside from performing domestic chores, commonly shared the beds of older monks.[124] Mountain priests (yamabushi), practitioners of the Shūgendō sect (a curious blend of esoteric Buddhism and Shintō), did not reside in monasteries, but they, too, acquired a reputation as boy-lovers.[125] The popular saying "Acolytes first, the mountain god second,"[hh] reflects the sense of priorities cynically attributed to the Buddhist clergy from at least the Muromachi period.[126]

The chigo, temple servant, or young priest as sexual partner

hh. ichi chigo ni sannō

appears very often in literature. Thus, we have love-poems from the tenth century on addressed from monks to acolytes, and both the *Konjaku monogatari* (Collection of tales old and new, early twelfth century) and *Uji shūi monogatari* (between 1212 and 1221) contain tales that allude to pederastic relationships.[127] The latter work, for example, contains a story about a Tendai abbot, Fujiwara no Zōyo (1031–1116), who falls in love with a young *sarugaku* (rustic noh) performer and asks the boy to become a priest so the two can spend all their time together. He comes to regret his decision, as the boy is less attractive in his new habit than before. He has the boy put on his old clothes and becomes sexually aroused, lamenting that he had ever made him a priest. "Now you can see," says the boy, "why I asked you to let me wait a bit longer, sir." The abbot has him remove the old costume and takes him into his private room. "What happened then," concludes the narrator, "I have no idea."[128]

A religious vow[ii] from the same period, registered by a monk named Samon Shūsei at the Tōdaiji Temple in Nara, also indicates widespread homosexual behavior in Buddhist monasteries. Containing five resolutions, it was composed in 1237, when its author was thirty-six years old.

FIVE VOWS:

Item: I will remain secluded at Kasaki Temple until reaching age forty-one.

Item: Having already fucked[jj] ninety-five males, I will not behave wantonly with more than one hundred.

Item: I will not keep and cherish[kk] any boys except Ryūō-maru.

Item: I will not keep older boys[ll] in my own bedroom.

Item: Among the older and middle boys,[mm] I will not keep and cherish any as their *nenja*.[129]

Interestingly, the commitment to Ryūō-maru does not prevent this monk from allowing himself five more partners in the future.

ii. *kishō*
jj. *okasu*
kk. *takuwaerubekarazu*
ll. *jōdō*
mm. *jōdō chūdō no aida*

The document ends with a pointed proviso that these vows are limited to the present lifetime and do not apply to future incarnations.

Clear references to male-male sex proliferated from the fourteenth century on. Monastic laws from the late Kamakura period (and perhaps earlier) suggest a concern about the disruptive effects of resident acolytes upon the contemplative life of the monks. One such reference occurs in a legal document issued by the Hōjō regent, Sadatoki, to a Kamakura Zen monastery in 1303.[130] Regulations issued by Ashikaga shoguns in 1419 and 1436 forbade monks to dress acolytes in gorgeous outfits. In 1463 the shogun Yoshimasa even ordered a certain temple to confine a beautiful acolyte held responsible for monks' "unruliness."[nn][131]

Artistic and literary depictions of homosexual relationships also proliferated during the fourteenth century. The *Chigo no sōshi* (Acolyte scroll), a ribald masterpiece about priests and acolytes, appeared in 1321 and is now in the possession of Sanpōin Temple (Figure 5).[132] Monastic records such as the *Inryōken nichiroku* (Daily record of the cool shady eaves, 1435–1493) make frequent reference to pederastic relationships.[133]

The first of what have been dubbed *chigo monogatari* (tales dealing with these monastic sexual relationships) was written around 1377 and followed by seven other such works during the Muromachi period.[134] Some scholars also find a subtle homoeroticism in such noh plays as *Kagetsu, Jinen koji, Tōgan koji*, and *Seigan koji*, all of which were written before 1423 and dealt with monk-acolyte relationships.[135] The *kyōgen* comic plays of the Muromachi period also sometimes featured homoerotic content.[136]

Katō Shūichi regards the development of "homosexual poetry and prose as one of the great contributions made by the Zen sect to the culture of Japan during the Muromachi period," citing the *Shinden shikō* of Shinden Shōben, the *Ryūsuishū* (1462) of Toshō Shūgen, and the *San'eki Shik-o* (ca. 1520) of San'eki Eiin. One of the *Ryūsuishū* poems runs as follows:

nn. *iran*

Fig. 5. Section from the "Acolyte Scroll" (*Chigo no sōshi*, 1321). A manservant applies clove oil lubricant to an acolyte's anus. Painting in the possession of Sanpōin Temple. Source: Philip Rawson, *Erotic Art of the East: The Sexual Theme in Oriental Painting and Sculpture* (London: Weidenfeld and Nicolson, 1973), p. 294.

> We passed the night in the same bed,
> And now looking at the pale moon at dawn through the window
> Our two shadows fall on the curtain
> A pair of mandarin ducks.
> I would celebrate the night's joy of love forever.
> Our temple is like Kimshan Temple on the Yang-tse.[137]

This classical Japanese poem,[oo] as Katō suggests, is clearly on the theme of love, not lust. Other Muromachi literature, however, deals with pederasty in a cruder fashion. Yoshida Kenkō's *Tsure-zuregusa* (Idle writings, ca. 1330) contains jocular stories about

oo. *waka*

Zen monks and their passion for acolytes.[138] The comic linked
verses[pp] of the priests Ikkyū (1394–1481), Sōgi (1421–1502),
Sōchō (1448–1532), and many others address similar themes.[139]
On a more refined level, Sōgi also wrote two manuals outlining
proper behavior for *chigo* lovers.[140] Priests and monks who were
illicitly married or involved with women, as were Ikkyū, Sōchō,
or the Hossō sect priest Satomura Jōha (1524–1602), also recorded their experiences with male lovers.[141] Priestly bisexuality
was apparently not uncommon. One Ikkyū poem begins, "Tired
of *nanshoku*, I embrace my wife[qq]...."[142]

Westerners first reached Japan in 1543. Their accounts of the
sixteenth and seventeenth centuries contain numerous allusions
to "sodomy" among the Buddhist clergy. The Jesuit missionary
Francis Xavier returned the hospitality of some friendly Zen
monks by railing against his startled hosts for their open indulgence in "the abominable vice of Sodom." In 1549 he reported
that "the evil is simply become a habit" among the Buddhist
clergy, who had sex with the boys sent them for education. The
priests "are drawn to sins against nature and don't deny it, they
acknowledge it openly. This evil, moreover, is so public, so clear
to all, men and women, young and old, and they are so used to
seeing it, that they are neither depressed nor horrified."[143]

The Jesuit Alessandro Valignano, in his *Historia del Principio*,
noting the "great dissipation" of the Japanese "in the sin that
does not bear mentioning," also singled out the Buddhist clergy
for attack: "[T]he bonzes teach that not only is it not a sin but
that it is even something quite natural and virtuous and to a certain extent reserve this practice for themselves."[144] Eager to
establish the tie between forbidden sexuality and their rival clerics, the Jesuits quickly accepted and publicized the supposed link
between homosexuality and the monk Kūkai. This legend was reported by Gaspar Vilela as early as 1571.[145]

Though emphasizing the Buddhist-homosexual link, however,
the Western missionaries seem to have regarded homosexuality

pp. *renga*
qq. *tsuma*

as somehow intrinsic to the Japanese character.[146] Even Japanese converts to Catholicism were regarded as prone to this supposed moral weakness. Valignano's *Catechismus* for Japanese converts (ca. 1580) specifically warns against such behavior.[147]

Westerners other than Roman Catholic missionaries also noted the prevalence of homosexual behavior in Japan. François Caron, a Franco-Dutch merchant who left Japan in 1641, singled out the clergy for comment: "Their Priests, as well as many of the Gentry, are much given to Sodomy, that unnatural passion, being esteemed no sin, nor shameful thing amongst them."[148] Fifty years later, the German traveler Engelbert Kaempfer observed that boy prostitution was common, "the Japanese being very much addicted to this vice."[149]

From all this material, we acquire some idea of the characteristics of monastic homosexuality. The typical relationship involved a monk and a boy serving as an acolyte or, in Zen monasteries, a postulant.[rr] These boys often came from ranking families and were either training to enter the clergy or receiving instruction in scripture and sutra-chanting as part of their education. Sometimes they were very young; among better-known religious figures, Hōnen (1133–1212) and Shinran (1173–1262) both entered at age nine, Ippen (1239–89), at ten, Eisai (1141–1215) and Nichiren (1222–82), at twelve.[150] A postulant might be placed in a Zen temple at age five. By the time he reached his teens, the boy may have developed a special relationship with an older monk, who would be referred to as the *nenja*.[151] The youthful partner would be called the *nyake*.[152] Both these terms were in use by the early twelfth century and appear in the reference work *Kojidan* (Talks on ancient matters, 1215).[153] By the seventeenth century the senior partner was called the "older brother"[ss] and the junior, the "younger brother";[tt] the relationship itself was called a "brother-

rr. *kasshiki*
ss. *anibun*
tt. *otōtobun*

hood bond."[uu][154] The pair ritually swore loyalty to one another and, at least in later periods, documented their relationship with a written oath.

Such bonds resemble the *qixiong-qidi* relationships of Fujian, described previously, or the *erastes-eramenos* relationships of ancient Greece.[155] These were also pederastic or transgenerational relationships—in the Greek case, the *erastes* (the adult "lover") was supposed to serve as a tutor, friend, and role-model for his *eremenos* (or adolescent "beloved")—but they differed in significant ways from the Japanese case. Because the ancient Greeks (although not, apparently, the Chinese) regarded oral sex between free men as an abomination and anal sex as an act that feminized (and therefore derogated) the passive partner, the *eromenos* was (at least in theory) never subjected to penetration (and, by implication, to "feminization").[156] Vase- and cup-paintings that show free men and adolescents having sex usually depict the inserter with his organ between the thighs of the standing boy—a technique called *diamerizēin* ("to do between the thighs").[157] There is, that is to say, no actual penetration of the boy partner.

In Japan, as the *Chigo no sōshi* makes plain, anal sex was the norm in monk-*chigo* relations, and the anal erogeneity of the insertee partner was even celebrated.[158] The following is a translation of the first section of the scroll.

> I think this occurred just after the Ninnaji [Temple] had been built. There was a venerable priest there, highly revered throughout the world. Influenced by the virtue of the Three Mysteries of the Dharma, his character and the effects of his incantations were renowned. Yet he was unable to abandon this Way [of sex with boys]. Although there were many beautiful youths around him, one in particular would lie with him in the most intimate fashion.
>
> But the ability to perform [sexually] has nothing to do with one's piety. He had apparently indulged too much, and so could not perform sexually to the extent he would have liked. In his heart, he yearned to [have intercourse with the youth] in the manner that the arrow of Shintō pierces the roofed mud wall. But his [penis] was like an arrow just brushing against the mountain [of the boy's buttocks]; penetration was out of the question.

uu. *kyōdai musubi*

The boy, saddened by this, diligently prepared [himself] each night. He would summon beforehand a youth named Chūta, the son of his nurse. [Chūta's] penis would still be soft as [his master] had him lubricate a dildo with clove oil and then insert it into his bottom. Up to this point Chūta would perform his services with complete diligence, but now his penis would be erect. He could not help but masturbate.^{vv} Blowing on the charcoal, he would warm the boy's bottom. Finally [the boy] would be called to [the priest's] bed. Being old, [the priest] went to sleep early, so there was not much time to embrace the boy before he went to sleep. Thus, without any delay, the old priest would insert his penis into the bottom of this boy who had prepared so well in advance. Such a sincerely devoted acolyte is without parallel. One must regard him as a priceless human being.[159]

Several paintings accompany this text. One depicts Chūta preparing the boy for his liaison using the dildo. The manservant is himself naked and in a state of sexual excitement. The captions translate as follows:

Chūta: This is hard to endure. You don't go [to the priest] until later, just before he retires. Do you really need me to perform this service for you already, while it's still afternoon? You're much too early.

Boy: Anyway, stick your finger in.

Chūta: Since I perform this service every night, I sometimes think, "Enough already!" I've already told you this confidentially. It's too much. You can't understand my feelings. You're insensitive. This time I'd like real satisfaction.

Boy: Well, how about sticking [the dildo in] one *sun*?

Chūta: I guess it can't be helped, can it? My thing gets erect, and there's nothing to do but masturbate. So my penis gets weak, and my wife reviles me. I'll endure it, though, and help you out.

  This smells good. [Excuse me for] talking to you [this way], Master, but isn't your bottom hard to please? You're very fond of your bottom, aren't you? Before you go to the honorable priest, I wonder if you'd let me stick *my* penis in.

The "sincerely devoted acolyte" is not, after all, entirely faithful to the old priest. The next illustration shows the manservant apply-

vv. *setsuri [senzuri] o zo kakikeru*

ing lubricant to the boy's anus. "Smear on that clove oil," reads the caption, "then screw me with your full five *sun!*"[ww] Another picture shows Chūta happily complying with the invitation, and the last illustration in the section shows the servant, now clothed, blowing a fire to heat the boy's buttocks for his subsequent encounter with the priest.[160]

In homosexual relationships of this type, the boys appear often to have served as surrogates for the females absent from the lives of the monks. Various Tokugawa-period jokes[xx] indicate the conflation of boys and women, and of the anus and vagina, in monastic society. In one, a priest on a religious retreat asks a friend to make him an *onyake* (artificial leather anus) for use in lieu of a boy. But he adds the request that it *taste* like a vagina.[161]

Some monks during the medieval period "shaved [their *chigos'*] eyebrows, powdered their faces, [and] dressed them in female garb."[162] In the fifteenth-century work *Gikeiki* (The tale of Yoshitsune), the hero spends some years as the *chigo*-lover of an abbot. During this period he wears cosmetics, wears his hair up in a girlish bun, blackens his teeth, and thinly pencils in lines over his shaven eyebrows. Similarly, when his beautiful wife is disguised as an acolyte, she is told, "It will seem natural for you to wear cosmetics."[163]

Although the boys looked rather like girls, they were not trained to imitate female behavior (as were, for example, *onnagata* in the kabuki theater of later centuries). Their speech was quite different from that of young women, and they cultivated arts (such as flute playing) that were regarded as exclusively masculine pursuits.[164] The acolytes exuded a unique, androgynous attraction that some men may have found more fascinating than feminine charms. Nevertheless, one must associate the evolution of the *chigo* role with the absence of women in the lives of the monks.

ww. *Sono chōji-yu o fude de tōtō to somete, go sun bakari hineri ireyo* (five sun equals six inches)
xx. *kobanashi*

Homosexuality Among the Samurai:
The Influence of Feudalism

Given the tenuousness of Japanese ties to the more homophobic traditions of continental Buddhism and the apparent absence of any indigenous taboo against male-male sexual contact, it is not surprising that the Japanese monastic environment should have produced such a highly developed and articulated homosexual culture. Once firmly established in a country whose elites had decisively embraced Buddhism in the ancient period, this culture was bound to influence lay society. The courtly age-structured homosexuality discussed earlier may well have been patterned on the priest-*chigo* relationships. And the sexual relationships among males in the martial or samurai class unquestionably came to be modeled in part on the traditions of monks and courtiers.[165]

The samurai, who during the twelfth and thirteenth centuries gradually came to dominate the country, had far fewer members during this period than the Buddhist clergy. Whereas the latter must have numbered in the hundreds of thousands, the military class constituted perhaps 6,000 men (out of a population of seven million) in about A.D. 1200.[166] It seems to have grown dramatically in the following century, however, and by the late sixteenth century the samurai population had reached the hundreds of thousands.[167] Thus, although the monastic and samurai traditions of *nanshoku* co-evolved, the former may have been the stronger and more influential until the fifteenth or sixteenth century.

Perhaps military, like monastic, society is by its very nature conducive to the formation of male-male sexual relationships.[168] Long periods in isolation in all-male environments encourage homosexual behavior. In given historical societies, the military emphasis on physical cultivation, as preparation for the battlefield, easily has led to glorification of the muscular male physique, such as one finds both in the homoerotic sculpture of ancient Greece or the work of such sculptors as Unkei and Kaikei in Kamakura Japan (1185–1333). Public celebration of the male body in art may even influence the construction of sexual desire.

Such military values as group solidarity, loyalty under conditions of extreme stress, and unquestioning obedience to authority might in some situations induce military men to engage in sex with one another and even to develop distinctive homosexual traditions. The problem can only be investigated in the context of the specific cultural and ideological environments surrounding such military societies.

It has been suggested that *feudalism* may encourage homosexual desire and behavior.[169] Feudalism, in the sense of a social formation based upon the rule of a hierarchically organized military class whose members exchange service for land, arose historically in both the West and Japan (from the twelfth century) in response to the collapse of centralized state institutions.[170] Strong men, directly governing manageable units of land and subject peasant populations through their own physical and mental attributes, constituted its leaders and heroes. Women's status declined with the evolution of feudalism; in the Japanese case, the system of primogeniture came to be applied from the fourteenth century and removed women from prestigious military and administrative positions they had sometimes held earlier.[171]

Strong men's traits, which represent the ability to survive in unstable conditions, may have acquired erotic significance to women and men alike.[172] Thus, the *Song of Roland* and other medieval European literary works celebrate the love of courageous warriors for one another above heterosexual love.[173] Among the samurai of Japanese feudal society, too, male-male affection was often eroticized, but only in the case of clearly defined status roles.[174] The "love of comrades" manifest among the bachelor knights of medieval Europe was conspicuously absent among the warrior class of Japan,[175] perhaps because such relationships might have conflicted with hierarchical feudal loyalties. A samurai treatise of the early Tokugawa period described *nanshoku* as "something both agreeable and disagreeable" because "[t]o throw away one's life [for one's male lover] is the ultimate aim of *shudō*. Otherwise it becomes something shameful. But then one has no life to give in service to one's lord—so it is both agreeable and disagreeable."[176] In other words, an unconditional commitment to a man other than one's lord made one less serviceable to the latter.

But the lord-retainer relationship itself often assumed an erotic character. This was not because the samurai universally embraced a code of honor inclining them toward unconditional loyalty to and love for their masters. Indeed, the best recent work on the early samurai emphasizes the conditional and self-serving character of samurai service.[177] During the civil wars of the late fifteenth and sixteenth centuries, vassals often turned against their lords in spectacular acts of betrayal, leading Japanese historians to refer to this period as one in which "inferiors overthrew their superiors" (gekokujo). Jesuit missionaries in sixteenth-century Japan, far from describing the samurai as faithful, dependable vassals, depict them as back-stabbers who "rebel ... when the opportunity presents itself"; as a result, "none of the lords ... are secure in their domains."[178]

Though it might have been observed in the breach, however, military society produced an exacting system of values. One of the most important elements in this system was the idea that loyalty to one's lord overrode loyalty to one's wife and children and even the obligations to one's parents. This, indeed, is one of the most significant Japanese modifications of Chinese Confucianism. From the fourteenth century it was commonly held that "[t]he relationship of parent and child is for one existence [i.e., incarnation]; the relation of husband and wife is for two existences; the relationship between lord and retainer is for three generations."[179]

There is ample evidence that some military men took such beliefs very seriously, selflessly struggling, for example, to reestablish masters' houses after their apparent annihilation by enemy forces.[180] Didactic tales helped to inculcate the values of uncompromising loyalty and duty (giri) in at least many young samurai. Such mens' feelings for their lords would have ranged from mere willingness to follow orders and obediently fight on their behalf and follow orders (what might be called "cold duty") to a genuinely passionate devotion ("warm duty"). Lords receiving the latter would be expected to reciprocate with affectionate attentiveness to their vassals' well-being.[181]

The erotic connotations of the idealized lord-vassal relationship are illustrated in the famous tale *Chūshingura* (The treasury of loyal retainers), which, though written during the early eighteenth century, reflects values that had been celebrated in samurai society for centuries. Popular in various dramatic interpretations (penned by bourgeois rather than samurai writers) since the mid-Tokugawa period, the story is based on an episode that occurred in 1703.[182] Provoked by the insolent remarks of an official in the shogunal palace, a daimyo (baron) from a small domain loses his patience and attacks the man with his sword. Because even unsheathing one's sword in the palace was a capital crime, the daimyo is ordered to commit *seppuku*, or ritual suicide. Forty-seven of his retainers then embark on an elaborate scheme to exact vengeance; a year later, they track down their master's foe, kill him, present his head before their master's shrine, then disembowel themselves.[183]

In single-minded pursuit of their aim, the conspirators do not hesitate to exploit or abandon their wives and children. Their sole aim is to requite their master's kindness by avenging his death. Although heterosexual love is depicted in the best-known puppet-play version of the story, it is shown as a sometimes tragic impediment to retainers' feudal duties. In the most moving scene in the play, the unfortunate lord, having been ordered to commit suicide, hesitates to slit his belly as he awaits the arrival of his chief retainer, Yuranosuke. Informed that he has not appeared, the lord expresses his sorrow that he "won't be seeing him again in this life. It's hard to leave him. But there's no helping it. I can wait no longer." [184] He says nothing to his wife, seated nearby.

Just as the doomed man plunges his dagger into his abdomen, his chief retainer rushes into the room. "Yuranosuke," exclaims the dying lord, "I waited for you as long as I could." The two men then express their joy at being able to look upon one anothers' faces one last time and, in their farewells, psychically agree that Yuranosuke will, with the daimyo's own dagger, wreak vengeance on this foe. "The story," writes sociologist Nakane Chie,

> bears some resemblance to a love affair. In Japan there is no love story comparable in popularity to [*Chūshingura*]. Men so much in-

volved in such a [lord-vassal] relationship have little room left for a wife or a sweetheart. I think that if he were involved to such an extent in this kind of man-to-man relation there would seem to be no necessity for a love affair with a woman. His emotions would be completely expended in his devotion to his master. I suspect this was the real nature of the Samurai mentality.[185]

Doi Takeo, a prominent Japanese psychiatrist, has also noted the homoerotic character of lord-vassal relationships depicted in kabuki dramas.[186] His work *Amae no kōzō* (The anatomy of dependence, 1971) suggests that the social inferiors' intense emotional dependence[yy] upon their superiors, so apparent in feudal literature, has survived in Japan to the present day. Doi closely identifies this dependence with homosexual feelings "in the broad sense," which, he maintains, remain far stronger in Japan than in the West.[187]

Homosexuality Among the Samurai: The Influence of Monastic Pederasty

Samurai attitudes toward sex would have been influenced not only by the idealized lord-vassal relationship or by the institutionalized devaluation of women. The existence of a pervasive monastic homosexual tradition would surely have encouraged warriors—who generally respected the Buddhist clergy and embraced many of their values—to regard the role-structured homosexuality practiced by the monks with particular tolerance and sympathy. They would then incorporate elements of that tradition into their own evolving culture.

Boys of samurai status often received education in monasteries and forged "brotherly bonds" with monks.[188] Alternatively, younger sons of samurai households might be placed in monasteries with the understanding that they pursue religious careers.[189] Accepting monk-acolyte sexual relationships as proper, and influenced by the erotics expressed in the writings of the Muromachi-period Zen poets, many adult warriors would have been socialized to experience and express a desire for boys. Boys serving as

yy. *amae*

menials or personal attendants in samurai retainer bands might easily have been drawn into sexual involvements with their masters, especially during long military campaigns, thereby acquiring martial skills and ultimately stipends or fiefs. As Ōta Kinjō noted in 1813, "During the time the country was at war [ca. 1467–1600], *nanshoku* became prevalent, and many strong and courageous warriors emerged from among the [warriors'] male sex-partners."[190]

With the restoration of peace to the country after the Battle of Sekigahara (1600), the object of sexual desire gradually shifted from the young soldier-in-training to the more effeminate boy-attendant. A picture scroll (*emaki*) of the Kyōhō period (1716–1735) painted by Miyakawa Chōshun vividly conveys the homosexual atmosphere such boys lent a contemporary samurai mansion. A high-ranking samurai, his son, and an entourage of twenty-eight servants and retainers are shown getting ready for an outing. Among the group is a youth dressed in female clothing, attended in his toilet by two other boys who are also seductively dressed and coiffured. A samurai in the center of the scene seems to gaze at these two boys. To their left, seated upon the stage, another youth is having his hair dressed in the fashionable Shimada style popular with courtesans. The attendant standing next to him wears the purple scarf of a kabuki actor. Near them another group centers around a boy who is choosing his kimono for the day, and at the left some other boys prepare tea. There is not one female in the painting.[191]

Biographical materials often refer to great men's involvements with youths and "beloved retainers."[zz] The list of shoguns, hegemons, and principal daimyo thought to have been sexually involved with boys reads like a *Who's Who* of military and political history; it includes shoguns Minamoto Yoritomo (1147–1199; r. 1193–1199);[192] Ashikaga Takauji (1305–1358; r. 1338–1358); Ashikaga Yoshimitsu (1358–1408; r. 1367–1394); Ashikaga Yoshimochi (1386–

zz. *chōshin*

1428; r. 1394–1428); Ashikaga Yoshinori (1394–1441; r. 1429–1441); Ashikaga Yoshimasa (1436–1490; r. 1449–1473); Ashikaga Yoshiteru (1536–1565; r. 1546–1565);[193] Tokugawa Ieyasu (1542–1616; r. 1603–1605; Tokugawa Iemitsu (1603–1651; r. 1623–1651); Tokugawa Tsunayoshi (1646–1709; r. 1680–1709); Tokugawa Ienobu (1662–1712; r. 1709–1712); Tokugawa Ieshige (1712–1761, r. 1745–1760); Tokugawa Ieharu (1737–1786; r. 1760–1786); and Tokugawa Ienari (1773–1841; r. 1786–1837).[194]

Warlords such as Hosokawa Masamoto (1466–1507); Hosokawa Takakuni (1484–1531), Hosokawa Fujitaka (1534–1610), Takeda Shingen (1521–1573), Oda Nobunaga (1534–1582),[195] Toyotomi Hideyoshi (1536–1598),[196] Toyotomi (Hashiba) Hidetsugu (1568–1595),[197] Uesugi Kenshin (1530–1578), Maeda Toshiie (1538–1599), Fukushima Masanori (1561–1624), Ogasawara Hidemasa (1569–1615),[198] and the great swordsman Miyamoto Musashi (1584–1645) are all known to have engaged in sex with boys.[199]

The relationship between Takeda Shingen and his lover Kōsaka Masanobu (or Danjō, 1527–1578) is particularly well documented. Kōsaka became one of the top generals in Takeda's army. Although he commanded the rearguard forces that rescued his lord at the Battle of Kawanakajima in 1561, he owed his post, his opponents charged, less to his martial skills than to his sexual connection to the daimyo. The relationship is recorded in their contract, written and co-signed in 1542, when Shingen was twenty-two and his partner, then named Kasuga Gensuke, sixteen. The text, which is preserved in Tokyo University's Historical Archive,[aaa] alludes to a third person with whom (despite his denials) Shingen seems to have had a sexual relationship:

Item: Although I have sometimes said to Yashichirō, "Let's have sex,"[bbb] he has refused me, saying, "I'm having stomach problems and am not feeling well."

Item: Yashichirō has never slept with me as my attendant in bed. To date, that has never happened. Not only have I never had sex

aaa. *Shiryō hensanjo*
bbb. *nanshoku o shiyō*

with him at night, but never in the daytime either. Especially now, I have no thought of having sex with him.

Item: Since I want to become intimate with you, from now on if you have any doubts about these things, I want you to understand that I do not plan to hurt you. If I should ever break these promises, may I receive the divine punishment of the Great Myōshin of the First, Second, and Third Shrines of the province of Kai, Mount Fuji and Shirayama, and particularly Hachiman Bosatsu, and all the higher and lower deities.[200]

Apparently Gensuke was jealous of Yashichirō and pressed Shingen for such a written promise. The document—a nice specimen of the "brotherhood contract"—suggests the seriousness with which both parties entered into *nanshoku* relationships.

Such documents are quite rare. As in the case of the Han emperors or Koryō kings, the great man's homosexual activities enter the historical record because they have some relevance to his public behavior—his distribution of gifts, lands, and offices. Thus, we know Yoritomo made his young lover, Yoshinao, an officer in the Imperial Guard and that Takauji lavished valuable swords on his boy.[201] Even Ieyasu was criticized for spending too much time disporting with boys.[202]

Major scandals and vendettas at the highest level can sometimes be traced to *nanshoku* infatuations overthrowing political judgment. Ashikaga Yoshimochi provoked rebellion by offering vast lands to his lover Akamatsu Mochisada, and his brother Yoshinori was slain in 1441 over his effort to similarly reward his own bedmate, Akamatsu Sadamura.[203] Oda Nobunaga may have met his end at the hands of Akechi Mitsuhide over a rumor that the latter's fief was to be transferred to the hegemon's favorite catamite page.[204] The Bitchū domain of Ukita Narimasa was thrown into turmoil in 1605 when the lord killed an innocent page, whose lover, Narimasa's nephew, then sought revenge.[205]

The second Tokugawa shogun, Hidetada, ordered his page and lover Koyama Nagato to commit *seppuku* in 1625 as punishment for Nagato's sexual affair with Naruse, the lord of Bungo.[206] The fief of the Nakatsu daimyo, Ogasawara Nagatane, was seized, cut

in half, and given to others in 1698 because the lord had appointed his bedmate, one Akimoto, his leading minister and had
allowed him to ruin the domain.[207] The ninth Tokugawa shogun,
Ieshige, and his successor, Ieharu, were accused in whispers of
appointing such controversial officials as Ōoka Tadamitsu and Tanuma Okitsugu partly on the basis of sexual favors.[208]

Such tales have survived because these relationships were relevant to politics. No doubt a myriad of tales about male-male love
involving no scandal, murderous vendetta, or colossal misjudg-
ment were simply forgotten soon after the principals died. Repre-
senting no exceptional or aberrant behavior, they did not become
the stuff of historical chronicles. Although we know next to nothing about the popular view of *nanshoku*, the historical record left
by the literate strata of society suggests that most people would
have inquired not why a given man *had* taken male lovers but
rather why he had *not* done so.

The Character of Pre-Tokugawa
Nanshoku

Let us conclude our discussion of pre-Tokugawa traditions of *nanshoku* by placing them in global perspective.

Two general types of male-male sexual behavior widely occur in
preclass societies: age-structured and gender-structured.[209] The
first involves adult males' use of younger males as the insertee
partners in oral or anal sex (or as the "passive" partners in intercrural sex). The second involves the establishment of a specific homosexual role, such as that of the cross-dressing shaman, whose adher-
ents may serve as insertee partners for interested men.

The Sambia of Melanesia provide one example of the first type;
among them, all boys are required to fellate older males on the
theory that without the ingestion of semen they will not attain
adulthood.[210] The *berdache* (cross-dressing shaman) traditions of
various preclass cultures in the Americas and Northeast Asia
provide examples of the latter type.[211]

Both age-structured and gender-structured homosexuality can

survive in more advanced, class-stratified societies. Among the Dorians of ancient Crete, ritualistic kidnapping and homosexual seduction of youths by older men constituted a rite of passage.[212] Similar customs appear to have prevailed among Celtic peoples.[213] Unmarried male adults among the Azande of the Sudan traditionally took boy-wives, who would perform wifely functions, service the men in intercrural sex, and, upon attaining adulthood, acquire their own boy-partners.[214]

Elsewhere, specific homosexual roles were constructed, to be fulfilled by a small number of specific males, often cross-dressers. In the ancient Near East, for example, male temple-prostitutes or cross-dressing eunuch priests performed the insertee role with male patrons.[215] The institution of the *hijra*, male cross-dressing devotees of the Mother Goddess, developed in India.[216] In China and Korea, as noted, actors, particularly those who performed female roles, often doubled as male prostitutes.

In pre-Tokugawa Japan, age-structured homosexuality flourished in monastic and military society. There was apparently no designated social role for the man who performed the insertee role throughout his life, but the youthful partner in male-male relationships was often (like the *berdache* or *hijra*) obliged to assume a feminine or androgynous appearance. Surely this tendency to feminize the younger partner resulted from the absence of women in the contexts that produced the first homosexual traditions.

The first developed tradition of *nanshoku* in Japan was that of the Buddhist monasteries. We cannot explain the monk-*chigo* relationship solely as the result of "situational" sexual behavior, for some individuals may have taken holy orders in part because they preferred an all-male environment and its sexual opportunities.[217] But surely many men who would otherwise have sought sex with females practiced it with boys in their absence. Heterosexual desire was evident in the construction of sexual objects made up, coiffured, and dressed much like women.

The emergence of the samurai *nanshoku* tradition can also be explained in part by the relative absence of women in martial society. During long military campaigns, warriors might become sexually attracted to young attendants and boys undergoing martial training. Ranking warriors might retain beautiful youths for sexual purposes, dressing them not as females but in conspicuously elegant, nonmartial attire.

Thus, we find in Japan on the eve of the early modern period two homosexual traditions that 1) emerged largely as the result of the lack of women; 2) were age-structured and seen as contributing to the younger partners' education or maturation; and 3) often required the younger partner to assume a female-like or androgynous appearance. These traditions were practiced by respected elites and legitimated by the strength of the Chinese tradition and by the Kūkai myth.

With the establishment of the Tokugawa shogunate and the subsequent growth of large towns and cities, a third, bourgeois *nanshoku* tradition emerged. Although males initially outnumbered females in urban environments, the homosexual culture they created owed as much to the enduring strength of the earlier traditions as to the undersupply of women. Aware of monastic and samurai traditions, men of common status in the Tokugawa period would naturally have regarded homosexual desire as normal and male-male sex as a permissible and attractive activity.

Chapter Two

The Commercialization of *Nanshoku*

Actors playing young men often received larger salaries
than those playing women. At that time, *shudō* was all
the rage in all the quarters of the town.

Tominaga Heibei, *Kei kagami*, early
eighteenth century

The New Order and the Rise of a Culture
of Prostitution

The period between 1568 and 1603 marks a watershed in Japanese history. During these three and a half decades, a nation that
had been divided for more than two centuries into numerous war-
ring feudal units was reunited under a form of central rule. Three
great warlords in succession achieved this reunification: Oda Nobunaga (1534–1582), Toyotomi Hideyoshi (1536–1598) and Tokugawa Ieyasu (1542–1616).

Each of these men understood the central conflicts in Japanese
society and in their attempts to deal with them produced radical,
far-reaching changes. Not all of their policies are pertinent to our
topic, but one—their effort to rein in the great majority of samurai and sever their links to the peasantry—was of extraordinary importance. It led to the rapid growth of castle-towns and
to the emergence of a huge bourgeoisie with a lively culture of
its own. This class developed a new *nanshoku* tradition quite distinct from the monastic or samurai traditions. For the merchants

and artisans of Tokugawa cities, male-male sex became largely a commercial transaction devoid of the commitments required by earlier traditions of male homosexuality.[1]

The emergence of the early modern bourgeoisie[a] is a complex phenomenon, but it may be explained, with some oversimplification, as follows.[2] By the sixteenth century Japan had become divided into more than 200 independent feudal domains whose barons (or daimyo) continuously warred with one another and with their own rebellious vassals. Alongside these conflicts within the ruling class, there were periodic local peasant revolts directed at daimyo or their officials. Lower-ranking samurai residing in villages might provoke rebellions by abusing the local peasantry; alternatively, they might make common cause with peasants in rising against their lords.

Both problems—samurai insurgencies and peasant uprisings— could be addressed by a policy of physically dissociating the classes, a policy Japanese historians call *heinō bunri* ("warrior-peasant separation"). During the sixteenth century, lords began to oblige their vassals to take up residence in close proximity to a castle that served as the lord's headquarters. This requirement allowed for closer supervision of the retainer band and reduced pressure on the peasants, who had hitherto been subject to the direct control of samurai village officials. Hideyoshi, who enjoyed national hegemony from 1582 to 1598, applied this policy on a national level beginning in 1591. He forbade peasants to own swords, making this weapon the badge of samurai status. All samurai (with the exception of those in a few domains) were to leave the villages or, in giving up their weapons, forfeit samurai status.

The warrior-peasant separation policy was also pursued by the Tokugawa regime after 1600.[3] Though it took decades to fully implement, it rapidly transformed the structure of Japanese society. Perhaps a million samurai (warriors including their families) came to reside in castle-towns.[4] This period of urban expansion has few parallels in world history.[5] In the mid-sixteenth century, only a handful of cities (including Kyoto and the port of Sakai) could

a. *chōnin*, lit. "townspeople" but connoting house-owning merchants or artisans

boast populations of over 50,000; by 1700, Edo had over a million residents, Kyoto and Osaka both numbered nearly 400,000 souls, Kanazawa and Nagoya both approached 100,000, and Sendai, Okayama, Kagoshima, Hiroshima, and Nagasaki each supported around 60,000.[6]

In most of these towns, the samurai constituted about half the population.[7] The implementation of the warrior-peasant separation policy required the labor of countless commoners[b]—initially (and paradoxically), for the most part, peasants who had migrated from the countryside to the town. Often they did so illegally, but the shogunate or local lords subject to the shogun were forced to rely upon such migrants in the construction and provisioning of the castle-towns. The samurai confined to such towns constituted a vast market, which inevitably came to support a large class of merchants, artisans, peddlers, construction workers, domestic servants, palanquin bearers, packhorsemen, entertainment workers, and other participants in an increasingly monetary, incipient-capitalistic economy.

The emergence of a vigorous bourgeois society, an unintended result of the separation policy, confronted feudal authorities with a range of new administrative and ideological problems. In theory, the samurai (from the shogun and daimyo down to the foot soldier) continued to constitute the ruling class. Supported by stipends (surpluses derived from the peasants as tax), men of samurai status staffed the shogunal and domainal administrations. By law, they could punish any commoner (non-samurai) for virtually any real or imagined impudence without consequence.

Tokugawa authorities, adopting Chinese neo-Confucian thought, conceived of society as a collection of hierarchically organized classes. The samurai, natural leaders of society, made up the highest class, monopolizing all positions of significant political authority. The peasants, whose labors fed and supported the samurai, came next in order, followed by artisans, who produced useful articles (though none so essential as food). At the bottom were the

---

b. *machikata*—a more inclusive term than *chōnin*, embracing propertyless workers as well as wealthy merchants

merchants, conceptualized as base persons whose only motive was to buy goods cheaply in order to sell them dear. These various classes were subject to different administrative systems, law codes, and systems of registration.

The regime attempted through elaborate sumptuary rules to enforce the dictum, *"Mi no hodo o shire!* (Know your place!)." Nevertheless, a wealthy merchant stratum appeared, and many samurai fell into poverty. A long era of peace (1639–1864) produced a decline in martial values and culture; the characteristic literary and artistic forms of this period—haiku poetry, kabuki drama, woodblock prints of the "floating world"—catered more to the tastes of the urban commoner class than those of the warrior elite. Commoners also created a new, bourgeois *nanshoku* tradition.

Men and women who migrated to the castle-towns during their formative decades may or may not have left villages where *nanshoku* was widely practiced or tolerated. But they would soon have learned, through exposure to samurai behavior, that the "natural leaders" of society were much given to homosexual behavior. And some commoners, in constructing their own homosexual tradition, sought legitimacy by emphasizing the samurai-*nanshoku* link.

"Nanshoku," according to the *Nanshoku yamaji no tsuyu* (Dew on the mountain path of *nanshoku*, 1730), "is the flower of the military class."[c8] The popular writer Ejima Kiseki (1667–1736) added, *"Nanshoku* is the pastime of the samurai. How could it be harmful to good government?"[9] Similarly, a character in the early seventeenth century *Denbu monogatari* (Tale of a boor) argues that "it is precisely because *jakudō* is so refined that the daimyo from great families, and priests of high rank and office, usually favor this way."[10]

Although the regime attempted to freeze class distinctions and regulate the minutiae of its subjects' lives, it made little effort to police individuals' sex lives. It tolerated male and female prostitution on a wide scale. Commoners interested in having sex with boys would have had few moral qualms about engaging in sexual

c. *Nanshoku wa bumon no hana*

activities associated with society's leaders, and they would have had ample opportunity to patronize male brothels in many castle-towns.

The demographics of these towns may have encouraged males to turn to one another for sexual pleasure. Samurai status was inherited from fathers by sons and daughters alike, but because the great majority of samurai were male, and because the cities required vast legions of (male) construction and transport workers, urban sex ratios (number of males per 100 females) were often very high. The sex ratio among urban commoners alone (the registered population, excluding samurai, clergy, and outcastes) often ranged from 110 to 140; in Edo (the most extreme case), it was 174 (340,277 males to 196,103 females) in 1733.[11] Samurai and commoner men alike lived in circumstances particularly lacking in opportunities for female companionship.

The stage was set for the emergence of one of the most extraordinary urban traditions of homosexuality in world history.

Much has been written about the relationship between urban growth and homosexuality. John Boswell, for example, has linked the "dissolution of urban society" of ancient Rome with the "steady restriction of sexual freedom" of the medieval period; he attributes the "reemergence of a distinct gay subculture in southern Europe" between the tenth and fourteenth centuries to the revival of major urban centers, which "consciously developed an atmosphere of liberty and tolerance."[12] His argument assumes that in agricultural society, limited cultural exposure promotes intolerance for minority groups such as homosexuals, and the mandate to marry and produce children discourages a "gay subculture." The more variegated atmosphere of the town permits its revival.

Boswell's view has been challenged on a number of grounds, including his assumption that a given society consists of a clearly defined heterosexual majority and a homosexual minority that receives more or less tolerance depending upon such factors as urbanization. Some have questioned his association of the city with homosexuality, pointing to the evidence of open homosexuality in nonurban societies or stressing that the most serious persecutions of men accused of homosexual behavior took place in such cities as Seville and Amsterdam.[13] Even critics of Boswell's view, however, have linked homosexual behavior to the privacy and anonymity afforded by urban life.[14] If we suppose that a given percentage of men in any society are sufficiently interested in homosexual contact to actively seek out sexual partners, it would seem to follow that the larger the population center, the greater would be the chance that such men will come to constitute a critical mass, producing a homosexual subculture such as we find in eighteenth-century London, Paris, or Amsterdam.[15]

Boswell's view seems inapplicable to the Japanese case, however. We know little about homosexuality in Tokugawa villages (where over 85 percent of the population lived), but there are numerous literary examples in which rural commoners patronize male prostitutes, either on sojourns to urban pleasure districts or as customers of traveling boy-actors.[16] By the end of the seventeenth century, male brothels could be found not only in the cities but also in large villages, post stations, and small temple-towns. It is not clear that agricultural villages displayed any less tolerance for *nanshoku* than did the great cities. Tokugawa cities, moreover, were very different from the urban centers of early modern Europe. Urban governance was handled not by guild councils but by a samurai bureaucracy; the cities were under tight feudal control and produced no sentiments of the *"Stadtlüft macht Frei"* variety. As milieux of sexual activity, urban centers naturally provided opportunities unavailable in rural society, and this variety may have helped alter attitudes. But there seems to have been no homophobia, rural-based or otherwise, that one could escape in liberating urban air.

Whereas church authorities in European cities sponsored or collaborated with pogroms against "sodomists," the Buddhist clergy of Japan lent moral legitimacy to *nanshoku*. In Europe, the rising bourgeoisie contemptuously linked homosexuality to ab-

solutism and aristocratic depravity; in Japan, the *chōnin* (bourgeoisie) eagerly accepted and engaged in "the pastime of the
samurai."[17] Even in the most tolerant of European cities, homosexual subcultures emerged shaped by the need for secrecy and
stealth. Homosexual networks existed from least the fifteenth century: in pickup streets, safe fields, parks, walks, even dark corners
of cathedrals, men cruised furtively for sexual partners. Molly-
houses provided more secure sites for homosexual contact.[18] In
Tokugawa Japan, however, such venues for discreet, anonymous
homosexual contact were unnecessary. Men made passes at boys
quite openly.[19] The public baths, where physical contact between
males was routine, afforded a particularly convenient site for such
activity.[20] *Sansuke*, male bathhouse attendants employed to scrub
bathers' backs, may have been available as prostitutes, just as were
their female counterparts.[d][21]

Perhaps the nature of urban life allowed some men who would
otherwise have married for economic and social reasons to remain
single, but there seems to have been little relationship between
marriage and homosexual involvements; as I will demonstrate in
Chapter 3, a buoyant bisexuality seems to have been the norm
among the townsmen.

These crucial differences between early-modern Europe and Japan
help to explain why the simultaneous growth of capitalism in the
two civilizations had such different effects. The rise of market
economies in Europe meant the political advancement of the
bourgeoisie and intensification of homosexual persecution in the
interests of the bourgeois family.[22] But the earliest stages of Japanese capitalism evolved under firm feudal (samurai) rule.[23] The
homosexual ethos of the battle camp remained strong within the
ruling class, and the commoner class, always firmly under feudal
control, was inclined to accept and adopt, rather than to reject or
condemn, ruling-class practices. Bourgeois critics of the aristoc-
racy in Europe during the Enlightenment contemptuously associated the latter with "sodomy" and "effeminacy" and used this pu-

d. *yuna*

tative link to discredit the political order.[24] But townspeople in Tokugawa Japan tended to regard samurai *nanshoku* as a legitimate, even admirable institution.

In developing their own homosexual tradition, however, commoner men did not typically reproduce the "brotherhood bonds" characteristic of the samurai. *Nanshoku* for them tended to mean the patronage of male prostitutes or the informal exploitation of vulnerable young males to whom the older partner owed no long-term commitment. By the early seventeenth century, *chōnin* entrepreneurs (including derogated samurai) were establishing some of the most extensive and elegant urban pleasure districts[e] ever known. For a price, one could spend several hours with a male or female partner without troubling oneself with long-term emotional commitments.

This was a rather novel development. Prostitution may be the world's oldest profession, but in Japan wide-scale, well-organized, *licensed* prostitution dates only from Toyotomi Hideyoshi's rule (1582–1598) or perhaps a bit earlier.[25] A money-based economy only came to flourish nationally in the Tokugawa period. Organized, large-scale *male* prostitution also dates from the late sixteenth century, although some male entertainers had long supplemented their earnings through commercial sex. Noh actors may have served theater patrons as catamites, and such entertainers as *hōka* and *kōwakamai* (street performers, including jugglers and acrobats) traditionally pursued this sideline.[26] Kitamura Nobuyo's *Kiyū shōran* (An amusing miscellany for your perusal, 1830) notes that "from ancient times, there were many *dengaku* actors, and later, *sarugaku* actors, who engaged in *nanshoku*."[27] Perhaps those referred to as "prostitute boys"[f] (as opposed to dancers, actors, and so forth) were retained by ranking samurai as early as the 1560s. The early Tokugawa text *Zoku buke kandan* (Idle tales of military families, continued) refers to two such boys belonging to the daimyo of Kai, who, during a battle with Oda Nobunaga, sent them away to safety. It notes that these "prosti-

---

e. *akusho* (lit. "bad places")
f. *shōō*

tute boys" of yesteryear were like "today's kabuki boys."[28] The *Inu makura* (Dog pillow), probably written around 1600 by Hata Soen (1550–1607), also contains references to male prostitutes.[g][29]

The commercialization of *nanshoku* greatly accelerated during the early Tokugawa period. The expansion of the market and the rise of the bourgeoisie (as an economic, although not political, force) produced both a vast labor market of male and female "sex workers" and a large demand for their services. Just as the Tokugawa period saw a transformation in the nature of class relations (from systems in which labor-power is exploited through the corvee, or lifetime, hereditary service, to forms resembling modern wage-labor), so it witnessed a *commodification* not only of heterosexual pleasure but of homosexual pleasure as well.[30]

Reflecting the emergence of new, proto-capitalistic class relations, this commodification of labor power impacted feudal samurai society in various ways.[31] The emergence of institutionalized, licensed prostitution may have weakened the samurai tradition of "brotherhood bonds"; from the seventeenth century it may have become more convenient for members of the military class to purchase sex from males or females without bothering with vows or contracts. It was said that the best customers of Edo's male brothels[h] were the retainers of the Shimazu daimyo of Satsuma.[32] Pleasure-quarter capitalists eagerly met the samurai demand for *nanshoku* prostitution, and these warrior patrons were soon joined by commoners keen to display their wealth and to indulge in a form of pleasure more typically associated with their "betters."[33]

Prostitution became closely associated with the kabuki drama, flourishing in city wards with or near kabuki theaters. It also took place in shrine precincts or on property near Shinto shrines owned by the priests.[34] In the great city of Edo, the wards of Daichi, Fukiya-chō, Kanda Hanabusachō, Kobiki-chō, Kōjimachi Tenjin, Negichō, Nihonbashi, Nuri Busshi, Sakai-chō, Shiba, Shinmei-chō, Shinmichi Nana-kenchō, Yoshichō, and Yushima Tenjin

g. *subari wakashū*
h. *kagema chaya*

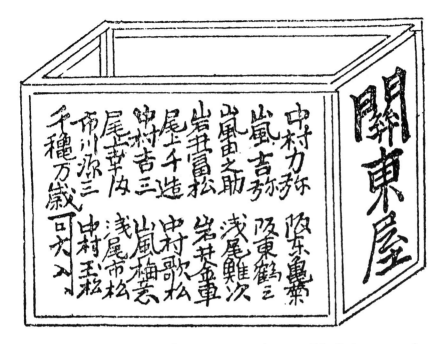

Fig. 6. Lantern sign outside the Kantō-ya, a teahouse in Edo, listing names of the male prostitutes employed. From a Tokugawa-period guidebook. Source: Uemura Yukiaki, *Nihon yūri shi* (Tokyo: Shunyōdō, 1929), p. 332.

featured *nanshoku* teahouses.[i] Ōe, Sakachō, and Dōtōnbori in Osaka and Shijō, Gienchō, and Miyagawachō in Kyoto provided the same services (Figure 6).[35]

Male prostitution was not only found in the "Three Cities."[j] Other large cities such as Nagoya, Sendai, Hiroshima, Sunpu (Fuchū), and Wakamatsu boasted teahouses in which patrons met actor-prostitutes, and male-male sex was for sale in over a dozen towns and post-stations in eighteen provinces from Mutsu to Aki.[36] Male prostitution particularly flourished in Kii and Sanuki provinces, home to large monastic communities. *Nanshoku* teahouses also operated in many small but well-trafficked towns. Up until the mid-eighteenth century, the small temple-town of

i. *nanshoku jaya*
j. *santō*: Edo, Kyoto, and Osaka

Seikenji, which lay near the Okitsu stop on the Tōkaidō highway, was famous for two attractions—medicinal plaster and boy-prostitutes. Engelbert Kaempfer, passing through the town with the Dutch mission in the 1690s, described the relationship between these two:

> On the chief street of this town were built nine or ten neat houses, or booths, before each of which sate one, two, or three young boys, of ten or twelve years of age, well dress'd, with their faces painted, and feminine gestures, kept by their lew'd and cruel masters for the secret pleasure and entertainment of rich travelers, the Japanese being very much addicted to this vice. However, to save the outward appearances, and lest the virtuous should be scandaliz'd, or the ignorant and poor presume to engage with them, they sit there, as it were, to sell the aforesaid plaister to travelors.[37]

Such wayside prostitution (like unlicensed female prostitution) was not officially approved; the hawking of medicinal plaster provided the boys with a convenient front. But many shogunate officials were probably inclined to overlook the infraction. Kaempfer expresses surprise that the commissioner[k] escorting the mission in its travels—normally a model of dignified impassivity—could scarcely contain his excitement at the sight of these boys and detained the whole procession half an hour as he enjoyed one's company.

Seikenji boy-prostitutes appear in fiction as well. The noh drama *Miidera* depicts a mother desperately searching for her son, a Seikenji boy-prostitute, who has been kidnaped by a priest of Miidera Temple, and a tale by Ihara Saikaku (1641–1693) describes how a samurai's orphaned son is forced to sell his body in the temple-town from age nine to fourteen.[38] A humorous travel tale of the 1780s, Hirajitsu Tōsaku's *Nikokuren pekidan*, depicts a master and servant sampling male brothels in Seikenji, but the trade seems to have subsequently declined. Meanwhile, the small castle-town of Shirakawa in Iwaki (southern Mutsu), frequented by samurai cavalcades en route to duties in Edo, was acquiring a reputation for its "call-boys."[l][39]

k. *bugyō*
l. *deyarō*

In his masterpiece, *Kōshoku ichidai otoko* (The life of an amorous man, 1682), Saikaku also wrote of a brothel featuring *tobiko* ("flying boys," or itinerant boy-prostitutes) in the village of Niōdō, near the ancient capital of Nara (Figure 7). Here the hero, Yonosuke, meets a youth who has been selling his body since childhood. After enjoying his services, Yonosuke asks him to recount the tale of his perambulations. The young man's story provides a list of male prostitution hot spots and reveals something of the instability of the lives of such boys. The boy began in Kyoto, working as a female-role actor on the stage while doubling as a prostitute, and later lived in Miyajima (Aki province) with a theater patron. After an interval serving as a daimyo's boy in Bitchū province, he found himself homeless, soliciting priestly customers at Konpira Shrine in Sanuki. He then plied his trade in the Anryū pleasure quarter in Sumiyoshi, between Osaka and Sakai; in the Kashiwara licensed quarters in Kōchi, Tosa province; and finally in Niōdō in Yamato province. At age twenty-four, he looks forward to the imminent expiration of his current contract.[40]

The organization of commercialized *nanshoku* varied from ward to ward and from city to city. In some Edo wards, men seeking male prostitutes patronized a standard "teahouse," or *chaya*, and asked the management to call in a boy-prostitute[m] rather than one of the resident female prostitutes.[41] In Edo's Yoshichō ward, teahouses were scattered among *kodomo-ya* ("children's shops") and the homes[n] of successful kabuki actors. Usually these boys were—at least in theory—apprentice kabuki performers living with wealthy actors and part-timing as prostitutes to help pay for their upkeep. Some were in fact full-time prostitutes. This form of organization resembles that of Beijing actor-prostitutes in the Qing period.[42]

Other teahouses, specializing in male prostitution, either housed actors in the building or called them in at customers' re-

---

m. *kagema*, or in Kyoto and Osaka, *wakashū*
n. *okiya*

Fig. 7. The rake Yonosuke, in Ihara Saikaku's *Kōshoku ichidai otoko* (1682), hurries into *nanshoku* teahouse near Nara. Illustration by Hishikawa Moronobu. Source: Teruoka Yasutaka and Asō Isoji, eds., *Ihara Saikaku shū* (Tokyo: Shōgakukan, 1971), vol. 1, p. 126.

quest; by the latter half of the period, all such teahouses in Edo maintained their own male prostitutes. In Osaka and Kyoto there were never any specifically homosexual teahouses, but customers could summon actors to "courtesans' teahouses."[o][43]

The pleasure quarters of the largest cities supported hundreds of male prostitutes. Yoshichō by itself employed over one hundred in the mid-eighteenth century; in the whole city, estimates Koike Togorō, there were six hundred boy-prostitutes alone.[44] A guide-book by Hiraga Gennai entitled *San no asa* (Three mornings, 1768) examined male prostitution in various locations and gave the following numbers for the male prostitutes in the Three Cities:[45]

Edo:

Yoshichō	67
Sakai-chō and Fukiya-chō	49
Yushima Tenjin	42
Shiba Shinmei-chō	26
Kōjimachi Tenjin-mae	19
Hatchōbori Daichi	11
Eimachi	10
Kobiki-chō	7
Ichigatani Hachiman-mae	7
TOTAL	232
Kyoto (Miyakawa-chō)	85
Osaka (Dōtōnbori)	49

No doubt this survey, enumerating fewer than four hundred male prostitutes, reveals only the tip of the iceberg.

The services of these prostitutes were rather expensive. Fees were set according to the prostitute's rank; just as there was what Ivan Morris termed a "hierarchy of courtesans," so there was a pecking order among the courtesans' male counterparts.[46] Saika-ku's works suggest that during the 1680s the most elegant male

o. *yūjo jaya*

prostitutes could command higher fees than could females. An ordinary actor-prostitute could be contracted in Kyoto for 43 *monme* of silver (in contemporary U.S. currency, roughly $32), and one of particular charm could fetch several times this amount.[47] A modern writer declares, "The Kyotoites, usually tightwads about everything, are said to have paid male prostitutes[p] 129 *monme* for one night of sex. This shows how deeply this period was overwhelmed by *nanshoku*."[48] At this time the highest-ranking courtesan[q] in Kyoto's Shimabara pleasure district charged only 58 *monme*, and a tryst with a common teahouse prostitute cost no more than 5 *monme*.[49]

By 1768, according to the *San no asa*, a three-hour session with a *kagema* (cross-dressing male prostitute) at a Yoshichō teahouse would cost, depending on the time of day and the quality of the boy, from 1 to 2.2 *ryō* in gold, the equivalent of 60 to 132 *monme* of silver.[50] Those employed by such houses were elegant imports from Kyoto or Osaka valued for their sophisticated dialect and manners. A comparably refined Yoshiwara *tayū* (courtesan), meanwhile, charged 130 *monme* of silver, and those of the next rank,[r] only 50.[51] At this time, a ranking samurai manservant might be paid the equivalent of 240 *monme* of silver per year; high-class prostitutes of either sex would have been beyond his reach.[52] He may, however, have been able to purchase less refined male prostitutes. *Kagema* at unlicensed teahouses in Hanabusa-chō and Hatchōbori charged fees (the equivalent of 7.5 *monme*, or about $10) comparable to those charged by women in similar teahouses.[53]

This sex industry was, as I have already suggested, closely connected to kabuki. Below, I will discuss the homoerotic atmosphere surrounding that theatrical form in itself; here I will simply elaborate on the intimate connection between the theaters and male prostitution. Kabuki playhouses and *nanshoku* teahouses were often located in the same wards; sometimes the teahouses

p. *yarō-atama*
q. *tayū*
r. *tenjin*

Fig. 8. Teahouse tryst between a young woman and a prostitute-actor. Print by
Katsukawa Shunshō, ca. 1785. Huguette Beres Collection, Paris. Source: Michel
Beurdley et al., eds., *Erotic Art of Japan: The Pillow Poem* (Hong Kong: Leon
Amiel, 1988), p. 256.

were directly connected to the theaters by passageways. Edo's Na-
kajimaya provided theater patrons with private rooms, within the
theater itself, to which they might invite their favorite actors.[54]
Hishikawa Moronobu (d. 1695) and other woodblock print artists
produced many works depicting these dalliances between theater
patrons—both male and female—and the performers (Figure 8).
As Donald Shively has pointed out, many such prints resemble in composition those depicting courtesans; like courtesans,
the kabuki youths sit behind latticed windows performing music
and calling out to passersby, who pause to inspect the available
merchandise.[55]

In kabuki's early years, according to Ihara Saikaku, the supply
of and demand for such youths was such that one could summon

an actor to a teahouse at any time of day and "entertain yourself with him exactly as you pleased."[56] Theater proprietors regarded prostitution the same way noh troupe heads had traditionally seen it—as a way of winning support from wealthy theater patrons. Fees do not seem to have been strictly set, but the proprietors would accept tips and gifts with exaggerated politeness.

But, as Saikaku explained, the rapidly growing cash economy radically altered the whole experience. In 1687 he wrote that actors were only available in the evening hours, that reservations had to be made days in advance for the more popular youths, and that patrons had to tip the actor's *attendants* many times what the tryst itself used to cost. The attendants did not even smile to indicate their thanks. Moreover, "[i]f you should delay slightly in paying your bill, you may find the long autumn night interrupted about ten o'clock by pounding on the door. 'He's got to appear on stage tomorrow. It is time he came home.' What a depressing thing to hear in the middle of love-making."[57] A Genroku-era (1688–1704) picture-scroll entitled *Kiku asobi* (Chrysanthemum play) depicts an even more abrupt disruption (Figure 9). Here a female attendant has entered the room where a customer lies with a boy-prostitute. Holding a burning incense stick—signifying that the tryst time is up—she gently pats the preoccupied gentleman on his back.[58]

By the late seventeenth century, the developing money economy had removed much of the romance and reduced the charm of sex with kabuki youths—at least in the opinion of writers such as Saikaku. Although the pleasure quarters allowed men of all classes more opportunities for homosexual sex, with more attractive partners, than ever before, such *nanshoku* was a radically different experience from the idealized relationships between monks and their acolytes or between samurai and their pages.

Most of our information about male prostitution comes from Edo, which boasted far more male teahouses than the other great cities. Yoshichō was the ward best known for such establishments, which appear to have reached their peak of prosperity half a century after Saikaku's death—specifically, from the Enkyō era, which began in 1744, to the Hōreki period, which ended in 1764. The

Fig. 9. Interrupted tryst with a male prostitute. The maid informs the brothel patron that his time is up. Unknown Hishikawa-school artist, Genroku period (1688–1704). Source: Fukuda Kazuhiko, *Nikuhitsu fūzoku emaki* (Tokyo: Kawade shobō), pp. 59–60.

teahouses are described in numerous guidebooks principally dealing with female prostitution.[59] Two guidebooks by the famous scholar Hiraga Gennai deal exclusively with male prostitution in Edo: *San no asa* and *Kiku no en* (Chrysanthemum garden, 1764).[60]

Such works, along with Saikaku's writings and other sources, give us an idea of the clientele as well. Some houses were frequented principally by Buddhist priests.[61] Wrote a diarist in the 1770s, "Buddhist priests wilt around male prostitutes."[62] It was said, "The one thing the Eight Buddhist Sects agree upon is the [fun to be had at] male brothels."[s 63] Samurai—their two swords visible in the background—also appear with male prostitutes in erotic art (Figure 10); they unquestionably constituted a large proportion of the patrons.

s. *Hasshū e kuchi o awaseru kagema jaya*

Fig. 10. Samurai with a female-role actor-prostitute. Utagawa school (early nineteenth century). Source: Charles Grosbois, *Shunga: images du printemps: essai sur les représentations érotiques dans l'art japonais* (Geneva: Nagel, 1964), p. 124.

Men of all walks of life patronized *nanshoku* teahouses. Literary sources refer to peasants, packhorse drivers, river forders, woodcutters, and fishermen.[64] Humorous anecdotes[t] of the period also depict peasants and domestic servants as customers in these houses.[65] But during the height of the teahouses' prosperity, perhaps the most typical patron was the foppish young bourgeois rake, dissipating his allowance (or his inheritance) on male and female prostitutes alike.

After the mid-eighteenth century decades of prosperity, the Edo teahouses fell into decline. The Tenmei era (1781–1788) was one of stagnation, and by the Tenpō era (1830–1843) only two houses and ten male prostitutes remained in Yoshichō. An 1833 document complains that compared to the 1750s, the number of male prostitutes in Edo was down by 90 percent. By the end of the period, only four wards (Yushima Tenjin, Yoshichō, Shiba, and Hatchōbori) remained famous for their male prostitutes.[66]

Possibly the decline of the male brothels was related to a general drop in demand for male prostitutes' services. Such a downturn could have resulted from a growth in more casual forms of male prostitution or from a tendency for men to turn to shop boys and other young subordinates for sex. Or it may have reflected a decline in men's sexual interest in youths, a trend related to various social and demographic changes.

Saikaku in the 1680s had declared Edo "a city of bachelors ... not unlike the monasteries of Mt. Kōya."[67] As noted previously, during the 1730s and 1740s there were about 170 males for every 100 females in the city. Good data is unavailable for the years from 1747 to 1832, but it seems clear that during this period the rate of urban-bound migration among peasant women soared.[68] In 1832 there were only 120 males per 100 females, and by 1844 there were only 111 males. In 1867—on the eve of the Meiji Restoration—the ratio finally balanced perfectly at 100:100.[69] These figures exclude the samurai population, which constituted about

t. *kobanashi*

half the urban total. Among the samurai, males always outnumbered females, and in the latter part of the period the marriage
rate among them decreased.[70] But the great increase in the non-
samurai female population in Edo may have served to diminish
men's desire for other males.

On the supply side, city government crackdowns on prostitution took their toll; in each of the three great reform periods (the
Kyōhō Reform, 1716–1735; Kansei Reform, 1787–1793; and
Tenpō Reform, 1841–1843) urban authorities attacked commercial sex, "lewd" art and literature, and extravagance in general.[71]
In 1842 all of Edo's teahouses were closed in the course of Mizuno Tadakuni's reform efforts, and the kabuki theaters of Sakai-
chō, Fukiya-chō, and Kobiki-chō were forced to move to a ward
on the city's outskirts, Saruwaka-chō, in a section of Edo known
as Asakusa.[72] (In Osaka, meanwhile, kabuki-troupe directors
were forbidden to send out boy-actors as prostitutes.)[73] Homosexual prostitution was not the main target of this movement, and,
like most elements in Mizuno's reform package, the ban does not
seem to have been wholly effective.[74] But it forced boy-prostitutes
to ply their trade more discreetly, under the guise of "tailors"[u]
and incense peddlers.[75]

Homosexuality and Bourgeois Culture

The new urban environment of the Tokugawa period, in which
human relations often came to rest ultimately upon a cash nexus,
constituted a "floating world"[v] of commercial sex. This milieu was
celebrated in new artistic forms: *ukiyoe* ("pictures of the floating
world"), *ukiyo-zōshi* ("novels of the floating world"), and the kabuki theater. Such manifestations of bourgeois culture revealed
an obsession with sex in all its variety. Any woodblock-print artist
worthy of the name produced erotic pictures (*shunga*, or "spring

u. *shitate*
v. *Ukiyo*, a term of Buddhist origins, originally connoted the transient material world. During the Tokugawa period it lost many of its religious associations
and came to refer to the fashionable, the up-to-date, and the erotic.

pictures")[w] in response to popular demand; among the better known were Hishikawa Moronobu (d. ca. 1695), Nishikawa Suke-nobu (1671–1751), Miyakawa Chōshun (1682–1753), Okumura Masanobu (1686–1764), Maruyama Okyō (1733–1795), Kitagawa Utamaro (1754–1806), Suzuki Harunobu (1724–1770), Ishikawa Toyonobu (1711–1786), Torii Kiyonaga (1752–1815), Katsushika Hokusai (1760–1849), and Keisei Eisen (1790–1848).[76] The production of such works was a vital part of the training of wood-block-print artists, and one authority suggests that on average one-fifth the oeuvre of such an artist consisted of *shunga* prints. In the case of Sugimura Jihei, it was closer to half the total.[77] Meanwhile, the greatest writers, such as Ihara Saikaku, Ejima Ki-seki, and Chikamatsu Monzaemon, chronicled life in the pleasure quarters, provoking one nineteenth-century Western student of Japanese literature to declare that Tokugawa popular works dealt "only with the most disreputable phases of human existence."[78] In our somewhat more tolerant era, we may find these views quaintly squeamish, but one cannot deny the prevalence of erotic themes, or at least bawdy, scatological humor, in much of the literary output of this era.

In this erotic art and literature, the *nanshoku* theme abounds. Visual depictions range from the subtle (e.g., men kissing or fondling fully clothed boys) to the explicit portrayal of sexual acts. Like other erotic art of the period, the more graphic homosexual-themed pictures are characterized by their detail and physiological realism, and the ribald captions accompanying much of the work suggest a great deal about sexual behavior of the time.[79] Usually the works dealing with *nanshoku* depict teahouse scenes in which samurai, commoners, or monks engage in sex with boy-prostitutes; often the presence of a girl or woman creates a bisexual atmosphere (Figures 11, 12, 13, 14, 16, 17, 19, 22 and 29).

Most erotic paintings and prints show both partners partly clothed; in the homosexual material, the insertee often wears female kimono, sports a female hairstyle and would—but for his

w. Other terms include *makura-e* ("pillow pictures") and *higa* ("hidden pictures").

Fig. 11. *Ménage à trois.* Youthful priest has anal intercourse with a youth copulating with a girl. Anonymous, mid-seventeenth century. Source: Phyllis and Eberhard Kronhausen, *The Complete Book of Erotic Art* (Hong Kong: Bell, 1987), vol. 1, illustration 32.

genitals—be taken for a woman (Figure 10). Indeed, in scholarly works on erotic art published in modern Japan, the censor's mutilation of such illustrations often makes them indistinguishable from prints showing patrons and courtesans.[80] In other prints, the insertee is dressed, coiffured, and apparently appreciated sexually as a young man (Figure 15).

As these erotic prints were reaching a mass audience, literature dealing with male-male sex was also becoming widely available, thanks to the spread of printing technology, the growth of the publishing trade, and (one must suppose) a growing demand for this kind of erotica. The period saw a virtual outpouring of such material, ranging from refined tales of samurai "brothers" to the

Fig. 12. *Ménage à trois*. A sexually excited man withdraws from a woman and prepares to mount a crouching youth. From Hishikawa Moronobu album *Koi no mutsugoto yonjū hachi te* (*Intimate Talks on Forty-Eight Kinds of Love*, 1678). Source: Fukuda Kazuhiko, *Ehon ukiyoe sen* (Tokyo: Kawade shobō, 1990), p. 57.

Fig. 13. Man relaxes with a male prostitute and a maid at a brothel in Kyoto's Miyagawa district. Kyōhō-era (1716–1735) print by Nishikawa Sukenobu. Source: Fukuda Kazuhiko, *Fūzoku ehon ukiyoe* (Tokyo: Kawade shobō, 1991), p. 28.

graphic sexual descriptions found in such works as the *Nanshoku yamaji no tsuyu*.[81] *Nanshoku* publishing history includes some significant firsts. The prototype tale of love-suicide,[x] *Mokuzu monogatari* (Tale of seaweed, 1640), detailed the true, tragic story of three youths involved in a love triangle and foreshadowed a genre that later immortalized *heterosexual* love-suicides.[82] And *Shudō monogatari* (Tales of *shudō*), appearing soon after the Meireki conflagration in Edo in 1657, "was perhaps the first illustrated book aimed at a mass market in Edo."[83]

Iwata Jun'ichi's bibliography includes 106 pre-Tokugawa works, 67 Meiji works (1868–1912), and 567 Tokugawa works, not count-

x. *shinjū*

Fig. 14. Brothel customer with female prostitute and young male companion. The latter is composing a poem included on the sheet of paper in other versions of this print. The poem compares the youth and the courtesan to the two guardian deities who stand on either side of Buddhist temples. Okumura Masanobu (early 1740s). Source: Richard Lane, *Images from the Floating World: The Japanese Print* (New York: G. P. Putnam's Sons, 1978), p. 79.

ing some 100 "actor-critiques."[y] [84] Thus, there are at least two or three extant books dealing substantially with *nanshoku* for each year of the Azuchi-Momoyama and Tokugawa periods, compared with one for every five years of the Kamakura and Muromachi periods. Many, if not most, of the best-known Tokugawa writers seem to have had ample personal experience with homosexuality; Matsuo Bashō, generally regarded as the greatest poet of the period, wrote several haiku on the subject.[85] They clearly reflect his own experience.[86] One is not even surprised to find a record of a well-known literary figure inviting a colleague to an outing at a male brothel.[87]

[y]. *yakusha hyōbanki*

is this titillation, or what? here for [handwritten marginalia]

Fig. 15. "Pardon me if I tear your ass. . . ." Kitagawa Utamaro (1753–1806) print showing a frustrated customer with a male prostitute. Source: Theodore Bowie, "Erotic Aspects of Japanese Art," in Bowie et al., *Studies in Erotic Art* (New York and London: Basic Books, 1970), illustration 95.

One of the first significant Tokugawa works to methodically discuss *nanshoku*, the *Denbu monogatari* (Tale of a boor), was written sometime around 1640. It is the first of a large genre of works referred to as "arguments on the relative merits of men and women."[z] Like similar Greek, Roman, medieval and Arab productions, this literature debates the comparative worth of males and females as men's bed partners.[88]

General reference works on homosexuality were not long in coming. In 1657 an anonymous Buddhist priest published a comprehensive manual of *shudō* entitled *Saiseiki* (Silkworm-hatching), with such chapter headings as the following:[89]

z. *danjo yūretsu ron*

How People Fall in Love; On the Exchange of Glances
How to Answer the First Letter; Favorable and Unfavorable Replies
On Not Talking Too Much; On Expressing Much through Letters
On Taking One's Leave to Return Home in the Morning
On Feeling Disgusted After One Encounter
On Serving as a *Nenja*
When the Feeling Changes
Style of Letters of Gratitude
On Bathing
On Food
On Winecups
Letters of Sympathy for Illness or Misfortune
On Corresponding Through a Messenger
On the Arts
On *Wakashū* Illnesses
On Various Matters of Etiquette
On the Supreme Lover's Sacrifice[aa]
On Rising in the Morning
On Kissing[bb]
On Ceremonial Robes and Pleated Skirts[cc]
On Outer Sashes
On Inner Sashes; On Fans
On Tissue Paper[dd]
On Towels
On Scented Bags[ee]
On Purses
On Bed Etiquette
On Cutting One's Nails
On Etiquette in Dress
On Smells
On Eyes
On Reading and Writing
On Hair; On Nose Hair
On Ears
On Folding Paper

aa. *dai-ichi shinjū no koto*
bb. *kōchū no koto*
cc. *kataginu hakama no koto*
dd. *hanagami no koto* (lit., "on nose-paper")
ee. *nioi fukuro no koto*

This work, with its emphasis upon etiquette (*tashinami*) and attention to the feelings of the *wakashū* (sexually attractive boys), seems to grow out of the ancient traditions of monastic and samurai homosexuality rather than the commercial *nanshoku* of the pleasure quarters.

Thirteen years after the appearance of *Saiseiki*, Kitamura Kigin (1624–1704), renowned scholar, poet, and mentor of Matsuo Bashō, produced his *Iwatsutsuji* (*Rock-Azaeleas*). This compilation of homosexual erotica, first published in 1713 and including stories and poems dating from the ninth century, has been called the first such collection in world literature.[90] Interestingly enough, it appears almost simultaneously with *Duanxiu pian*, the Chinese anthology of historical material on homosexuality mentioned in Chapter 1.

During the decade after 1682, the Osaka novelist Ihara Saikaku—probably the greatest prose writer of the period—produced his major works. Nearly all of these refer at least in passing to *nanshoku*, and in some, notably *Nanshoku ōkagami* (The great mirror of *nanshoku*, 1687), it is the unifying theme.[91] Homosexual relationships are also celebrated in Yamamoto Jōchō's *Hagakure* (Hidden by leaves), published by a disciple in 1716.[92] Ejima Kiseki's *Keisei kintanki* (Courtesans forbidden to lose their tempers, 1711) and Hiraga Gennai's *Nenashigusa kōhen* (*Nenashigusa*, volume two, 1768) carry on the *nanshoku* versus *joshoku* theme.[93]

Hiraga (1726–1779) was a prominent *Rangakusha* (scholar of "Dutch"—i.e., European—learning) and botanist who conducted experiments with asbestos and electricity. He was also one of the most popular writers of the late Tokugawa period and a regular patron of the male brothels referred to as *kodomo-ya*. His friend, the leading scholar Ōta Nanpo, recorded that "when [Gennai] had money, he hurried to spend it in Yoshichō on the pleasure-boys.[ff] There he would spend days at a time, and that is why he glorified *nanshoku* in *Nenashigusa*."[94]

Ōta refers to the first volume of this work, which is worth summarizing as an example of the lighter, satirical *nanshoku* literature

ff. *gandō*

of the period. It begins in hell, where a twenty-year-old novice monk[gg] has just arrived after wasting away for love of the popular actor Segawa Kikunojō. His crimes include squandering his superior's fortune, selling the brocade curtains of his temple's altar, and pawning a precious statue of Amida Buddha—all to finance his trips to Sakai-chō to purchase Kikunojō's favors.

The devils accompanying the hapless monk observe that he has sinned against his superior. They note, however, that nowadays the clergy patronize courtesans and ignore the monastic dietary rules, "so this monk's passion for actors seems a comparatively minor sin."[hh][95] They suggest a slight reduction in the youth's punishment. However, Enma, the king of hell, will not be persuaded to apply lenient treatment. "His sin," he declares, "may seem minor, but it is not." He lists the evil effects of homosexual passion, ranging from hemorrhoids to political rebellion, and orders that henceforth *nanshoku* is to be strictly forbidden.

Another deity of the netherworld politely suggests that *nanshoku*, though not harmless, is not nearly as dangerous as lust for women. Noting that even in death the monk has brought with him a portrait of Kikunojō by the painter Torii Kiyonobu, he suggests that the assembled gods and devils have a look at the famous performer. Enma reluctantly agrees that the portrait be shown but declines to examine it himself "since I hate looking at *wakashū*."[96] But when the beauty of the revealed portrait elicits gasps of admiration from all present, Enma cannot help but open his eyes. He immediately falls in love with the image and, in his excitement, tumbles down from his throne.

The king of hell at once declares his determination to leave the netherworld for Japan, where he will seek out the actor and "share his pillow." Only with difficulty can the others dissuade him from this plan; instead, they persuade him to procure the actor through the services of the Dragon King, who will arrange Kikunojō's death by drowning. Satisfied, Enma lifts his ban on *nanshoku* and releases the monk from hell.

gg. *bōzu*
hh. *bōzu no yarō-gurui wa sono tsumi karuki ni nitare*

Meanwhile, unaware of all this, Kikunojō and his friend Yaegiri, another female-role actor, plan a boat outing with some companions on the Sumida River. The Dragon King, hearing of this, commissions a water-sprite[ii] to manage the drowning. Water-sprites, according to folklore, can pass through the human anus and are known to be lovers of youths.[jj] [97] On the appointed day, Kikunojō and his friend rent a boat and row out onto the Sumida River, drinking sake and composing poetry. When someone suggests that they hunt for clams on a sand bar, Kikunojō remains in the boat to complete a poem. The water-sprite, disguised as a handsome, twenty-five-year-old samurai, floats by in a boat of his own and, through glances and fragments of exchanged poetry, easily wins an invitation to board the actor's boat. Soon Kikunojō has fallen deeply in love with the stranger, and the two make love in the moonlight.

At length, however, the "samurai" breaks into tears. He has, despite his mission, become thoroughly smitten with Kikunojō and is now unable to execute the mission given him by the Dragon King. He confesses all and declares his willingness to die rather than drag the actor into hell. Kikunojō, however, refuses to allow his strange lover to die in his place and attempts to throw himself into the river. The water-sprite prevents him, and, as the two wrestle, Yaegiri reappears. Having overheard everything, he offers, out of love for Kikunojō, to drown in the latter's place. Before he can be restrained, he disappears over the side of the boat. The water-sprite also vanishes, and the other friends return to the boat and escort the forlorn Kikunojō home, but the final illustration of the book shows the water-sprite, having returned to his original grotesque form, looming over the water in the distance (Figure 16).[98] In the next volume we learn that Enma, displeased with the sprite and the lesser prize of Yaegiri, condemns the former to haunt the human world, possessing the bodies of young men and arousing homosexual passions within them.[99]

Three thousand copies of this work were sold within a year of its publication; it was, for the time, a remarkably popular novel.[100] It also seems fairly representative of *nanshoku*-themed

ii. *kappa*
jj. *wakashū-zuki*

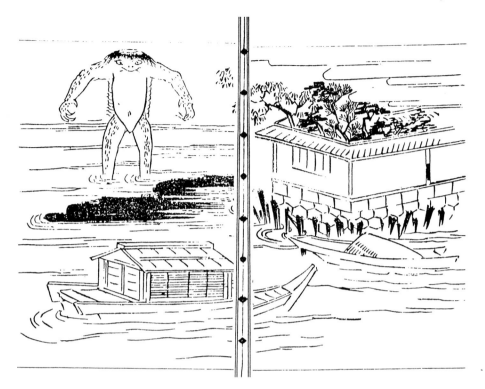

Fig. 16. The water-sprite (*kappa*). Passionately fond of young men, he penetrates them through the anus and inflames them with homosexual desires. From Hiraga Gennai's novel *Nenashigusa* (1763). Source: Hiraga Gennai, *Hiraga Gennai shū*, ed. Miura Satoshi (Tokyo: 1971), pp. 206–207.

fiction. Other works also include satirical arguments against homosexuality, and associate it with holy men and divine beings. Violence appears as a natural concomitant of *nanshoku* in Saikaku's *Nanshoku ōkagami*, Yamamoto Jōchō's *Hagakure*, the anonymous *Denbu monogatari*, Ueda Akinari's *Ugetsu monogatari*, Takizawa Bakin's *Kinsei bishōnen roku* (Record of beautiful youths in the modern age, 1829–1842), and elsewhere.[101] As in *Nenashigusa*, actors based upon real-life people are prominent characters in the writings of Saikaku and Kiseki.

As noted in Chapter 1, actors and entertainers in China and Korea were closely associated with prostitution. Perhaps such a connection was once universal; in Shakespeare's England, too, boy-actors were alleged to "play the Sodomite."[102] What seems to distinguish the Japanese case is that the government's regulation of the kabuki theater indirectly strengthened the association between actors and male prostitution.

The origins of kabuki have been described by many Western scholars, so I will provide only a brief sketch here.[103] As a dance-drama form, it probably dates to the 1603 performances of one Okuni, a former shrine priestess, in Kyoto. Because Okuni's troupe consisted primarily of female performers, her art was referred to as "women's kabuki,"[kk] but she was often joined by male performers. As often as not males would play female roles and vice-versa, causing quite a sensation. Among Okuni's most popular skits was one in which, dressed as a handsome man, she trysted with a prostitute (also played by a woman) in a teahouse.[104]

Because the performers engaged in prostitution, it was perhaps inevitable that quarrels over them should lead to violence and hence to shogunate regulation. Okuni was banned from performing at Ieyasu's camp at Suruga in 1608. From 1612 or earlier, Okuni's kabuki was rivaled by a theatrical form called *wakashū* ("youths'") kabuki. The companies consisted entirely of young men and boys playing both male and female roles. This was not new, of course; there had been no actresses in noh, either, although in the latter the erotic element was muted. In "youths' kabuki," eroticism took center stage. Many early performances dealt with homosexual themes. By this time the word *wakashū*, originally designating a male no longer a child[ll] but not yet a full-grown man,[mm] had come to suggest an adolescent who excites a man's sexual interest.[105]

By 1617, both women's and youths' kabuki had been introduced to the shogun's capital, Edo. A series of violent incidents, however, led the regime to ban women's kabuki in 1629. The prohibition had to be repeated in 1630, 1640, 1645, and 1646, indi-

kk. *onna kabuki*
ll. *kodomo*
mm. *yarō*

cating that the ban was not entirely effective; eventually, however, the stage in all but a few rural areas was left to all-male performances. Thus, just as actresses were first beginning to appear on the stage in England, France, and Germany, they were being removed from the Japanese theater.[106]

The authorities did not stop at banning actresses. Female impersonation was also banned in 1642 on the grounds that too much blood had been spilled in rivalries over the young female-role actors.[107] "Men," ordered an Edo city commissioner, "must not imitate women and behave seductively."[108] The all-male troupes, at least for the time being, could present only all-male plots. Small wonder that *nanshoku*-themed plays constituted a major part of the repertory. Tominaga Heibei's *Kei kagami* (Mirror for actors, early eighteenth century), notes, "In the plays[nn] of former times the theme of *shudō* often occurred. Principal actors playing young men often received larger salaries than those playing women. At that time, *shudō* was all the rage in all the quarters of the town."[109] The fact that *wakashū* performers' wages were higher than those of other actors suggests that audiences found youths' kabuki particularly fascinating.

The plot of one such play, entitled *Ujigami mōde* (A visit to the family shrine), may seem banal to modern audiences but is of some historical interest in indicating audience tastes. A daimyo, leading a large procession, visits his family shrine. Roguish onlookers drool over his handsome pages but are frightened off by the lord's attendants. Attention shifts to the lord's young bed partner, who learns to his chagrin that a rival page has replaced him in the master's affections.

The daimyo, having retired to a room within the shrine, calls the jilted page, planning to have him summon the catamite who has eclipsed him. The page, however, stomps off in anger, as do all the other members of the party when called by the daimyo. He is left alone with his horse, wondering why his whole staff has suddenly become so hostile.[110] The play affirms that sexual relationships between high-ranking samurai and their manservants

nn. *kyōgen*

were common and implies that even a daimyo was expected to observe certain basic rules of etiquette within such relationships. Its humor (reminiscent of Muromachi comic drama) lies in the depiction of a household thrown into utter disorder because of the injured feelings of a mere pageboy.

Audiences, like the rogues depicted in this play, drooled over the beautiful youths. Predictably, the young actors were blamed for provoking the same kind of violent incidents that had earlier been associated with actresses and female-role actors. The shogunate thus lashed out at them as well, banning them from the stage. However, cooler heads prevailed, and the prohibition against cross-dressing actors was reconsidered. The latter were allowed to return to the theater in 1644, and in 1652 the youthful male-role actors were allowed back as well. Henceforth, however, the players of adult male, female, and youth roles alike were obliged to adopt the standard male hairstyle of the time, with the forelocks shaven back to the crown of the head. Thus, all actors, regardless of their age or dramatic specialty, had to appear either as adult males or as a curious hybrid.[111] The new dramatic form, called "adult men's kabuki,"[oo] has endured to the present day.

Although the theme of *shudō* grew less important in the kabuki repertoire, it by no means disappeared. Mature dramas with significant *nanshoku* subplots include Chikamatsu Monzaemon's *Mannengusa shinjū* (Stonecrop love-suicide, 1708), *Oman Gengobei Satsuma uta* (The Satsuma song of Oman and Gengobei), and *Shinjū yoi no kōjin* (Love-suicide on vigil night, 1721). Nanboku Tsuruya's dramas *Sakura hime azuma bunshō* (Eastern documents of the cherry-blossom princess, 1817), *Chigogafuchi hana no shiranami* (White waves of the flowers of Chigogafuchi, 1817), and *Asakusa reigenki* (Account of the Asakusa miracle, 1829) also depict male-male sexual relationships.

This brief survey of the homoerotic content of popular culture suggests that *nanshoku* enjoyed a high level of "social tolerance"

oo. *yarō kabuki*

in Tokugawa urban society. "Tolerance," as employed by John Boswell, implies "public acceptance of personal variation or idiosyncrasy in matters of appearance, personality or belief."[112] But it does not necessarily connote general *approval*; indeed, as I have shown, *nanshoku* provoked ambivalent feelings in some. In the following chapters I will examine the structure of typical male-male relationships and the attitudes toward them reflected in popular literature, philosophical texts, laws, and medical writings.

Chapter Three

Tokugawa
Homosexual Culture

The Way of Men, the Way of Women—there's no difference.

> The monk Gengobei, in Ihara
> Saikaku's *Kōshoku gonin onna* (1686)

Those who like female prostitutes dislike youths; those who like youths revile female prostitutes.

> Hiraga Gennai, *San no asa* (1768)

The homosexual tradition of Tokugawa Japan represents a culmination and merger of several traditions—monastic, samurai, bourgeois—encouraged by the emergence of large towns and cities, disproportionately populated by males. Although the intellectual climate featured some anti-sensual trends (in Buddhism) and some pro-family, pro-procreative elements (in Confucianism and Nativism, or Kokugaku), it never produced a strong current of hostility to male-male sex. In the course of Japanese history, broad social, economic, political, and ideological changes shaped *nanshoku* to service elite institutions: the imperial court, the monasteries, feudal hierarchies. In each case, men in positions of power came to desire the youths serving at the base of the respective institution: the boy-attendant at court, the acolyte in the monk's cell, the valet or footboy in the battle camp or samurai mansion.

In the Tokugawa period, as money increasingly mediated human relations, a new locus of power—the merchant class—produced its own objects of desire, whose sexual services could be purchased, for specified periods of time, for cold cash. Relationships with such partners involved no commitments nor any rejection of male-female relationships; the *nanshoku* tradition of

94

Tokugawa Japan was essentially part of a bisexual eros. Its structure mirrored not only male-female relationships but, even more significantly, the relationships between older and younger, superior and inferior, and master and servant stressed in the neo-Confucian tradition.

The Prevalence of Bisexuality

In the overwhelming majority of references to *nanshoku* in Tokugawa Japan, men do not appear to pursue an exclusively homosexual lifestyle. From the daimyo who divided his attentions between pages, mistresses, and wives to the bourgeois rake who shuttled between Yoshiwara courtesans and Yoshichō "pleasure-boys,"[a] Tokugawa men seldom viewed *nanshoku* and *joshoku* ("the way of women") as mutually exclusive categories. The daimyo, complains the heroine of Saikaku's *Kōshoku ichidai onna* (1685), "are busy with their formal duties, and with boy-attendants[b] nearby day and night, they fall in love with them. They also feel a deep affection for their women [such as secondary wives and mistresses], but neglect their [main] wives."[1]

Richard Cocks, director of the English East India Company factory in Hizen in the 1610s, recorded that the local daimyo's brother, Matsuura Nobumasa, was keen on both women "& bogering boyes."[2] Lesser samurai behaved the same way. The author of *Inu makura*, expressing his fastidious tastes in his lists, refers constantly to sex with *wakashū*. But in his catalogue of "Disagreeable Things" he includes "A woman who falls asleep on you after making love."[3] His readers would have found no contradiction in such references. One episode in the kabuki play *Narukami Fudō Kitayama zakura* (Kitayama cherry-blossoms of Narukami and Fudō, 1742), by Tsuuchi Hanjurō, Yasuda Abun, and Nakada Mansuke, nicely illustrates the bisexual tastes expected of the robustly amorous, swashbuckling *rōnin* (masterless samurai). The hero, Danjirō, lingers in an antechamber awaiting an audience with a lord. Retainers of the household come to attend him. First

a. *gandō*
b. *maegami* (lit. "forelocks;" boys before their *genpuku* ceremony)

Hidetarō, a delicate boy of twelve or thirteen, enters to offer him tobacco. A delighted Danjirō compliments him on his beauty and asks about the progress of his martial training. The boy replies that he has been studying archery but has not yet learned to ride a horse.

Danjirō thereupon offers to instruct Hidetarō in horseback riding. When the boy enthusiastically accepts the offer, the stalwart squeezes the boy between his thighs, explaining, "Press tightly against the flanks of your mount, thus." Embracing the boy, he rocks him back and forth suggestively, but when he attempts a kiss, Hidetarō panics and runs off. Danjirō laughs, bows to the audience, and facetiously pronounces his own conduct "shameful."

Next a woman of the house arrives with tea. Danjirō badgers her as well, making several vulgar jokes that play on the slang use of the term "tea" to refer to sex with a prostitute. She, too, abandons him in disgust while he faces the audience and quips, "That's two cups of tea I've been denied!"[4]

Clearly, this samurai hero is equally amenable to having sex with boys or with women. So too, apparently, were many commoners, particularly the young libertines glamorized in much of Tokugawa popular literature. Even characters particularly attracted to other males are often open to heterosexual adventures. In the following *kobanashi* (humorous anecdote), an Osaka man who frequents the male brothels of Sakamachi is persuaded to try women for a change:

> "Hey, you only like male prostitutes, and only go to the Sakamachi [section of Osaka], but why don't you try Shinmachi for a change? You can change your mood there by doing it with a high-class courtesan."
> He was so well persuaded that finally he just had to go to Shinmachi with his friend. So they started out, but on the way they passed by a night-soil man, causing the one who liked boys to remark,
> "Hey, I really think I'd better go to Sakamachi."
> "Why? We're almost there at Shinmachi!"
> "Yes, but with that smell I'm just pining to make love to a boy."[5]

Although the Sakamachi patron never makes it to the courtesan brothel, the anecdote suggests an atmosphere thoroughly conducive to bisexual behavior.

The young rakes in Saikaku's works are generally bisexual. Four wealthy youths in one of his stories

> did nothing but have sex from dawn to dusk. One day they would visit Morokoshi, Hanasaki, Kaoru, and Takahashi in Shimabara. The next day they would make love to Takenaka Kichisaburō, Fujita Kichisaburō, and Mitsuse Sakon in Shijō Kawara. Making no day-and-night distinction between the Way of Youths[c] and the Way of Women,[d] they indulged in various pleasures.[6]

Shimabara featured courtesans, whereas Shijō Kawara was known for its prostitute-kabuki actors.

Saikaku's most memorable character, the Casanova-like merchant Yonosuke (short for Ukiyonosuke), patronizes both male and female brothels. He reaches age fifty-four having dallied with 3,742 women and 725 young men, numbers that probably represent the sexual fantasies of many men of the time.[7] Although Yonosuke's sexual history is of heroic proportions, he is merely a contemporary man-about-town writ large. It is altogether possible that one trip to the *nanshoku* teahouse per five to the courtesan brothel may have been the standard routine of many a wealthy urban rake.

If Yonosuke is basically a hedonist, other Saikaku characters seem to develop genuine emotional ties to members of both sexes. A widower contents himself with a boy after the loss of his beloved wife; a young husband and father dies of love for an actor; and many men lose their wives and children ("whom they still love") because of homosexual infatuations.[8] Much of the *nanshoku*-versus-*joshoku* literary genre is written from the point of view of such men.

Marriage was thus no barrier to homosexual involvements, including those pursued quite openly. A beautiful wife in *Nanshoku ōkagami*, for example, attempts to arrange a tryst between her husband and the actor he loves.[9] "There are some married men who also love boys," notes the author of the *Denbu monogatari*.[10] Even a formal "brotherhood bond" did not necessarily pre-

c. *shudō*
d. *nyōdō*

clude heterosexual involvements. Yamamoto Tsunetomo coun-
seled samurai youths to "avoid following the two ways" simultaneously, but his is a particularly demanding and purist vision of
shudō.[11]

There are many literary examples of men or youths involved in
homosexual affairs who also develop relationships with women. In
Saikaku's Kōshoku gonin onna (Five amorous women, 1685), a
temple acolyte enters into a passionate relationship with a girl.
Having committed a terrible crime, the girl is put to death, and
the boy wishes to follow her to the grave. He is only dissuaded
from doing so by monks who remind him that his "older brother,"
presently away on a journey, would object to his suicide.[12] The
implication is that the "older brother" will forgive his partner's
heterosexual affair, but he might instead respond to such a situation with outrage. In Chikamatsu's Mannengusa shinjū (Stonecrop
love-suicide, 1708), the character Yūben, a Mount Kōya monk, reviles his nineteen-year-old "younger brother," Kumenosuke, for
having an affair with a girl. He had been willing to die for Kumenosuke, Yūben declares, but now he will break off all ties:

> "I misjudged you, you little monster. I never dreamt you had such an
> evil character. What did you mean when you swore the intimacy of
> brothers with me? Have you forgotten ... how I insisted that the
> most important part of a younger brother's[e] behavior was to refrain
> from creating a scandal and bringing disgrace on his brother? ...
> How hateful of you! How unworthy! How degrading!"[13]

The younger partner could also insist upon his lover's constancy.
The Denbu monogatari suggests that "brotherhood contracts"
might specifically prohibit the "older brother" from having relationships with other youths or with women. The very fact that
such clauses were considered necessary indicates that bisexuality
was common but that some "younger brothers" resented sharing
their partners with women.[14]

Literature also provides examples of monks who proceed from
homosexual to heterosexual involvements with little apparent difficulty. In Saikaku's Kōshoku gonin onna, the monk Gengobei,

e. wakashū

who until age twenty-six has had no sexual contact with women
and has devoted himself entirely to *jakudō*, ultimately falls into a
relationship with a young woman. "*Nanshoku, joshoku*—there's
no difference," he happily reflects.[f][15]   *check*

Nanboku Tsuruya's kabuki drama *Eastern Documents of the
Cherry-Blossom Princess*, mentioned in Chapter 1, treats the
question of clerical bisexuality in particularly novel fashion. Here
a priest and his "younger brother" acolyte plan to commit double
suicide. The boy leaps to his death, but the priest, reconsidering
at the last moment, goes on living in his temple. Seventeen years
later, he encounters a woman who, he discovers, is the reincarna-
tion of his former male lover. He finds her attractive and seeks to
seduce her as well, but she repulses his advances and in the process accidentally kills him. Thus, the reincarnated acolyte finds
revenge for the faithlessness of his "older brother."[16]

Erotic art suggests that the bisexual *ménage à trois* was the ultimate sexual fantasy of many Tokugawa men (Figures 11–13, 17–
18, 20). A Hishikawa Moronobu print entitled *Patterns of Flower
and Moon* (Figure 12) shows a sexually excited man with a woman
and youth. He has apparently just withdrawn from the woman;
meanwhile the youth, buttocks bared, positions himself for intercourse. "The one Way isn't so exciting, but there's nothing more
enjoyable than having both kinds of sex!" declares the man.[g] Here
the woman's vagina is the "flower," the youth's bottom the
"moon."[17]

In Figure 17 a samurai divides his attentions between a boy and
a partly clothed girl. Figure 19, by contrast, shows a courtesan apparently irritated by the neglect of the man having sex with a boy-
prostitute in her presence. Sometimes a husband or lover catches
his woman in bed with a youth, then joins them, anally penetrat-
ing one or the other.[18] In Figure 20, however, a man finding his
mistress in bed with a female-role actor masturbates the youth
while having intercourse with the woman. The youth copulating
with a girl while being sexually enjoyed by a monk seems to have

f. *Nanshoku joshoku no hedate wa naki mono*
g. *Hito michi ni tedate ni omoshirokaran ni, ni iro made no tanoshimi wa
nani tomo tatoe ga tarame*

Fig. 17. *Ménage à trois*. Print by Sugimura Jihei (late seventeenth century) showing man having sex with a youth while embracing girl. Philip Rawson, *Erotic Art of the East: The Sexual Theme in Oriental Painting and Sculpture* (London: Weidenfeld and Nicolson, 1973), illustration 224.

been a popular motif; the clergy were often satirized for their supposedly insatiable lusts (Figure 11).[19]

One must not, however, ignore the evidence for the existence of exclusively homosexual men. Such terms as *nanshoku-zuki* (*nanshoku* enthusiast)[h] and "youth fanatic"[i] generally refer to bisexual men like the shogun Tsunayoshi, who, although somewhat more attracted to other males than were most men, also engaged in sex with women. But at times these terms seem to refer to men who

h. synonymous with *wakashū-zuki*, *shudō-zuki*, etc.
i. synonymous with *wakashū-gurui*, *yarō-gurui*, etc.

Fig. 18. *Ménage à trois* in a brothel. The boy, lying on his back, complains that the patron will not let him sleep. Isoda Koryūsai print (1770s). Note the similarity to Figure 20. Source: Fukuda Kazuhiko, *Fūzoku ehon ukiyoe* (Tokyo: Kawade shobō, 1991), p. 47.

completely reject heterosexual behavior. In the *Denbu monoga-tari*, the term *jakudōgata* ("one [who follows] the way of youths") is contrasted to *nyodōgata* ("one [who follows] the way of women"); this seems roughly comparable to the modern concep-tion of a "homosexual" (or at least to a man attracted to younger males). The dialogue also refers to a man who, hopelessly ob-sessed with youths, "envies men able to follow both ways."[j][20]

Sometimes these men are depicted as dedicated misogynists. Hiraga Gennai's *San no asa* declares categorically, "Those who like female prostitutes dislike youths; those who like youths revile

j. *futamichi kakuru hito o sonemi*

Fig. 19. Neglected, angry young woman entreats man to withdraw from boy-prostitute. Print by Nishikawa Sukenobu, Kyōhō era (1716–1745). Source: Fukuda Kazuhiko, *Ehon ukiyoe sen* (Tokyo: Kawade shobō, 1990), p. 30.

female prostitutes."[k][21] Gennai himself, according to Ōta Nanpo, often visited Yoshichō and the "southern wards" of Edo, with their *nanshoku* teahouses, but never went to Yoshiwara, with its female prostitutes.[22] His biographers claim the scholar was not simply a *shudō-zuki* but an *onna-girai*, or "woman-hater."[l] Men identified as such, like similar characters in Ming-Qing or even in English Augustan literature, find any contact with the female sex revolting.[23]

In one of Saikaku's stories, two elderly men of this type live next door to a husband and wife who often quarrel. Overhearing the argument, they "egg the husband on by pressing their faces

k. *jorō-zuki wakashū o iyagari, wakashū-zuki jorō o soshiru*
l. *joshiki-girai* ("hater of sex with women") is synonymous with this term

Fig. 20. *Ménage à trois*. Man, discovering mistress with female-role actor, has intercourse with her while masturbating him. He is about to apply some of his saliva to the youth's penis to heighten the sensation. Print by Suzuki Harunobu (1725–1770). Source: Lawrence E. Gichner, *Erotic Aspects of Japanese Culture* (New York: n.p., 1963), p. 45.

against the wall and shouting, 'Beat her to death, mister, and replace her with a sandal-boy!'" When women or girls happen to pass by, one of these woman-haters rushes out wielding a broom and shouting, "Such filth! Disgusting! Get out of here!" (Figure 21).[24] In another Saikaku tale, a man notes that his traveling companion is carrying two funeral urns and inquires whose ashes they hold. His comrade explains that one holds the ashes of his young male lover and that he is carrying them to Mount Kōya for burial. The other holds the ashes of a woman who was betrothed to a friend but who died before the marriage could take place.

> "He asked me to take her remains with me on this trip."
> His companion laughed.

"What a fool you are! Just because a woman has turned to ashes does not make it right for a lover of boys to hold her in his arms."

The young man immediately realized the error of his ways and threw the woman's ashes into a muddy creek where they sank beneath the plantain and lotus leaves.

"What a pair of woman-haters we are!" he exclaimed. After that their conversation became even more friendly.[25]

Equally striking examples appear in Ejima Kiseki's *Seken musuko katagi* (Characters of worldly young men, 1715). One merchant's son in this work is described as "from the very first ... a woman-hater: all his life he remained unmarried, in the grip of intense passions for a succession of handsome young boys."[26] The son of a wealthy moneylender, meanwhile, shows no interest in his father's trade but devotes all his time to sumo wrestling. His parents obtain a wife for him, but he never enters her room, declaring that sex with a woman saps a man's strength. An illustration in the text shows him practicing with his wrestling cronies as maidservants look on. "Women disgust me!" he declares. "Take the maids back into the house" (Figure 22).[27]

There is even some evidence for a popular stereotype linking *nanshoku* and effeminacy. The term *yowa-yowa* (after *yowai*, "weak") alluded to effeminacy; Saikaku wrote that whereas *shudō* once meant something "rough and powerful,"[m] the *wakashū* of his day were all expected to be *yowa-yowa*.[28] The term *yatsushi* (rendered by one translator as "namby-pamby") seems to have connoted "fawning," "made up," and "affected" in the manner of male prostitutes and some kabuki actors.[29]

In *Nenashigusa*, Hiraga Gennai implied that men of the imperial capital were especially effeminate. "The Kyoto male, however manly the beard he may sport, lisps: 'Oh gracious dear me! Isn't that simply scandalous what you just said?'"[30] The dialect was considered elegant, and boy-prostitutes everywhere were encour-

m. *arakenakirri*

Fig. 21. Illustration from Ihara Saikaku's *Nanshoku ōkagami* (1687). A woman-
hater threatens a party of women passing his house. Source: Munemasa,
Matsuda and Teruoka, eds., *Ihara Saikaku shū* (Tokyo: Shōgakukan, 1972),
vol. 2, p. 454.

Fig. 22. Magojirō, a woman-hater in Ejima Kiseki's *Seken musuko katagi* (*Characters of Worldly Young Men*, 1715), practices wrestling with his comrades. "Women disgust me!" he declares to the maids at left. Print by Nishikawa Sukenobu. Source: Howard Hibbett, *The Floating World in Japanese Fiction* (Tokyo and Rutland, Vt.: Tuttle, 1975), p. 149.

aged to emulate it.[31] Kyotoites were much sought after as male prostitutes; the Russian admiral Golovnin noted during his forced stay in Japan (1811–1813), "The province of Kioto ... is celebrated for the beauty of its male inhabitants and furnishes the greater part of the youths" for "the abominable vice."[32]

Not only prostitutes but also their patrons were sometimes portrayed as effeminate. An illustration in the *Nikokuren pekidan* shows a certain Kakukuni, a regular customer at the male brothels along the Tōkaidō highway, as a sissified figure with tiny eyes and mouth, a foppishly towering hairdo, and a kabuki-style cloth covering his shaven forehead. His servant, Kakubei, who also patronizes Seikenji's male prostitutes, shoulders his master's jumbo knapsack. His broad face, smiling in stupid contentment, seems to contrast with his spindly arms and legs.[33] These figures probably represent popular stereotypes (Figure 23).

The *Denbu monogatari* provides a rather detailed portrait of the "youth fanatic"[n] in the early seventeenth century: "First of all, he wears a backless, well-starched, hempen tunic, and at his shoulders and waist, he sports colored paper and poem-cards. He wraps himself in a thick cotton loincloth° knotted high [on the belly]." The *nanshoku* enthusiast is not merely effeminate and eccentric, however; he is also unclean and unkempt: "His face is blacker than the 'old man' noh mask, and his neck and forehead are grimy. He doesn't cut his nails, and his hair is as reddish and wild as an orangutan. Even if he sometimes puts it up, bundling it up with cut straw or used ribbons, lice come crawling out, and [his head] smells of boils."[34]

This negative and hostile image seems to describe the unruly masterless samurai, who were particularly associated with the love of boys. One does not find such references to uncleanliness in later years. This description indicates, at any rate, the existence of a popular stereotype of the *nanshoku-zuki* as early as the 1640s.

n. *wakashū-gurui*; same as *waranbe-gurui* and *wappa-gurui*
o. *fundoshi*

Fig. 23. Kakakuni and his servant, Kakubei, travel the Tōkaidō in search of homosexual brothels in Hirajitsu Tōsaku's *Nikokuren pekidan* (ca. 1785). Illustration by Jichōsai. Source: Oliver Statler, *Japanese Inn* (New York: Arena Books, 1976), p. 159.

The Active-Passive Dichotomy

Most sources suggest that a limited interest in *nanshoku* did not set one apart from society as a whole—as long as one followed the rules. Principal among these was the precept that the older partner always assumed the "active" (inserter) role, even if his status in the feudal hierarchy was lower than that of his partner. The only exception to this basic rule occurred when the older man was an actor or prostitute servicing a customer, in which case he would usually assume the identity of either a younger male (an adolescent youth or young adult) or a female.

This emphasis upon the assumption of fixed roles, even by men of only slightly different ages, mirrors the emphasis on natural hierarchies found in Japan from the most ancient times and encouraged by imported Confucian concepts.[35] If one of the Confucian "Five Regulations" specifies that "Between friend and friend there is fidelity," another insists that "between elder and junior there is precedence."[36]

In the Tokugawa period, as in the medieval period, the preferred homosexual act was anal sex. There is little reference to any other homosexual act in the erotic art and literature of the time, and such references as do occur contemptuously dismiss the alternatives. A work printed in 1661, for example, reflects contemporary taste in reporting a curious bit of folklore. The Buddha himself, having condemned partners in oral sex as "beasts in men's flesh," witnessed intercrural sex, mutual masturbation, and anal sex, concluding that the latter, though defiling the active partner and painful for the passive partner, was nonetheless most suitable for his own monastic community.[37]

The *Kōbō Daishi ikkan no sho*, or *Book of Kōbō Daishi*, mentioned in Chapter 1 was probably written in Satsuma a few years before the beginning of the Tokugawa era. It contains sections on hand signals exchanged between acolytes and their priestly suitors, on observations of boys in the course of seduction, and on techniques of anal intercourse.

1. There is a method called *skylark rising*. The ass is raised in the air like a skylark rising in the sky.

2. Always keep "cut plums" on hand in case you want to attempt insertion without saliva.

3. There is a method called *turned-up soles*. Place the acolyte's legs on your shoulders and penetrate him from the front.

4. There is the method called *reverse drop*. Insertion is from above the turtle's tail, and should be accomplished gradually.

5. There is a method called *summer moat*. Press the boy's ass to the moat of your belly as you enter. The method is painless, even for a young acolyte.

6. There is a method called *dry insertion*. Moisten only slightly with saliva, then penetrate. The method causes severe pain.

7. The method for initiation is called *tearing the hole*. In this method, a man with a large penis penetrates in one thrust without lubrication. This method causes severe pain.[38]

By including the latter two "methods" in this definitive list, the author seems to legitimate them.

Terms and symbols for sex between males usually refer to anal sex as well. The chrysanthemum[P] was not only the emblem of the imperial family but also the principle symbol of *nanshoku* because of the supposed resemblance of the inner part of this flower and the anus.[39] (See the pattern on the quilting in Figures 11 and 24.) Much of the terminology for male homosexual behavior also contains anal illusions. *Kiku no chigiri* ("chrysanthemum tryst") and *kiku asobi* ("chrysanthemum play") both meant homosexual intercourse, as did the curious expression *ketsumatsu* ("anus-marriage").[40] One term for a daimyo's male sex-partner, *kongō*, may be written with various combinations of the Sino-Japanese characters; one set ("golden" plus "strength") is ambiguous, but other combinations ("golden buttocks," "nearby buttocks," and "hospitable buttocks") leave no doubt as to the *kongō*'s role.[41]

allusions

A common term for male prostitute, *okama* (literally, "pot"), refers to the buttocks but can also mean "bathtub," a coincidence Tokugawa humorists readily exploited.[42] Ishikawa Masamochi, for

p. *kiku*

example, in recalling a disappointing trip to a male brothel, compares the boy-prostitute who refuses to have anal sex with him to a bathhouse closed for repairs.

> Karamaru [the popular writer Tatsuya Jūzaburō] invited me to go out and buy *kagema* with him, but when I started doing it with the *wakashū*, he couldn't bear it because of his hemorrhoids. So: *sashiatari nan to sentō no hairi guchi kama hason ni tsuki kyō yasumi* ([The sign] over the door of a certain bathhouse says, "For the time being due to damage to the *kama* we're closed today.")
>
> It's just like the sign over the bathhouse entrance, "Because of damage to the *kama*, we're closed today." You just return home, carrying your towel; for the time being, there's nothing you can do about it. When the *kama* is damaged, whether it's the bathtub or the *kagema*, it's a bother![43]

Jippensha Ikku's works feature humor in a similar vein. In *Hizakurige*, the character Kitahachi accidentally breaks the thick iron plate that heats an innkeeper's bathtub and has to pay damages. His companion Yajirōbei tells him not to be downhearted, insisting he has actually gained by the transaction. "Puncturing the pot for two *shu* [in copper coins] is cheap! You'd never get off so cheaply in Yoshichō!"[44] At this time, a cheap *kagema* in Edo charged twice this amount.

Some male prostitutes were called "tight holes,"[q] and the term *nyake*, written with the characters for "youth," and "spirit," could mean either anus, male prostitute, or coquettish boy.[45] The terms "fine hole"[r] and "rough hide"[s] referred to boys who had not yet experienced anal sex.[46] The phrase "passing through the back door"[t] was synonymous with homosexual sex.[47]

In literature, where homosexual acts are described at all, they involve anal sex; a boy in *Nanshoku ōkagami* muses that, like the firefly, he makes his living with his butt.[48] *Inu tsurezuregusa* (Idle thoughts of a dog, 1670), a guide to male brothels by Kiyo-

---

q. *subari; subari wakashū*
r. *uiana*
s. *arakawa*
t. *uramon tsūkō*

mizu Shunryū, provides a rather explicit discussion of this topic; he clinically distinguishes, for example, between types of *waka-shū* anuses.[49] The *yakusha-hyōbanki* (actor-critiques) sometimes evaluated young actors' anuses as *kiku hiroshi*, *kiku sebashi*, and *kiku warushi*—i.e., loose, tight, and "bad" chrysanthemums.[50]

Artificial rawhide anuses, lubricants such as clove oil, and a powdered root called *nerigi*, or *tsūwasan*, were marketed during the period by the famed Yotsumeya sex shops and in outlets in wards featuring male prostitution, such as Edo's Yushima Tenjin.[51] A *senryū* (humorous poem) runs:

> *Tenjin no*
> *uramon de*
> *tsūwasan*[52]
>
> [Sold at]
> Tenjin's back gate—
> tsūwasan

Apparently there was such a shop selling the ointment—but, of course, "back gate" has a double meaning here.

The *Morisada Mankō* (Morisada's dirty book, 1837–1853), a massive work on manners by Kitagawa Morisada, describes *tsūwasan* as follows: "Also called *nerigi*. A white powdered medicine used with saliva for *nanshoku*, or when deflowering [female virgins]. Sold at certain houses in Kyoto's Miyagawa-chō."[53] Bookshops also sold texts, such as *Makura bunko* (Pillow library, Bunsei era, 1818–1829), instructing one how to produce homemade sexual lubricant from egg white, arrowroot starch, and a glue plant called *funori*.[54] Sometimes the latter term was used synonymously with *nerigi*; another *senryū* runs:

> *kagema no*
> *mizusake yōshin ni*
> *toku funori*
>
> [When] deflowering
> a *kagema*, carefully
> daub on *funori*[55]

Insertee partners were also urged to eat *konnyaku* (a firm gelatin made from the paste of devil's tongue, which was thought to clean the rectum in passage).[56]

As already noted, erotic pictures dealing with homosexual subject matter generally depict anal intercourse between an adult male on the one hand and a youth, boy, or actor on the other. The only exception to this rule seems to have been the depiction of two copulating adults in humorous art.[57] (In Figure 2, Raijin, the god of thunder, is shown being buggered by the illness-preventing god—perhaps as punishment for having brought flood or drought.)[58]

Some depictions emphasize the violence of the inserter. In one Utagawa school print, a samurai, grimacing in pleasure, couples with a female-role actor in a teahouse (Figure 10). It seems he has wasted little time on preliminaries; his two swords are laid aside, but he has not even disrobed. His stance, facial expression, complete physical control over his partner, and size of his organ all emphasize his dominant role.

Other works convey an atmosphere of tender mutuality. In one print, a man having sex with a boy (significantly, on a chrysanthemum-pattern quilt) manipulates his partner's penis, which seems to respond (Figure 24).[59] The youth in Figure 25 obviously is as sexually excited as his partner. Another print depicts a brothel patron cuddling a boy while taking him from behind; the response of the boy, who clutches tissue paper, is not clear (Figure 26). An Utamaro work shows a teahouse patron, sporting a formidable erection, peering with frustration at the forbiddingly constricted fundament of a "young man" (as opposed to boy or female-role actor) partner; "Pardon me if I tear your ass," reads the caption. A courtesan, meanwhile, peeks in and offers her own services (Figure 15).

Attitudes toward both heterosexual and homosexual anal erogeneity in early modern East Asia differed markedly from attitudes in Europe.[60] In the Christian West, anal sex was in general viewed

Fig. 24. Customer having sex with, and masturbating, male prostitute. Quilt features pattern of chrysanthemums (*kiku*), which symbolize anal sex. Source: Lawrence E. Gichner, *Erotic Aspects of Japanese Culture* (New York: n.p., 1963), p. 42.

with a horror of feces and the anus itself grounded, in Arthur N. Gilbert's opinion, in a complex of values developed from antiquity out of Judeo-Christian tradition. The "anal function," he maintains, citing the writings of Saint Paul, Dante, Martin Luther, and Jonathan Swift, "became a symbol of evil, darkness, death, and rebellion against moral order."[61]

One must wonder how deeply these linkages influenced the mentality of the ordinary premodern European peasant, but various developments over the last few hundred years may have strengthened the "anal-evil" association. The psychoanalyst San-

Fig. 25. Woodblock print showing a sexually excited male prostitute with *murasaki-bōshi*; his partner steps out for a minute. Yoshida Hanbei, 1705. Source: Fukuda Kazuhiko, *Ehon ukiyoe sen* (Tokyo: Kawade shobō, 1990), p. 36.

dor Ferenczi suggested that during the past few centuries the intensified "sense of cleanliness" has resulted in "the *repression of anal eroticism*" and thus also in an increasingly harsh proscription of homoerotic desire.[62] Gilles Deleuze and Felix Guattari suggest that only with the emergence of capitalism has it become necessary to thoroughly exclude the anus "from the social field"; it was "the first organ to be privatised" in order for the phallus to emerge as the "despotic signifier" fetishized in much the same way as money is in capitalist society.[63]

Whereas these scholars link the repression of anal eroticism to specific historical processes, Freud regarded it as an inevitable result of toilet training (some form of which presumably has existed in all historical societies). The infant finds pleasure in withholding feces until "through accumulation there result violent muscular

Fig. 26. Customer with boy-prostitute. From painted scroll by Nishikawa
Sukenobu (1671–1751). Source: Phyllis and Eberhard Kronhausen, *The
Complete Book of Erotic Art* (Hong Kong: Bell, 1987), vol. 2, illustration 310.

contractions"; the parent (or "nurse," in Freud's example) must
train him or her to resist such pleasure. This "first forbidding"

> which comes to the child, i.e., the forbidding of obtaining sexual
> pleasure from anal activities and its products, is of immeasurable sig-
> nificance for its entire development. The little child through such an
> occasion must get an inkling of an environment antagonistic to his in-
> stinct stirrings, must learn from these strangers his own nature, and
> then accomplish the first repression of his pleasure possibilities. That
> which is "anal" from then on remains a symbol of everything that
> must be pushed aside, to be cut out of life.[64]

Whatever the validity of these psychoanalytic or historical ex-
planations of the rejection of anal erogeneity in Western society,
they seem incapable of explaining the veritable celebration of
things anal in preindustrial Japanese society. Here the anus and
defecation carried far fewer negative or fearful associations; indeed, early Japanese culture allotted the anal function a certain
respect, even reverence.

In the eighth-century text *Kojiki*, as well as in the ancient chants (*norito*), defecation[u] is listed along with various taboos, such as parent-child incest and breaking down divisions between rice fields, as sources of impurity. Such defecation probably refers to excretion in improper places for purposes of effecting malevolent magic.[65] The antics of the Sun Goddess's mischievous younger brother, Susano-o, include such behavior; he hurls excrement about in the Palace of Heaven, shocking the various deities, although his sister makes excuses for him.[66]

Pani-yasu-biko-nō-kamī and Pani-yasu-bime-nō-kamī, deities of earth or clay, were said to be born out of the anus of the goddess Izanagi.[67] Matsumura Takeo writes that he knows of no other people with divinities produced from excreta.[68] In the same text, the food goddess, Opo-gē-tu-pime-nō-kamī, prepares food from her nose, mouth, and rectum to feed the god Susano-o, and upon her death, a key foodstuff, soy beans, originates from her anus.[69]

During the medieval period, courtly society produced technically superb paintings of "wind-breaking contests" depicting bare-buttocked, elite men competing to expel gas directly into one another's faces while judges look on.[70] Such works were no doubt intended as humor, but those portraying the *gaki* (hungry ghosts) had a gloomier purpose. *Gaki* were thought to be souls doomed to roam the earth consuming human waste products; the decomposition of dung was attributed not to bacterial activity but to these *gaki*. Religious paintings show them hovering near defecating humans, getting ready to eat the product.[71] They reflect, in William R. LaFleur's words, "the intellectual shape of an era in which shit was still largely a substance whose physical properties and transformations were still matters of primary curiosity."[72]

Much of Tokugawa popular literature reflects this fascination with anality.[73] Indeed, even twentieth-century literature abounds in what might strike the Western reader as rather gratuitous references to anal functions. Tanizaki Junichirō's lengthy, elegant novel *Sasameyuki* (translated into English as *The Makioka Sisters* and arguably the greatest novel by one of Japan's greatest modern

u. *kusoto*

novelists) tells us much about the sisters' stomach problems, concluding, "Yukiko's diarrhea persisted through the twenty-sixth, and was a problem on the train to Tokyo."[74] Contemporary children's television programming and advertisements not infrequently feature coils of shit that speak and behave like human beings; educational book publishers provide comics for toddlers on the theme of *unchi* (shit)—on the theory (I am told) that small children's natural interest in feces should be explored rather than repressed.[75] Perhaps this "feces-friendly" attitude reflects the fact that in Japan and China human waste was traditionally seen not as a disagreeable if inevitable by-product of existence but as a valuable commodity.[76] As the Jesuit Luis Frois put it in the late sixteenth century, "We pay a man to remove the night-soil; in Japan, it is bought and money or rice given for it."[77] Such differences help to account for the differences in the two societies' views of anal intercourse.

As noted previously, references to homosexual acts other than anal intercourse are rare. In *Nanshoku ōkagami* a male prostitute satisfies his customer with intercrural sex,[v] but there is no way of knowing how common this was.[78] Mutual masturbation may have been considered acceptable behavior; a dictionary of obsolete obscene expressions includes a word for "mutual stroking."[w][79] Depictions of this practice among boys occur in Chinese erotica, but I have seen no Japanese examples.[80] One does find illustrations of men *unilaterally* fondling other men's genitals (Figures 20 and 24).

Homosexual kissing[x] also appears conspicuously in literature and erotic art. Throughout East Asia, kissing is viewed as an extremely intimate act; to this day in Japan, it is considered rather scandalous for heterosexual (to say nothing of homosexual) cou-

---

v. *himitsu no sumata*; "the secret technique"

w. *aikake*

x. *kōchū; kuchi o suu* (lit., "mouth-sucking"), *kuchi yose, kōchū no chigiri, shita no kyoku* ("tongue-pleasure") and many other expressions (see Sasama, *Kōshoku engo*, pp. 247–248)

Fig. 27. Customer kissing a male prostitute. In *Nanshoku yamaji no tsuyu* (1730). Nishikawa Sukenobu. Source: Ōmura Shage, ed., *Nanshoku yamaji no tsuyu* (Tokyo: Nichirinkaku, 1978).

ples to indulge in it publicly. It was viewed not as heterosexual foreplay but as an expression of passion during the height of heterosexual intercourse.[81]

It is significant, therefore, that men in literature, upon meeting handsome youths for the first time, attempt to kiss them[82] and that *shunga* show men kissing each other both before and during sex (Figure 27).[83] Figure 28 depicts a rare sight: two fully mature adult men, one of them heavily tattooed, kissing while in a state of obvious sexual excitement. And in Figure 29, two gangsters kiss one another while simultaneously having sex with a courtesan.[84] As noted in Chapter 2, the work *Saiseki* (1657), a comprehensive handbook of *shudō* etiquette, includes a section on kissing. Vendors even sold toothpicks carved with popular actors' crests to make theatergoers feel as though they were kissing their favorite performers.[85]

Although some cultures may find the very notion of oral contact

Fig. 28. Sexually aroused adult men kissing. Source: Friedrich S. Krauss, *Sei fūzoku no Nihonshi* (Tokyo: Kawade bunko, 1988), p. 4.

with another's saliva repugnant, the Japanese clearly felt no such revulsion. In one Saikaku tale, the secret admirer of a young samurai, seeing the boy spit into a river, scoops up the saliva and consumes it. This episode is intended not to disgust the reader but to evoke admiration and create an erotic atmosphere: "May the saliva I just drank," prays the admirer, "remain in my mouth forever, so that I can always enjoy its nectar-like flavor!"[86]

I find absolutely no Tokugawa-era evidence, however, for homosexual oral sex.[87] There is at least one medieval reference: The fourteenth-century *Chigo no sōshi* includes a scene in which a priest engages an acolyte in analingus while the latter fellates him. The caption over the priest runs, "How delicious, although a bit bitter."[y] "This is nice too," replies the boy, "if a bit salty."[z][88]

y. *Ara umaya, chito nigaku sōrō.*
z. *Kore mo yoku sōroedomo, chito shihaba yuku sōrō zoya*

Fig. 29. Bisexual *ménage à trois* with two men kissing. Kitagawa Utamaro, ca. 1801. Source: Fukuda Kazuhiko, *Fūzoku ehon ukiyoe* (Tokyo: Kawade shobō), p. 75.

Such activity presumably continued to take place into the early modern period, but the absence of comparable Tokugawa material indicates a reluctance to depict male-male oral-genital contact.

Perhaps *shunga* artists of the Tokugawa period avoided the topic of male-male fellatio for technical reasons. Prints dealing with heterosexual themes depicted cunnilingus more often than fellatio, probably because of the difficulty of reconciling two key conventions of *shunga* art—the massive penis and the tiny female mouth—necessary in a representation of the latter act. This factor might explain in part the absence of pictorial depictions of male-male oral sex; the passive partners in homoerotic art also tend to have dainty mouths.

But if such sexual activity often occurred and met with the degree of tolerance extended homosexual anal sex, one would expect to find works in which one male's penis is at least close to another's mouth. I have seen nothing of this sort, however; the closest approximations are depictions of men masturbating youth's penises with hands lubricated with saliva (Figure 20).

The lack of reference to male-male oral sex is striking, not only because this is the principle form of homosexual activity in some cultures but also because its absence constitutes the only clear break in the symmetry of male-male, male-female, and female-female sexual acts depicted in *shunga*.[89] Insofar as it was physically possible, men engaged in the same sexual activities with other males as they did with women: *shunga* show them kissing, masturbating, and having anal sex with members of both sexes. Female couples, for their part, are shown kissing, fondling one another's genitals, and coupling through the use of double *hari-kata* (dildo) (Figure 30).[90] Men performed cunnilingus, women performed fellatio, and female couples engaged in cunnilingus, but there is no evidence that males sought oral contact with one another's sex organs.[91]

The Object of Desire

Tokugawa literature on *nanshoku* usually expresses the viewpoint of the "older brother," or male-brothel patron whose homosexual desire focuses upon attractive younger males. An examination of male-male sexual desire during this period, therefore, should begin with an inquiry about what sort of partners the former seem to have preferred. I will also consider the feelings of those who attracted the interest of such men: boys in general, youthful or young-looking actor-prostitutes, and young manservants.

Boys and Youths

Such terms as *wakashū-zuki*, *shudō-zuki*, and *nanshoku-zuki*, which were generally interchangeable, referred to males with a general preference for younger male partners and indicated the prevalence of age-graded homosexual relationships in Tokugawa Japan.[92] The ideal partner for the "older brother," or paying cus-

Fig. 30. Katsushika Hokusai (1760–1849) print, showing lesbian sex with double-headed *harikata*. Source: Michel Beurdley et al., eds., *Erotic Art of Japan: The Pillow Poem* (Hong Kong: Leon Amiel, 1988), p. 189.

tomer, seems to be a boy between fifteen and eighteen. This period was regarded as one of transition from childhood to adulthood; the initiation (*genpuku*) ceremony could be performed any time within this interval. Perhaps because the average life expectancy during the period was only about fifty, boys were encouraged to assume full adult responsibilities at an early date. There seems to have been little concern about shielding teenagers from sexual experience, including the sexual advances of their elders, unless the latter became obnoxious or violent.[93]

Thus, the publisher's afterword to the *Iwatsutsuji* (1713), a collection of homoerotic literature, urges adult readers to share the volume with young male friends: "We hope that men will read the book with youths who are not yet enlightened about this way of love, and that it will be a source of pleasure to many."[94] By "youths," the editors probably meant teenagers. An early seventeenth-century work called *Shiratama no sōshi* (The white ball book) suggests that a male was considered most suitable as a homosexual sex partner from age seven to twenty-five, during which time he would develop from a child[aa] to a youth[bb] to a man.[cc] [95] These categories roughly correspond to the more poetically defined stages given in the *Wakashū no haru* (Springtime of youths): from age eleven to fourteen, the boy was a "blossoming flower";[dd] from fifteen to eighteen, a "flourishing flower";[ee] and from nineteen to twenty-two, a "falling flower."[ff] Sixteen (fifteen by Western reckoning, as the Japanese regarded babies as one year old at birth), was thus the boy's "springtime."[96] Saikaku also declares that sixteen "is the age when youths are most attractive to other males."[97] References to such youths often contain melancholy overtones; the poem on a Toyonobu portrait of a beautiful youth holding a small flower cart runs, "The days of young men are as numbered as those of the cherry blossom."[98] It is surely no accident that the samurai is also often compared to this flower. In the latter case, the tragedy is death in battle; in the former, the inevitable onset of age and ugliness.

The terminology of male prostitution also expresses the preference for boy partners. Some *nanshoku* teahouses were known as "children-shops,"[gg] and the suffix -*ko* (child) was included in the terms for various male prostitute types: "sex child,"[hh] "stage child,"[ii] "cross-dressing child,"[jj] "working child,"[kk] etc. The

aa. *kodomo*
bb. *wakashū*
cc. *yarō*
dd. *tsubomeru hana*
ee. *sakari-bana*
ff. *ochiru hana*
gg. *kodomo-ya*
hh. *iro-ko*
ii. *butai-ko*
jj. *kage-ko*
kk. *tsutome-ko*

term *chishi* ("seedling" or "little boy") also referred to a young catamite.[99]

In ancient Greece, according to Dover, "once the beard was grown, the young male was supposed to be passing out of the ero-menos stage."[100] In Japan, by contrast, the transition was marked by the adoption of a new hairstyle and mode of dress at the *gen-puku* ceremony. The growth of facial hair cannot be controlled, so the Greek boy's evolution out of the sexually passive role could not be delayed, but the timing of the Japanese boy's transition could be determined by his parents or his lord. The rite of passage might occur any time between ages thirteen and seventeen.[101]

Between about age ten and the time of the *genpuku* ceremony, a boy's head would be partly shaven. First, the crown of his head would be shorn, leaving conspicuous forelocks, or *maegami*. (This term was also used to refer to the boy himself at this stage.) Some-what later, these forelocks would be reshaped; the hair at the tem-ples would be cut at right angles. This hairstyle was known as "cornered forelocks."[ll] Finally, the entire pate and crown of the head would be shaven; this was the adult hairstyle. Thus, the two lovers in Figure 31 are clearly distinguished as a *maegami* and an adult. *Genpuku* literally means something like "first clothing," and at this point the youth would also receive his first adult robe, dis-tinguished by its rounded, closed sleeves.[102]

Bashō celebrated the appeal of the *maegami* in a haiku poem:

> *Maegami mo*
> *mada wakagusa no*
> *nioi kana*

> Doesn't the boy
> with his forelocks
> still bear the
> fragrance of fresh
> grass?[103]

But a poem of 1693 indicates that, as he aged, the *maegami* lost much of his sexual attractiveness:

ll. *sumi-maegami*; the youth himself was also referred to by this term

Fig. 31. "Older brother" and "younger brother" with long forelocks in bed. From the *kanazōshi* work *Iro monogatari* (1620s or 1630s). Source: Asakusa Haruhiko, ed., *Kanazōshi shūsei* (Tōkyōtō, 1983), vol. 4, p. 189.

genpuku wa
shudō no ue no
tonseisha

Genpuku means
retirement from
[the insertee role in] *shudō*[104]

Jippensha Ikku's *Hizakurige* seems to illustrate this rule. The ne'er-do-well duo of Yaji and Kita begin as sexual partners. Yajir-ōbei, "a proper merchant," becomes enamored of a boy named Hananosuke, the apprentice of a traveling actor. After he ex-hausts his small fortune on this boy, the two flee Yaji's hometown to Fuchū (Sunpu). Soon Hananosuke undergoes the *genpuku* cer-emony and assumes the adult name Kitahachi. Yaji and Kita undergo many adventures in this long novel, but after the *gen-puku* ritual there is no mention of any sexual contact between the two men. Indeed, they compete in pursuing women.[105]

The ending of a male's availability as an insertee partner at *gen-puku* contrasts with practices found among certain ancient Euro-pean peoples, including some Dorian, German, and Celtic tribes, and among some Melanesian cultures. As mentioned in Chapter 1, in these societies the male rite of passage marked the *begin-ning* of his availability as an insertee and often of his residence in a "men's house," where the older inmates routinely had sex with the younger.[106] Some Japanese practices of the Tokugawa period may hint at an ancient Melanesian-style ceremony. At the *gen-puku* ritual, which dates to at least the seventh century A.D., a formal male headdress (*eboshi*) would be placed on the young man's head by an "*eboshi*-father"[mm] who thereafter served as a role model, teacher, and guardian.[107] In village society, the boy, after undergoing the rite, would take up residence in a "young men's house"[nn] until his marriage.[108] Such institutions also ex-isted in ancient China.[109] I find no evidence, however, for ritual-

mm. *eboshi-oya*
nn. *wakamonoyado; wakashū-yado*

ized, initiation-related pederasty in either Japan or China. The Sino-Japanese term *saibi*, which means homosexual anal sex and is written with the characters "to plant" and "tail," recalls the notion, common in some other societies, that anal sex with a boy confers manly qualities upon him and indeed is essential for his growth. An obscure passage in the *Kojiki*, meanwhile, thought by some to represent advice about heterosexual intercourse conferred upon the initiate during *genpuku*, may in fact refer to homosexual anal sex.[110] In any case, if such ritualized pederasty once occurred in Japan, the practice had long been forgotten by the Tokugawa period.

Men seem to have been rather universally drawn to beautiful youths. But how did boys respond to the adult male's advances? Certainly one finds literary examples of youths sexually harassed by men they despise; in Ishikawa Masamochi's *Hida no takumi monogatari* (Tale of a Hida craftsman, 1808) the hero, Yamabito, continually attracts such unwanted attentions.[111] Yamamoto's *Hagakure* recommends that a youth cut down an obnoxious suitor. However, it is the poor qualities of the suitor, rather than the reception of homosexual interest, that meet with disgust.[112]

But literature also commonly portrays *nanshoku* as an emotionally rewarding experience for the boys pursued. For example, they may be deeply touched by love letters from male admirers.[113] They frequently take the initiative in offering themselves to men who attract them.[114] Some lack an older lover but pine for one. In one Saikaku tale, the thirteen-year-old page of a daimyo, who shares the latter's bed but does not love him, declares that "if one day someone should tell me he loves me, I shall risk my life for him."[115]

In ancient Sparta, boys lacking male lovers apparently suffered embarrassment.[116] In Japan such relationships met with more ambivalence, but Saikaku notes that "a youth with no male lover is like a maiden without a betrothed"°°—i.e., the object of pity.[117] Elsewhere, discussing the disfiguring effects of smallpox, Saikaku suggests that girls suffer little from their pockmarks; after all, if

oo. *nenyū no naki maegami wa enpu motanu onna no gotoku*

they have large dowries, they can always find a mate. "The unfortunate ones," he declares, "are the boys [who have been smitten with smallpox]. Their figures are no different from those of other boys, yet because of a few facial scars they are doomed to go through life unloved by men."[118]

Kenneth Dover suggests that in ancient Greece, the adult lover in a homosexual relationship (*erastes*), who could easily buy a male prostitute or slave boy, was obliged to court his beloved youth (*eromenos*), impressing him with his qualities before winning his sexual favors. The boy, who could also find sexual outlets in prostitutes and slaves but who knew nothing of heterosexual courtship, may have been flattered by such attentions and have found satisfaction in "being welcomed *for his own sake* by a sexual partner of equal status."[119] Youths depicted in Tokugawa literature express a similar pleasure at receiving the attentions of worthy men.

In classical Athens, according to David Halperin, "the youth was expected to submit ... to the enflamed desire of his suitor solely out of the feeling of mingled esteem, gratitude, and affection (*philia*)."[120] *Nanshoku* handbooks in Tokugawa Japan exhorted *wakashū* to respond to sincere advances with *nasake* (a Buddhist term meaning selfless compassion) and to pursue the relationship with *giri* (honor and duty).[121] Thus, in agreeing to a homosexual relationship, a youth may have felt he was demonstrating his moral worth.

Actors and Male Prostitutes

The tremendous popularity of kabuki was rooted in the sexual fascination produced by its actors, particularly by *onnagata*, or female-role specialists. One early-nineteenth-century print, however, suggests that some men preferred to play the active role with more mature partners. In this depiction, a specialist in heroic warrior roles crouches down upon a samurai patron's penis backstage. The fact that an *onnagata* sits nearby, nonchalantly applying makeup, makes the patron's sexual choice all the more striking.[122] But men are far more frequently depicted dallying

with *onnagata* or *wakashū*. The homosexual atmosphere of Tokugawa kabuki, centering on the latter actor types, lingers even in
modern Japan; Mishima Yukio's short story *"Onnagata"* reflected
his own attraction to the female-role specialist.[123]

Urban audiences expressed their enthusiasm for these actors in
ways that would be familiar to fans of contemporary rock 'n' roll
stars. They organized fan clubs, often on a ward basis; fiercely
loyal, they would bar any member who patronized another actor's
performances.[124] They circulated posters bearing their thespian
hero's image and attended his performances in groups, chorusing
their devotion. They purchased "actor-critiques"[pp] that publicized
not only his dramatic skills but his physical charms as well.[125] (The
latter, however, were stressed less and less over time as kabuki
became a more refined and sophisticated art form.) Most important, the devotees patronized the theater often enough and paid
sufficiently high ticket prices to make some actors very wealthy.
In the 1660s, Yoshizawa Ayame became the first actor to earn
over a thousand *ryō* per year—quite a salary for someone who,
in officialdom's eyes, was little better than an outcaste.[126]

Women as well as men became enamored of these performers,
including the *onnagata*, but men with a sexual interest in the actors seem to have constituted the bulk of early theater audiences.
Thus, the homosexual appeal of the kabuki actor was not the
subtle homoeroticism of the noh *chigo* character but a brash, provocative sensuality that drove male (and female) spectators wild
with desire. Men viewing plays, according to the *Yarō mushi*
(*Yarō* bugs, ca. 1660), "become weak-kneed and call out, 'Gosaku!
Good! Good! I'll die!'"[127] "The men in the audience," wrote Asai
Ryōi in his *Tōkaidō meishoki* (Famous sights along the Tōkaidō,
1660), "became utterly intoxicated with [the actors'] beauty and
lost all hold on themselves: slicing flesh out of their own thighs
so they could hardly walk or mangling their arms with wounds as
proof of manly love, they produced one more ludicrous cripple
after the next."[128] (One performed "flesh-gauging"[qq] as a pledge

pp. *yakusha-hyōbanki*
qq. *kanniku*

of homosexual devotion.)[129] The wealthier of such men rented special raised seats concealed by screens, where they would invite their favorite performers between acts to exchange drinks and arrange for later trysts. Or they might meet actors in their dressing rooms, despite prohibitions against such visits.[130]

There are many references to monks selling temple treasures and samurai pawning their weapons to purchase the favors of these actors; the *Hagakure*, for example, records the following incident, which occurred in Hizen in the seventeenth century:

> Among the pageboys in Lord Mitsushige's retinue, one Tomoda Shozaemon was in attendance. A rather wanton fellow, he fell in love with a leading actor of the theater by the name of Tamon Shozaemon and changed both his name and crest to that of the actor. Completely abandoning himself to this affair, he spent everything he had and lost all his clothing and furnishings. And at length, when he had exhausted all his means, he stole Mawatari Rokubei's sword and had a spearman take it to the pawnshop.
>
> The spearman, however, spoke up about this matter, and at the investigation both [the page] and [the actor] Shozaemon were put to death.[131]

As noted in Chapter 2, the authorities attempted to prevent such incidents by reducing the kabuki performers' sex appeal. After banning women from the stage, they sought to diminish the attraction of youth- and female-role actors by forcing them to shave their forelocks. These were to a large extent the measure of feminine and adolescent male beauty; indeed, descriptions of characters in classical literature seldom allude to any physical attribute other than lovely hair.[132] By denying youth- and female-role actors this adornment, the authorities intended, according to the *Tōkaidō meishoki*, "to make them unsightly to look at,"[133] and for a time, indeed, the shaven-crowned actors proved a turnoff for Tokugawa audiences. The *Edo meishoki* says they looked "like cats with their ears cut off." Even so, "it seems that later they were not thought so ugly."[134] "True," wrote Asai Ryōi,

> it made them look odd and too old for their years, but because of the way they carried themselves they were still far from being without charm. The curtain goes up; all decked out, they strut across the walk-

way—they are really bewitching. From the boxes cheers go up; "Look, look, the visitation of Amida [Buddha]!" while from the pit comes a chorus of catcalls, "Whose piece of work are you?"[135]

Actors were obliged to maintain these shaven pates and at times even had to report to an inspector, who would ensure that their forelocks were less than a half-inch long.[136] Forbidden to use wigs, they soon hit upon the device of placing purple scarves[rr] over their foreheads; officials permitted this, presumably because they found the effect suitably unerotic, but (testifying to the malleability of the libido) the purple scarf itself soon assumed erotic connotations.[137]

The fact that all kabuki actors, regardless of age or theatrical role, were now obliged to sport the same hairstyle had important implications for male prostitution. Hitherto this had been the preserve of boys and youths, but now that the boys looked older, the post-*genpuku* males looked comparatively younger. According to the *Nanshoku ōkagami*, "It used to be that no matter how splendid the boy, it was impossible for him to keep his forelocks and take on patrons after the age of twenty. [But after 1654,] since everyone wore the hairstyle of adult men, it was still possible at thirty-four or thirty-five for young-looking actors to get under a man's robe. How strange are the ways of love!"[138] Just as the lines of gender blurred upon the kabuki stage, so faded the lines of age. In this fantasy world, appearances were much more important than biological realities.

In marked contrast to the entertainers on the stage, numerous boys and youths did little more than prostitute themselves. The term for such prostitutes, who were not registered with urban authorities as legitimate actors, was "unregulated boys."[ss] Formally banned in Edo and Osaka in 1689, they seem to have proliferated even as the actors of the kabuki theater acquired greater artistic sophistication and respectability.[139] Such boys would often be trained to entertain their patrons with music, dancing, or simple

rr. *murasaki bōshi*
ss. *seigaiko*

party tricks. The brothel handbooks mentioned in Chapter 2, *San no asa* and *Kiku no en*, suggest that some Edo establishments specialized in cross-dressing prostitutes, whereas others featured boys and young men in normal male attire. In his *Okimiyage* (Souvenir, 1693), Saikaku describes a teahouse in Osaka's Dōtōnbori district, where a posted roster of employees listed a variety of prostitute types for all customer tastes:

1. Hanayama Tōnosuke, 14 years old. Fair complexion, lovely eyes. Recites *kodayu* tunes.
2. Iwataki Isaburō, 16 years old. A skillful dancer, sings *nage* tunes, and naturally imitates the manners of a woman.
3. Yumekawa Dairoku, 15 years old. A good drinker, who can keep up with anyone. Plays *shamisen* well, and is the most attractive of those dressed like traveling performers.[tt]
4. Matsunokaze Kotonojō, 17 years old. Good at making shadow figures, and can also spit water from his mouth to write characters on the wall. In juggling, he rivals Shio no Chōjirō.
5. Fukakusa Kankyūrō, 17 years old. In his manner of speaking, he closely resembles the late [*wakashū* role actor] Suzuki Heihachi. He has no special skills but is wonderful in bed!
6. Yukiyama Matsunosuke, 19-year-old *yarō*. When he sits in the room, it is easy to mistake him for a real stage-actor.[140]

Of these boys, Isaburō dresses as a woman, Kankyūrō as a *wakashū* and Matsunosuke as a *yarō*. In this story, Matsunosuke seems most popular with the male customers.

Various itinerant entertainers and pleasure-ward employees—officially registered as shampooers, privy cleaners, or peddlers of aloes-wood perfume or fans—also served as homosexual prostitutes in Tokugawa cities.[141] In Edo's Yoshiwara, those referred to as *otoko no geisha* ("male geisha"), *hōkan* (jesters), or *taikomochi* (drummers) often performed bawdy dances or strip-teases for customers in the courtesan brothels.[142] Wealthy and sophisticated customers such as the young rakes in Kiseki's *Seken musuko ka-*

tt. *tabiko*

tagi (Characters of worldly young men, 1715) liked to surround themselves with these youths and sometimes employed them as personal servants.[143]

The lives of these entertainers were, of course, often harsh. They typically entered the profession as a result of desperate poverty. Destitute parents offered sons to teahouse proprietors, and although the purchase and sale of human beings[uu] had been outlawed early in the period, one might be placed, as early as age eight, by one's parents or guardians into a slave-like indentureship lasting up to ten years. Many boys from poor families in the Osaka-Kyoto region were handed over to agents of Edo brothels.[144] These boys would be unlikely to receive any of the advance payment. Thus, boys were subject to exactly the same type of exploitation as were girls. A song popular in Kyoto during the Genroku era depicts a teahouse courtesan lamenting the fact that her father, a palanquin bearer, and mother, a miller, have sold all four of their children into prostitution. An older and younger sister are both prostitutes, and the younger brother is now a *kagema*.[145]

Upon placement, the boy would be physically conditioned to his new trade. His rectum would be dilated by insertion of wooden implements of increasing dimensions several times a day for a month or more.[146] He would be fed and perhaps trained to some level of skill as a performer. Those showing promise as *onnagata* were taught to imitate women. They were encouraged to live as women, rooming and bathing separately from male-role actors and observing female etiquette in their speech and table manners. They were even expected to squat while urinating. Many of them probably developed a female gender identity.

By law, actors were confined to the theater wards, just as courtesans were constrained from leaving the pleasure quarters. The wealthiest did in fact obtain houses elsewhere in the city, but only clandestinely through agents. In public they were ordered to wear broad, face-concealing sedge hats, and from the Tenpō Reform period the shogunate actually referred to them in official documents with the suffix *-hiki*, normally applied to animals![147]

uu. *jinshin baibai*

To the psychological damage of such treatment were added constant threats to the actor-prostitute's health. The sources constantly refer to the problem of hemorrhoids, and both syphilis and gonorrhea were rampant during the period. The male prostitute's best hope was that a rich, attractive patron would buy out his contract, establishing him as an independent artist in the theater world or merely taking him on as a dependent in mutually agreeable circumstances.

Saikaku provides several sensitive depictions of the boy-prostitute's lot. In one of his tales, a boy named Handayū must entertain customers all night long, then perform on stage the next day:

> The previous day, for example, he was forced to drink from sunset to late at night with a stubborn country samurai who took a liking to him, and today he had to work again, with seven or eight pilgrims on their way to Ise. Sleeping partners were decided in secret by drawing straws, and as luck would have it he was assigned to a repulsive old man, even though there were others he actually found attractive.[148]

Day after day he must sleep with coarse men who have never brushed their teeth or who smell of sweaty deerskin socks. All his fees are pocketed by the innkeeper.

This is a fictional treatment of the actor-prostitute's life, but biographical details of real actors confirm its credibility. Nakamura Chūzō, a popular youth-role actor of the Tenmei era (1781–1788), first performed on the stage at age ten. He was treated like a slave by the master of his troupe, and his troubles culminated when, at age sixteen, he angered a patron with whom he had forged a "brotherhood bond." This "elder brother" hired five men to seize Chūzō, gang-rape him, and beat him senseless. After this episode, another patron bought Chūzō's contract and sponsored his successful theatrical career.[149] Thereafter he even counted among his patrons Yanagisawa Nobutoki, the daimyo of Kōriyama.[150]

The experience of some actors and male prostitutes may have been less harsh. Studies of male prostitution in the modern world suggest that a substantial number of those who practice it do so for reasons of pleasure as well as profit, and this was probably true in Tokugawa Japan as well.[151] The actor Kikunojō, as depicted in *Nenashigusa*, seems genuinely attracted to other men and willing to serve them sexually.[152] The artist Torii Kiyonaga, himself a female-role actor in the kabuki theater, specialized in depictions of man-boy sex, perhaps expressing a positive attitude toward his own experience.[153] Even Saikaku's male prostitute, Handayū, finds some compensation in his job: "What made it possible to forget the agony of the job were those moments when he saw the love-lorn faces of men and women gazing after him on his way home and could hear their countless cries of admiration. It filled him with a sense of pleasure and pride in his own beauty, and this alone made him willing to bear his bone-grinding regimen."[154]

Handayū actually derives a sense of self-worth from his popularity as a sexual object. One imagines such feelings would be all the more intense in youths of untouchable social origins.

Manservants

Any handsome manservant was apparently fair game for a *nan-shoku-zuki* employer, but some were employed specifically for sexual purposes: Priests and monks had their *chigo*, ranking samurai had their hired bedmates,[vv] daimyo retained their "golden buttocks"[ww] or "lord's goods,"[xx] and townsmen could procure male sex partners through employment agencies.[yy] The Tokugawa shoguns themselves found lovers among their pages: Ieyasu slept with Ii Manchiyo, Hidetada with Niwa Nagashige and Koyama Nagamon.[155]

Probably the most extraordinary example of master-manservant sex can be found in the *Sannō gaiki* (Unofficial history of the three rulers), the biography of Tokugawa Tsunayoshi. This eccentric but brilliant shogun, known for his excesses, reportedly maintained sexual relationships with more than one hundred handsome youths, including many selected by a special officer appointed in

---

vv. *yoru no tomo*; lit. "night companions"
ww. *kongo*
xx. *gomotsu*
yy. *hito-yado* or *kuchiire*

1693.[156] Some were confined, like concubines, to the women's quarters of the shogunal palace, but more than twenty of the favorites were housed in a special dormitory at the mansion of Tsunayoshi's chamberlain (and onetime lover), Yanagisawa Yoshiyasu: "Some had wives, others not. They were under regulations concerning their travel to the castle every day, their return from the castle, their rising, eating, studying, and so forth. . . . There were four men in charge of watching them. They waited for an evening call."[157]

There is also some evidence for sexual relationships between teachers and students, although the pedagogical element in *nanshoku* seems to have been minor in comparison to that in Greek *paiderastia*.[158] A Harunobu print depicts a tutor interrupting his lesson to couple with his boy pupil.[159] The poet Bashō seems to have been sexually involved with several of his disciples, including Tsuboi Tokoku. In his *Saga nikki* (Saga diary, 1691), Bashō described his feelings for this youth:

> In dreams I called out something about Tokoku, and awoke in tears. . . . For me to have dreamed about him must surely be a case of what they call a "dream of longing." He was so devoted to me that he travelled all the way to my home in Iga Ueno to be with me. At night we shared one bed, and we got up and lay down at the same time. He helped me, sharing the hardships of my journey, and for a hundred days accompanied me like my shadow. Sometimes he was playful, sometimes sad—his solitude impressed itself deep in my heart. I must have had such a dream because I cannot forget him. When I woke I once again wrung the tears from my sleeves.[160]

Transgenerational homosexuality remained widespread in monastic institutions, where the priest-acolyte bond continued to have a pedagogical as well as sexual function, but such relationships were frowned upon in other institutions of learning.

Egalitarian Homosexual Relationships

As shown earlier, the two partners in a *nanshoku* relationship typically differed not only in age but also in social rank. Japan was not unique in this role-structured homosexuality; Michel Foucault, writing of European classical antiquity, referred to the "principle

of isomorphism" between "sexual relations and social relations."
In ancient Greece, he notes, sexual relations "were seen as being
of the same type as the relationship between a superior and a subordinate, an individual who dominates and one who is dominated,
one who commands and one who complies."[161]

Homosexual relations between such partners were accepted
not only because they suited the existing class system but also because they did not seem to threaten established gender roles. But
what of relationships that defy Foucault's "principle of isomorphism"? Eva Keuls writes that in ancient Athens, a relationship
in which men alternated sexual roles would have constituted "a
rebellion against the social order. A mutual sex relationship between two adult men of approximately the same age and social
standing negates the use of sex as the underpinning of a power
structure, be it that of man over wife, man over prostitute, or
adult male over young boy."[162]

Thus, even in ancient societies where homosexual relationships
were widely tolerated, the insertee role in the adult male was
viewed with fear or hostility. Some have suggested that such a fear
is universal in preindustrial, including non-Western, societies.[163]

However, one must question the applicability of such theses to
Japan. Although adult males apparently preferred boys as homosexual partners, one also finds references in the literature to relationships between social equals of comparable ages. Such relationships do not seem to have been perceived as a challenge to the
existing social order, nor does one find any particular fear of
male sexual passivity.

In Tokugawa Japan, the insertee was often an adult. As noted
above, kabuki actors could sometimes "get under a man's robe"
even midway through their fourth decade, and so, no doubt,
could common male prostitutes. Yonosuke, Saikaku's hedonistic
merchant, has sex at age fourteen with a twenty-four-year old itinerant prostitute.[zz][164] The *Fumoto no iro* (Eros of the foothills,
1768) records how a male prostitute[aaa] named Ogiya Yashige
stayed in the business until age sixty![165]

zz. *tobiko*
aaa. *iroko*

Manservants employed for sexual purposes were not necessarily boys, although they might be obliged to assume a boyish appearance; as noted, the initiation ceremony could be delayed or even postponed indefinitely. A poem written in 1709 implies that a sexual relationship between a lord and page might last a lifetime:

> *Itsumademo*
> *koshō mo gomotsu*
> *dono mo dono*
>
> Forever and ever
> the page still the favorite
> the lord still the lord[166]

Homosexual relationships, of course, often developed between boys or adolescents of equal status, and these might endure into adulthood. Saikaku, in a rather burlesque chapter of his *Nanshoku ōkagami*, describes two nine-year-olds involved in a "brotherhood-bond"; more plausibly, he depicts about a dozen such relationships between samurai teenagers.[167] But where he specifies age, the partners are usually separated by several years: a sixteen-year-old and an eighteen-year-old, a fifteen-year-old and a twenty-year-old, a sixteen-year-old and a nineteen-year-old. In such relationships, the formal attainment of adulthood meant little; both partners might have undergone the *genpuku* ceremony, or both might retain their long forelocks.

However, if only one of the partners had undergone the initiation ceremony, he would surely have been considered the "elder" (hence, "active") member of the pair. Such relationships could endure for a long time, even into the twilight years. One scholar suggests that Kōsaka Danjō remained "the lover and constant companion to [warlord Takeda] Shingen throughout his life"; if so, Danjō was still sharing Shingen's bed at age forty-eight.[168] In one of Saikaku's fictional examples, two samurai named Toyoda Haemon and Mondo Takashima, having been lovers since Haemon was nineteen, have for many years co-managed an apothecary specializing in hemorrhoid medicine. Haemon is now sixty-six, Takashima sixty-three.[169]

Most significant, relationships among social equals of comparable ages might begin after both men had reached adulthood. Perhaps the best literary example of such a relationship—what Eva Keuls calls "a true homosexual relationship"—is found in the tale entitled *Kikuka no chigiri* ("The Chrysanthemum Vow") in the *Ugetsu monogatari* (Tales of moon and rain) by Ueda Akinari (1734–1809). The story is set in the fifteenth century to increase its exoticism but probably reflects a contemporary conception of ideal male-male relationships. A "scholar" named Hasebe Samon, whose age is not given, lives with his aged mother in the town of Kako (modern Kakogawa) in the province of Harima. When Akana Sōemon, a samurai from Izumo, comes passing through and suddenly falls ill, Samon kindly nurses him back to health. Their mutual feelings deepen. "As one [heart], honored by one another and happy to be together," they forge a "brotherhood bond." The relationship is open and honorable; Samon's mother is much pleased to have gained another son.

There comes a day when Akana, fully recovered, must leave to avenge his former lord. (As always, feudal obligations must transcend personal feelings.) He promises, however, to return on the night of the Chrysanthemum Festival. Samon waits up until late on the night of the festival, having prepared a feast for his friend's homecoming. As midnight passes, his mother retires. Samon's heart sinks—but then to his joy, Akana's figure appears in the distance. Strangely somber, the samurai enters the house but eats none of the delicacies offered. He is dead, a ghost lingering on earth only to fulfill his "chrysanthemum vow." Moved by Akana's loyalty, Samon hastens to Izumo, where, boasting that he is Akana's "younger brother," he avenges his lover's death.[170]

The homoerotic content of this short, strangely moving tale seems unmistakable, and Iwata Jun'ichi includes it in his *nanshoku* bibliography. Though few pieces of Japanese fiction have been so often translated into Western languages, it is amazing that even well-annotated translations of this story overlook the sexual elements.[171] True, there is no explicit mention of sex between the two, but Samon's feelings and actions represent far more than ordinary friendship; the terminology used to describe the pair's relationship has sexual overtones; and the title itself contains terms clearly associated with homosexuality. *Kiku* (chrysanthemum) is an important symbol of *nanshoku*; *chigiri* refers either to the brotherhood "vow" or to a "tryst."

Some relationships began as intimate friendships between boys and men but were not sexually consummated until the boy had reached adulthood. Yamamoto Jōchō's *Hagakure*, seeming to echo Plato's *Symposium*, suggests a five- to six-year courtship period so that the partners can test one another's faithfulness.[172] By the time this period was over, the younger partner would probably have passed out of adolescence.[173]

One therefore finds evidence of egalitarian homosexual relationships during the period. However, even relationships between adults of equal status and only slight age differences took the form of a "brotherhood bond" forged through a "brotherly oath."[bbb] The consequent establishment of a distinction between an "older brother"[ccc] and "younger brother"[ddd] probably rested on a range of factors in the partners' interaction. This is, again, a reflection of deep-rooted Confucian concepts. The *Kikuka no chigiri* tale gives a striking example. Samon and Akana are both adult men, separated in age by only five years. Having fallen in love, they "at length made a brotherly oath. Since Akana was five years older, he became Samon's 'elder brother,' according to [the rules of] etiquette."[174] The long-established rules of such "brotherhood bonds" entitle Akana, as the elder partner, to various courtesies and deferential treatment from his "younger brother" and establish his role as the active partner in their sexual relations. In the tale of Haemon and Takashima, too, the "older brother–younger brother" distinction appears: Takashima, who makes himself up to look like a pre-*genpuku* page to please Haemon, is clearly supposed to be the "passive" partner.[175]

It seems likely that most men attracted to *nanshoku* never became involved in such stable, egalitarian homosexual relationships. One of Saikaku's characters, for example, voices some thoughts that "most people try to avoid thinking about." The

bbb. *kyōdai keiyaku* or *kyōdai chigiri*
ccc. *anibun, anikibun, nenja, nenyū, kyūyū*
ddd. *otōtobun, wakashū*

best homosexual partners, he declares, are *not* those with whom one shares "mutual feelings of affection" and must "support in a crisis"; rather, "professional youths"[eee] are the finest. One need not consider their feelings. They are purely sexual objects.[176] By contrast, another character in the same work, having enjoyed sex with a thousand boys over twenty-seven years, regrets that his *nanshoku* experiences have lacked real affection; with only a few of the boys, he laments, has he "shared a sense of honor[fff] and masculine pride."[ggg] Relationships such as that of Akana and Samon were probably rare, if not beyond most men's imaginations.[177]

Social Status and Sexual Roles

Even homosexual relationships between social equals conformed to an active/passive model. More surprising, in relationships involving men of different class or status groups, the older "brother" might actually be a social inferior. In one of Chikamatsu's plays, for example, the page of a certain samurai, courted by four different men, must choose a lover from among them. Three of the eager suitors are samurai officers. The fourth is a manservant[hhh] working in the same household as the page. The samurai hopefuls jeer the servant's suit, but the page's (biological) brother, speaking on the latter's behalf, declares, "In this Way there are no rank distinctions!"[iii 178]

All men, that is to say, are capable of sincere love for a *wakashū*, and youths may choose to respond even to the advances of a humble suitor.[179] The *Chikusai monogatari* (Tale of Chikusai), written around 1621 by the physician Tomiyama Dōya, describes how a rough-hewn Kyoto commoner, visiting Kitano shrine, catches a glimpse of a beautiful aristocratic youth discussing poetry with some comrades. He immediately falls in love and cannot restrain himself from approaching:

eee. *wake no wakashū*
fff. *giri*
ggg. *iki*
hhh. *chūgen*
iii. *Kono dō ni kōge wa nai*

[T]aking hold of the curtain enclosure, he lifted it and without the slightest trepidation or hesitation knelt respectfully on the white sand of the garden. Those who were inside the closure judged from his bearing what it was he wished. "It certainly seems to me that he has come here thinking to present himself to our Lord. True sentiment indeed does not depend on birth. Even that frightful, rotting plum tree flowers with double blossoms. Although in appearance he seems uncouth, pity him from the generosity of your heart."

The noble listened and without saying a word offered the fellow his cup. "Ah, your kindness is more than I deserve," said the rough-hewn fellow, "an honor for me while I live and glory to my name after I die. What more could I desire?" They then exchanged three cups.[180]

Soon the aristocratic youths leave in their palanquins, but the love-smitten fellow composes an amusingly inept love-letter, which fully reflects his "uncouth" background, and sends it after the noble he will never see again.[181]

The author of this work depicts such passion as altogether natural, and the young nobleman's friend seems to regard the suitor's "true sentiment," if not his bearing or appearance, as entirely appropriate. Similarly, an Okumura print depicts an impoverished samurai entertaining a visiting youth who seems to be of higher social origins. The warrior is shown carving up his treasured flute to use as firewood to prepare tea for his guest. The picture is meant to be satirical; it alludes to the plot of a noh play in which a poor samurai cuts up his treasured bonsai trees for firewood when visited by a high official. The humor of the print resides in the fact that the samurai here is motivated not by respect for an officer but by lust for a beautiful boy.[182]

One finds actual historical examples of social inferiors' taking the active role in consummating sexual relationships with a superior. Tokugawa Iemitsu, the third shogun of this line, was sexually involved with his "older brother page,"[jjj] Mizuno Narisada, and, according to the *Genkan nikki* (Diary of the Genna and Kan'ei eras), another personal attendant[kkk] named Sakabe Gozaemon.[183] The latter had been close to Iemitsu from childhood; four years

jjj. *nenyū no koshō*
kkk. *kinjū*

older than his lord and physically attracted to him, he took the "older brother" role in the relationship. "In his case," according to Koike, "it was a homosexual relationship[III] in which Iemitsu, as the 'younger brother,' offered himself physically, giving pleasure to Gozaemon, the 'elder brother.' The 'younger brother' Iemitsu was forced to bear the pain of the passive partner in this act."[184]

The relationship ended in tragedy: The sixteen-year-old Iemitsu killed his twenty-one-year-old manservant for a real or imagined offense while the two and other retainers were relaxing in a bathtub. Nevertheless, the example proves that sexual relations did not always conform to social relations. The insertee, or passive, role was not exclusively taken by class or status inferiors; it was generally regarded as the role of youth—even aristocratic youth.[185]

III. *nandō kankei*

Chapter Four

Social Tolerance

Why don't we debate the issue? Is the Way of Women
truly vulgar, and the Way of Youths really more refined?
Let's see whose logic is superior, and be tolerant
towards the weaker argument!

Denbu monogatari (ca. 1640)

Cold and hot seasons, day and night come in turn. No
one can control how the spring blossoms or autumn
leaves fall. So how can anyone criticize either the Way
of Men or the Way of Women?

Hiraga Gennai, *Kiku no en* (1764)

The ancient Greeks regarded eros as a powerful creative drive independent of any specific erotic object. Similarly, most Japanese
of the Tokugawa period probably viewed sexual desire (*iro*)[a] as a
force that might become focused upon either women or men.[1]
The object of desire was less of an issue that the volatile nature
of *iro* itself. *Iro* inhered in all human beings, even the greatest, and
had the potential to inspire them to great deeds or, alternately, to
lead them astray. Ieyasu himself, the founder of the Tokugawa
shogunate, was described by the Osaka scholar Nakai Shūan
(1693–1757) as "a sage who could not control his sex life."[b][2]

Only the holiest and most disciplined of Buddhist priests were
thought capable of overcoming sexual desire and faithfully observing the Buddha's command to abjure all sexual activity. The rest
of the clergy, it was widely assumed, would yield to temptation
with male or female partners. The positive attitude toward sexuality found in the indigenous Shinto faith may have worked to relax

a. written with the same character as *shoku*, as in *nanshoku*, and also meaning "color"

b. *nema o osamaranu shōnin*

the negative view of the body and of sex expressed in the Buddhist sutras; it may also have helped to produce a tolerant attitude toward individuals in whom "human feeling" (*ninjo*) sometimes overcame religious vows or "duty" (*giri*). In any case, Tokugawa views about the potency of *iro* are most poignantly expressed in tales about monks and priests.

Nanshoku—which might be rendered "a man's male-oriented eros" or "a man's male-directed eros"—was thus usually seen in itself as a normal form of sexual desire. But, like all forms of *iro*, it was a mysterious and complex phenomenon, sometimes danger- ous and base, sometimes ennobling and refined. Thus, a discussion of popular attitudes toward male-male sex cannot be reduced to the simple observation that it was tolerated. It was in fact sub- jected to various criticisms. Whereas a samurai's adoration and patient courtship of a younger man might have been associated with the highest values of the ruling class, a monk's unrestrained passion for a kabuki actor might be depicted as ruinous and con- temptible. Tokugawa commentators expressed concern about the potential effects of homosexual passion upon (heterosexual) mar- riage, procreation, personal finances, physical and mental health, social order, and the maintenance of the status system.

Acceptance and Criticism

Men's sexual desire for other males, as long as it conformed to the rules described in the previous chapter, was regarded as one of the typical weaknesses of the flesh. *Nanshoku* was an inclination common to all men, but some were more vulnerable to it than others. This attitude is reflected, for example, in the similarity of the terms *nanshoku-zuki* ("*nanshoku* enthusiast" or "*nanshoku*- lover") and *sake-zuki* ("alcohol-lover"—i.e., heavy drinker). Pa- rents would counsel their sons to avoid potentially ruinous homo- sexual involvements, but the context of such advice suggests that they probably did not expect absolute abstinence from male-male sexual contact. When Hori Chikayoshi, daimyo of Iida, drew up his testament[c] in 1636, he exhorted his son and heir, Chikamasa,

---

c. *yuigon*

to take care in his diet, spurn tea and liquor, and avoid "both the way of women[d] and the way of men.'"[e] It would have been difficult to abjure all such enjoyments; Chikayoshi was probably advocating restraint and moderation in all of them.[3]

In this document, heterosexual and homosexual indulgence are represented as equal dangers and placed on a par with excess caffeine consumption. Elsewhere the exhortation to avoid pederasty appears alongside homiletic warnings to pursue military preparedness and to avoid frivolous pastimes. Oda Nobunaga, upon granting part of Echizen province to Shibata Katsuie in 1575, advised him to avoid falconry, to "stockpile weapons and supplies," to "not be greedy," to "stay away from young boys," and to "abstain from theatricals, parties and promenades, and other such diversions."[4] *Nanshoku* (like tea, liquor, falconry, and parties) was a pleasurable distraction, which might divert one from one's work— a natural temptation one should indulge in only sparingly.

Hiraga Gennai, in his *Kiku no en* (Chrysanthemum garden, 1768), argued that the coexistence of *nanshoku* and *joshoku* is as natural as the alteration of the seasons or the differing tastes in food and drink: "People with a sweet-tooth[f] rarely overdrink, while heavy drinkers dislike the sweet taste of bean-jelly.[g] Cold and hot seasons, day and night come in turn. No one can control how the spring blossoms or autumn leaves will fall. So how can anyone criticize the differences between *nanshoku* and *joshoku*?"[5]

Surely there were some who, for one reason or another, found *why?* male-male sex objectionable, but they are often depicted as uncultured, boorish people. Gennai writes: "In a Yoshiwara guidebook, there will be a graded list [of actor-prostitutes] of each [theatrical] season in Sakai-chō and Kobiki-chō. It's appreciated by men of the world[h] everywhere. But won't some others despise it—foolish, ignorant louts—people who don't understand this thriving thing?"[i][6] For the benefit of such culturally deprived men, Gennai

d. *nyōdō*
e. *nandō*
f. *mochi-zuki*, lit. "lovers of rice cake"
g. *yōkan*
h. *yo no hito*
i. *kono sakan naru koto o shirazaru guchi muchi bonbu*

lightheartedly describes the *nanshoku-jaya* experience, including its thrills and frustrations:

> Stroking his patron's arm, [a male prostitute] will strike a dreamlike pose, as though he is himself reaching heights of ecstasy. He'll make endless, capricious vows,[j] and address you with the most intimate names. [Tears] will appear about the eyes on his dazzled face. *Aara,* that's strange! Is this some apparition? A group [sent from] his manager![k]
>
> *Yai!* Those of you who love sweets might find this amusing. But don't laugh. It'd be the gravest mistake not to eat up all those crumbs. You might start taking a liking to wine![7]

In other words, just as those with a sweet tooth can become fond of alcohol, so all males are potentially vulnerable to the attractions of their own sex.

Among young men, in particular, a passion for boys or other youths was regarded as normal. In the tale *Nenashigusa,* summarized in Chapter 2, a devil argues that the monk's sentence in hell should be reduced because of his "youthful spirit,"[l] and Enma ultimately pardons him on the grounds that *nanshoku* is "something apt to happen in young men."[m][8] And in the story's sequel, the water-sprite invades the bodies of youths, inflaming them with homosexual desires.

Older men's attraction to youths may have been regarded as less natural and less acceptable. Yamabito, the handsome young hero of Ishikawa Masamochi's *Hida no takumi monogatari* (Tale of a Hida craftsman, 1808), is repeatedly approached by two elderly men depicted as "evil and perverse."[n][9] Yamabito complains of one of these unwanted suitors, "Although an old man he loves pleasure and makes all sorts of advances to me."[10] Pederastic interests seem to have been frowned upon even in men approaching thirty. In Saikaku's *Kōshoku gonin onna* (1685), for example, a

---

j. *mura no seigen*
k. As noted in Chapter 2, trysts were often abruptly interrupted by teahouse servants or messengers from drama troupes.
l. *wakage*
m. *wakai mono no arisō na koto*
n. *kokoro higamitaru nejikebito*

young girl, having admired the monk Gengobei from afar, makes her way to his hermitage, hoping to seduce him. He is absent, but she enters the dwelling and discovers an open book dealing with *nanshoku*. "So," she observes to herself, "he still hasn't given up this passion!"[o][11] She does not seem surprised that the monk remains sexually active despite his religious calling; rather, she finds it odd that a man nearly thirty years old continues to prefer sex with boys. When the poet Bashō, at age twenty-nine, wrote, "I used to enjoy *shudō*,"[p] he may have been implying that he had since outgrown this stage.[12]

The charge that one is not acting one's age is not, however, damning, and occasional forays into the world of *nanshoku* teahouses by men of any age were probably condoned by society. The "brotherhood bonds" described in Chapter 1 also met with tolerance. Surely there were exceptions. Monks, as already noted, may have met with a degree of public contempt for breaking their vows of sexual abstinence, the Kūkai legend notwithstanding, and parents may have discouraged young sons from entering into homosexual relationships. In one of Saikaku's *Nanshoku ōkagami* tales, a youth involved with a martial-arts teacher has to meet him in the evening when his father is at work. He fears his parents' reaction but is unconcerned with "society's censure."[q][13] Elsewhere a mother appeals to her boy's attendant to shield him from homosexual involvements—even though the boy himself is eager to enter into such an affair.[14]

However, the terms "accept" and "approve"[r] occur very often in this text; for example, Saikaku writes that "people easily accepted"[s] the homosexual relationship of two young samurai.[15] In Ueda Akinari's short story *Kikuka no chigiri* (The chrysanthemum vow, 1768), a mother expresses joyful approval when her adult son enters into a "brotherhood bond" with another man, and in some literary works family members help broker homosexual relation-

o. *iro*
p. *ware mo mukashi wa shudō-zuki*
q. *yo no soshiri*
r. *miyurushi*
s. *hito mo yasashiku miyurushikeru*

ships.[16] In Ishikawa's *Hida no takumi monogatari*, the mother of
fifteen-year-old Yamabito is anxious to forge such a bond between
the Hida craftsman and her son, and in Chikamatsu's play *Shinjū
yoi no kōjin* (Love-suicide on vigil-night, 1721), a seventeen-year-
old's older brother helps him to choose from among four male
suitors.[17]

But if *nanshoku* was widely tolerated, it was not necessarily regarded as exemplary behavior. Engelbert Kaempfer, as noted
in Chapter 2, referred to "the virtuous" of Japanese society as
being "scandaliz'd" by boy-prostitution.[18] But let us examine a
few blanket condemnations of *nanshoku*, based upon its alleged
unnaturalness.

In 1676 the poet Kitamura Kigin wrote, "It has been in the nature of men's hearts to take pleasure in a beautiful woman since
the age of the male and female gods, but to become infatuated
by the blossom of a handsome youth, not being a woman, would
seem both wrong[t] and unusual." He adds, however, that "people
have a natural curiosity about the unusual."[u] [19] A character in the
Denbu monogatari expresses a similar opinion: "Other males are
useless as love-objects. Men have been fond of the way of women
since ancient times."[20] And the king of hell, in *Nenashigusa*, initially remarks, "The only thing I absolutely cannot understand in
this corrupt world is *nanshoku*. The way of husband and wife is
yin-yang nature,[v] and if it's shameful for a monk [to follow this
way], then neither should he ever fuck another man!"[21]

All of these statements are made tongue-in-cheek, however.
Kitamura's appears in the preface to his volume of homoerotic
poetry, the *Denbu monogatari* reference is countered with a spir-
ited defense of *nanshoku*, and in Hiraga Gennai's work, as we
have seen, the lord of the netherworld himself falls in love with
the actor Kikunojō. One might expect to find the "nature argu-

t. *ayashiku*; could be rendered "dubious" or "suspect"
u. *mare naru mono wa warinaku mima hoshiki*
v. *in-yō shizen*

ment" articulated more seriously by neo-Confucian intellectuals or by Nativist (*Kokugaku*) scholars, both of whom emphasized the individual's obligation to enter into heterosexual marriage. As noted previously, the former had little to say on this matter; Hayashi Razan, for example, simply found it "interesting." But among Nativist scholars, Miyahiro Sadao (1797–1858) seems to have upheld "male-female intercourse as a principle," indeed a religious duty, and implied that bisexual behavior in the male would lead his wife to "give birth to bad offspring."[22] He compares homosexuality to sowing grains improperly and reaping a bad harvest. Not surprisingly, Miyahiro also condemned the practice of sending young boys to Buddhist monasteries, where they would not be allowed the "natural" use of their penises.[23]

All in all, though, the nature argument does not amount to much; it has been raised in many societies, including those that tolerate male-male sexuality. In the latter, the very prevalence of homosexuality seems to contradict the argument and to support the "naturalness" of such behavior. Thus, whereas the Athenian in Plato's *Laws* regards homosexual pleasure as "contrary to nature," the pseudo-Aristotilean *Problemata* explains that "some men are effeminate by nature."[24] It goes so far as to hypothesize that some of the semen in such men passes naturally from its place of origin into their rectums, which it sensitizes for sexual enjoyment.[25] The Japanese folklore of the *kappa*, or water-sprite, seems to represent a similar effort to explain homosexual inclinations; as noted, the sprite intrudes through the anus, takes possession of the body, and awakens a passion for *nanshoku*.[26] More commonly, the laws of karma were invoked to explain both heterosexual and homosexual desires.[27]

The nature argument against *nanshoku* was less compelling than specific, practical concerns. Men inclined toward homosexual behavior might neglect to marry women, for example. In societies influenced by Confucianism, failure to marry constitutes a lack of filial devotion. "Filial piety is the most important thing for children," declares the critic in *Denbu monogatari*. "Do you think that parents are happy when, after they have taken the trouble to finally arrange a good marriage for a son, he tells them, 'I only like youths. Please find a youth for me—I despise women'? Or when he marries in order to please his parents, but then greets his bride with, 'I'm a boy-lover'?"[w] [28]

Much of the *Denbu monogatari* is in fact devoted to the defense of brides and women in general. The critic of *nanshoku* obliquely attacks male homosexuality as a disparagement of women's worth, and indeed the "way of youths"[x] spokesman reviles the female sex on traditional Buddhist and Confucian grounds. The critic responds with an extraordinary review of the role of great women in Japanese and continental history, from the Buddha's wife, Yashodara, to Heian authoresses, to Hōjō Masako.[29] Though he does not suggest that women-hating is an integral feature of *nanshoku*, the fact that this issue arises in the debate indicates that misogyny and male-male sex were to some extent linked in popular conception.

Men enamored of youths might also be criticized for frittering away the family fortune in pursuit of such relationships. The anti-*nanshoku* debater in *Denbu monogatari* comments: "There are some married men who also love boys. But don't they as a result ignore their wives and children, wasting away their wealth and property? They turn the keys of their treasure-storehouses over to their boys. And haven't you heard about men who leave their fortunes to youths instead of to their wives and children?"[30] The *Hagakure* refers to various men who come to financial ruin because of homosexual involvements, including a pre-*genpuku* page who, "infatuated with an actor,"[y] sells off his clothes and other possessions and ends up stealing in order to finance his trysts.[31]

Other charges leveled at homosexual behavior refer to its effects upon the "passive" partner, particularly the pain the "younger brother" is presumed to experience and the potential risks to his health. The critic in the *Denbu monogatari* charges that boys used for anal sex "suffer from hemorrhoids and become bow-legged. When their parents inquire, 'Why do you walk as though you were

w. *wakushū-zuki*
x. *jakudō*
y. *yarō-gurui ni*

being stuck with a bamboo cane?' they can't explain what's ailing them. They just blush with embarrassment. Pitiful! Then too, they contract incurable diseases, which even the springs of Arima and Totsukawa cannot cure."[32] In a similar vein, King Enma in *Nena-shigusa* deplores *nanshoku* on the grounds that it has increased the numbers of hemorrhoid-sufferers taking the cure at the hot springs of Kinosaki in Tajima and Sokokura in Hakone.[33]

In his *Shikidō kinpishō* (Compendium of sexual secrets, 1834), the scholar Nishimura Sadao discounted the health hazards involved in homosexual intercourse. Rather than emphasizing hemorrhoids or the pain the passive partner might experience, he stressed the flexibility of the anus: "Even though it is narrow at first, the creases around the anal opening indicate that it can accommodate [a penis] of any size—more than a vagina can. It is commonly stated that a vagina has forty-eight folds. The anus has more than that, and since the pubic bones are not in the way, larger things will fit into it."[34]

As for health risks to the active partner, Nishimura admitted that contact with feces might produce disease. But he downplayed the dangers by citing a bit of folklore.

> I myself am in the dark about this Way, but here is something I heard from someone who practices *nanshoku*.[z] One should avoid withdrawing one's turtle-head[aa] covered with feces—something which is called "a headband."[bb] To prevent this, when you are about to withdraw your turtle-head, you should strongly pinch [your partner's] buttocks. Because of the pain, he will automatically droop down.[cc] If you withdraw at that point, you probably will not acquire disease from the "headband."[dd] I haven't tried this myself, but it's an interesting theory.[35]

All in all, health and hygiene arguments do not seem to have been very prominent in the discussion of male-male sex. Indeed,

z. *nanshoku-ka*
aa. *karisaki*; a common euphemism for the foreskin
bb. *hachimaki*
cc. *omowazu shiri o shibomu*
dd. *hachimaki no uree nashi to ka ya*

some believed that such sex had potential curative properties for the inserter. Just as intercourse with a menstruating woman was thought to cure venereal disease, so anal sex with boys was thought to provide a cure for the degenerative nerve disease beriberi.[36]

Fears about the potentially corrosive effects of sexual desire in general upon mental health outweighed concern about the physical aspects of male-male sex. Ueda Akinari's story *Aozukin* (The blue hood, 1776) reflects such anxiety. In the tale, set in a village in Shimotsuke, a highly learned and virtuous abbot returns from a pilgrimage to a distant temple, bringing back with him a good-looking thirteen-year-old boy. Soon he is so enraptured with the boy that he neglects his duties; when the boy falls ill and dies, he is inconsolable. Refusing to cremate or inter the corpse, he goes mad: "He played with the boy just as he had done while the youth was alive. Then, refusing to allow the body to rot and decay, he sucked the flesh and licked the bones until he had utterly devoured it. 'The abbot has turned into a devil,' the people in the temple said, and all fled."[37] Later, he begins to haunt the cemetery, searching for fresh cadavers to eat.

A Zen priest of great virtue learns of the mad abbot and, to the relief of the villagers, leads him from insanity to salvation. The priest explains the abbot's madness by referring to his uncontrollable passion for the boy:

> It must be owing to his past karma.[ee] After all, his constant piety, his devotion and his service to the Buddhas were the epitome of reverence, so he would certainly have been an ideal priest had he not taken in the youth. Quite likely, once he descended into the sinful path of love and lust,[ff] he was changed into a demon, and he fell victim to the flames of the fires in the hell of delusion.[38]

But here the phrase "sinful path of love and lust" seems to refer to an immoderately passionate attachment to an acolyte rather than to homosexuality itself.

Other criticisms of homosexual behavior dealt specifically with

ee. *kano no inen*
ff. *aiyoku no meiro*

its supposedly disruptive effects upon the social order. In the
Denbu monogatari, for example, the critic of *nanshoku* declares
that these relationships often result in violence. During the early
seventeenth century, when it was written, bloodshed involving homosexual rivalries and love triangles was particularly common
among young samurai, and quarrels over kabuki actors often produced disorder.[39] The *Iro monogatari* (Erotic tales, ca. 1670) records that "recently the scoundrels[gg] called 'youth fanatics'[hh] have
been very troublesome, and all the damage they have caused
would make a good story."[40] As I will later show, the authorities
were especially concerned about the explosive aspect of many
male-male relationships, including love triangles and instances of
unrequited love.

Even popular uprisings, such as the "smashings"[ii] that periodi-
cally occurred in the great cities from the early eighteenth century, were sometimes linked to homosexual fascination. Often it
was rumored that the mass movements were led by "beautiful
youths"[jj]—apparitions whose identity could not be determined.[41]
Perhaps with such associations in mind, the writer Takizawa Bakin
depicted the beautiful youth as a vaguely evil being in his *Kinsei
setsu bishnen roku* (A record of recent rumors about beautiful
youths, completed in 1848).[42]

The very status system underlying the social order might be
threatened by homosexual passions. As noted previously, "older
brothers" or male-brothel patrons might shower their lovers with
extravagant gifts, leading to financial ruin. Moreover, low-born
prostitutes and actors might exploit their sex appeal to topple
their betters. The popular work *Edo meishoki* (Famous sights of
Edo, 1660) points out that, even though the male prostitutes associated with the kabuki theater all come from "extremely base"
family backgrounds, they are nevertheless "respected by the stupid"—including those with substantial wealth: "[T]hey flapped
about like kites and owls and, going into the presence of the ex-

gg. *kusemono*
hh. *wakashū-gurui*
ii. *uchikowashi*
jj. *bishōnen*

alted, befouled the presence; and these were scoundrels who, saying insolent things as it pleased them, ruined men and held them
in contempt; moreover, they polluted the highborn on the sly."[43]
The regime shared this concern as it strove, with little success, to
prevent such interclass mixing and to implement sumptuary laws.

Nanshoku and the Law

If society in general was tolerant of *nanshoku*, so was the ruling
class, partly out of very pragmatic concerns. Although the rise of
absolutism in both early modern Europe and Ming-Qing China
has been linked to mounting repression of homosexuality, the
Tokugawa regime, described by the English merchant Richard
Cocks in 1614 as "the greatest and powerfullest Terrany, that
ever was heard of in the world," undertook no such campaign.[44]

Part of the Tokugawa rulers' genius, indeed, was their ability to
use pleasure to divert the energies of samurai and commoners
alike from potentially rebellious action. Denied fiefdoms and the
glory of battle and having little prospect of fortune or advancement, the samurai could dissipate their energies and meager
incomes in licensed brothel districts such as Edo's Yoshiwara. Nationally, twenty-four such districts were officially approved by the
shogunate, and unauthorized pleasure quarters[kk] were generally
tolerated by the authorities.[45] In certain urban spaces, such as riv-
erbanks, the approaches to bridges, theaters, baths, and teahouse
brothels, prostitutes were traditionally allowed to operate with little official interference.[46] On temple and shrine lands, which were
separately administered, bans on public performances and commercial sex were often administered less strictly than elsewhere.[47]

True, samurai were discouraged from entering these demi-
mondes. The *Buke sho-hatto* (Laws for samurai households, 1615),
a basic legal document defining proper samurai behavior, warned

---

kk. *okabasho; kakurezato* ("hidden villages"); *kakuremachi* ("hidden wards").
The first of these terms is written with characters suggesting "hill places" but is
derived from the phrase *hoka basho* ("other places," i.e., pleasure wards other
than the officially licensed ones). In the Osaka-Kyoto area, the term *hoka basho*
itself was used.

that "lasciviousness"[ll] could ruin the state,[mm] and individual samurai mansions strove to control their retainers' behavior through
such devices as curfews.[48] As noted previously, the shogunal regime occasionally launched reform movements that included
measures to discourage prostitution, paying particular attention to
the moral conduct of the warrior class. Samurai were banned from
using Edo's public bathhouses,[nn] for example, after a violent incident involving a samurai official and a bathhouse prostitute[oo] in
1600.[49]

But the Tokugawa shoguns generally seem to have expected
the warriors to release some of their sexual tensions in the flourishing pleasure quarters of the castle-towns. They would swagger
through the licensed quarters, clearly distinguished as samurai by
their long and short swords, but they would conceal their personal
identities under broad wicker hats. They also frequented the
theater districts, drawn to the performances as well as to the inns
specializing in male prostitution. It was said that the best customers of Edo's male brothels[pp] were the retainers of the Shimazu daimyo of Satsuma.[50]

By the eighteenth century the authorities were conceptually
coupling the *nanshoku* brothel districts with the courtesan wards
as "bad places."[qq] Among the many sections in the collections of
ofuregaki (edicts) is one containing proclamations concerning
"Kabuki Drama, Prostitutes, Male Prostitutes and *Bikuni*."[rr][51]
Not only theater-related male prostitution but also the content of
the plays and even the sensual twang of the *shamisen* accompanying the performances were regarded by Confucian scholars as
deleterious to morals.[52] "The sound of the shamisen," warned
one eighteenth-century Kyushu moralist, "is enough to put lewd
thoughts into the mind of a saintly priest with years of Zen medi-

ll. *kōshoku*
mm. *bōkoku*
nn. *sentō*
oo. *yuna*
pp. *kagema chaya*
qq. *akusho*
rr. *Kabuki shibai yūjo yarō bikuni nado. Bikuni* in this instance means a kind
of prostitute dressed as a nun.

tation behind him."[53] From the time of the fifth shogun, Tsunayoshi (r. 1680–1709), kabuki performances were in theory off-
limits to the samurai. After the Ejima-Ikushima scandal in 1714
(described in Chapter 5), official opposition hardened further.

Such attitudes had not always prevailed. In the formative decades of kabuki, the art form had indeed received high-level support. The third shogun, Iemitsu, often invited the troupe of Nakamura Kenzaburō to perform in Edo Castle, and in 1635 powerful
daimyo treated the ruler to plays performed by their own *wakashū*
pages. During this period, Matsudaira Naonori, a daimyo of Yamato province, kept a diary of his own theater visits.[54] Even after
samurai had been forbidden to attend the performances, artists
produced woodblock prints clearly depicting two-sworded warriors in the audiences, and high-ranking samurai still numbered
among avid kabuki fans.[55]

Despite Tsunayoshi's distaste for kabuki, his own top minister
and intimate, Yanagisawa Yoshiyasu, kept a theatergoing journal,
and the latter's grandson Nobutoki patronized actors, collected
actor prints, and held performances at his own mansion in Kōriyama until 1772.[56] In any case, official hostility to samurai involvement with kabuki probably stemmed from concerns about class
mixing and the weakening of military discipline rather than the
homoerotic qualities of this dramatic form.

The shogunate itself, after all, lavishly patronized the older
drama form of noh from the days of Ieyasu. The stateliness of
this theatrical tradition seemed to satisfy Confucian aesthetic requirements, but it, too, was surrounded by a homoerotic atmosphere and associated with male prostitution.[57] Just as Ashikaga
Yoshimitsu had fallen in love with the noh performer Zeami and
his art, Tsunayoshi enthused about noh, even acting in performances himself, and he took lovers from among the thespians.
So, apparently, did another powerful aficionado of the art, the
eleventh shogun, Ienari (r. 1786–1837).[58] Unlike kabuki actors,
noh performers were not officially despised but rather received a
pseudo-samurai status, and samurai were positively encouraged to
patronize noh.[59]

The regime paid less attention to the moral conduct of the

common classes. Merchants, artisans, and their employees were denied access to political power and were continually reminded of their fourth-class status, but they could squander their wealth in a "floating world" where money alone lent prestige.[60] In one of Chikamatsu's plays, a rich businessman expresses the arrogance prompted by familiarity with the pleasure quarter and his own wealth. Visiting a teahouse, he learns from the manager that his favorite courtesan, Koharu, will be entertaining a samurai client that evening. Undeterred, he proposes a *ménage à trois*: "I'll take Koharu and the samurai, too!"[ss][61]

For the common people patronizing them (although not, to be sure, for the prostitutes), wards specializing in commercial sex constituted islands of democracy in an extraordinarily class-conscious society. For the ruling class, they provided a safety valve. The so-called *Ieyasu no ikun* (Legacy of Ieyasu, ca. 1616) summarizes the thinking of shogunate officials. Acknowledging that "courtesans, dancers, catamites, streetwalkers, and the like always come to the cities and prospering places of the country," causing various social problems, the document suggests that "if they are seriously repressed, serious crimes will occur daily."[62] Two centuries later, the Russian naval captain Golovnin noted the same official ambivalence: "The government does not indeed approve of [this abominable vice], but it adopts no vigorous measures to suppress it."[63]

Despite such mixed feelings, by strictly controlling commercial sex, both heterosexual and homosexual, the authorities in fact used it for their own ends. Consciously or not, the Tokugawa government pursued a program of what might be called "repressive desublimation."[64] I borrow the term from Herbert Marcuse, who suggested that the "pre-established harmony between individual needs and socially-required desires, goals, and aspirations" in modern Western society has resulted from the "mobilization and administration of the libido."[65] Through such means a "happy consciousness" can be generated even in an "unfree society."[66]

Tokugawa Japan was an extraordinarily repressive place; the

ss. *Samurai gurume ni Koharu dono morauta*

status quo imposed rigid limits on personal advancement; punishment for rebellion was demonstratively cruel. But at the same time urban life was deeply colored by the "happy consciousness" cultivated in the pleasure quarters. The regime, though occasionally cracking down on pornography and prostitution, more typically tolerated commercial sex, probably on the theory that subjects diverted by the attractions of the "floating world" would be less likely to demand political or social change.[67]

As the seat of shogunal power, Edo was supposed to serve as a model of urban order. Thus, the regime took careful steps to insure that the masses' level of discontent did not reach a boiling point. About 340 urban uprisings[tt] occurred nationwide during the Tokugawa period, most of them during and after the Tenmei era (1781–1788).[68] But Edo residents seldom rose up, even during critical famine years, partly because the regime organized effective relief programs to placate the most impoverished.[69] Urban authorities appear to have consciously pursued a policy of "bread and circuses"—or rather, relief rice and brothels.

Of course, some laws did govern sex in general and *nanshoku* in particular; adulterous relationships involving married women[uu] were severely proscribed, and female prostitution carefully regulated. Gregory Pflugfelder has argued that the shogunate was less concerned about male homosexuality than about heterosexual crimes. In dealing with offenses involving a homosexual aspect, such as the kidnapping of boys for purposes of prostitution, the regime applied no special punishment for the homosexual connection.[70] Authorities dealt with transgressions such as male-male rape and participation in an attempted homosexual love-suicide[vv] no differently than analogous heterosexual offenses.[71]

Perhaps the earliest edict[ww] of the period to mention homosexuality, issued in Edo in the fifth month of 1648, has at times been interpreted as a general ban on male-male sex.[72] The text, how-

tt. *uchikowashi* ("smashings")
uu. *mittsū*
vv. *shinjū*
ww. *ofuregaki*: general hortatory pronouncements directed to urban populations, often repeated and specifying no specific punishment

ever, suggests a more modest purpose. "One must not," it reads, "make outrageous *shudō* propositions, or lose one's head over *wakashū*."[xx][73] Another edict, issued in the fifth month of 1653, apparently repeats an earlier law which targeted both partners: "These days *shudō* has appeared in the city. As in the past, to make or even to accept *nanshoku* propositions is strictly forbidden."[74] Although the latter law seems quite categorical, it is not clear whether it and many others like it pertain to the samurai or to the entire Edo population. It seems doubtful that the regime intended to ban all homosexual behavior in samurai mansions and commoner households; as noted, Iemitsu, the ruling shogun at the time, openly preferred male sex-partners. Rather, such laws probably applied only to public behavior, including solicitation of male prostitutes.[75]

Boy-prostitution, though widespread, was never specifically legitimated through a licensing system such as that applied to female prostitutes. Kabuki theaters received licenses from urban authorities, but the actors were forbidden overnight visits to patron's homes, and even the kabuki teahouses were occasionally penalized for sponsoring male prostitution.[76]

Several documents, each dated 1689, demonstrate that male prostitution was not always tolerated by Tokugawa authorities. They involve the apparent arrest of a man named Kazen, owner of a shop in Sakai-chō, one of Edo's centers of male prostitution.

(1) Sworn Confession, with Seals Affixed:

I, with base intentions, employed an actor[yy] named Shōzen, when I absolutely should have been obeying the law. This time I give thanks that I have been pardoned [for this offense], but hereafter [I acknowledge] that I must never employ any type of actor or ordinary incense-peddler.[zz] No violation of this law, even the employment of one such person, will be tolerated.

Those affixing their seals will report any evil deeds occurring hereafter.

---

xx. *Shudō no gi ni tsuki mutai nari koto o moshikake wakashū-gurui shi majiku koto*
yy. *yarō*
zz. *kōgu-uri* (a type of male prostitute)

Seals thus affixed:

Sakai-chō Yoshibei Shop: Kazen

[6 other persons]

Second Year of Genroku, Year of the Snake, Sixth Month, Eighteenth Day

(2) Sworn Confession, with Seals Affixed:

I, with base intentions, sent my son Shōzen to serve as an actor[aaa] with Kazen of the Yoshibei Shop in Sakai-chō, when I absolutely should have been obeying the law. This time I have been pardoned, but especially since [Shōzen's] master [Kazen] frees me [from the contract I had made on behalf of my son], and [since my son] is placed back into my care, I express deep gratitude. Hereafter [my son] will absolutely not work as any type of actor or incense peddler, nor [practice prostitution] independently.[bbb]

No violation of [this law] by the person in question will be tolerated. Those affixing their seals will report any evil deeds occurring hereafter.

Seals thus affixed:

Sakai-chō Yoshibei Shop: Kazen, Employer of Shōzen

Second Year of Genroku, Year of the Snake, Sixth Month, Eighteenth Day

(3) Sworn Confession, with Seals Affixed:

I did not send out actors to any theater, but invited patrons of actors to my home. From long ago there have been laws [against this], and all the more hereafter one must not call actors. Actors of the theater and their employers must strictly obey the law, and if they violate it and go somewhere [for a tryst], or if I invite actors' patrons to my home, committing evil acts when I should obey the law, those affixing their seals [below] must quickly report what they see and hear. Or if I hire any type of incense-peddler or actor outside the theater, [the signatories] must quickly report what they see and hear.

If the [rules listed] above are violated, the main actor[ccc] must report this. Those affixing their seals will report any evil deeds occurring hereafter.

Seals thus affixed:

Sakai-chō Rihei Shop: Main Actor Matazaburō

Second Year of Genroku, Year of the Snake, Sixth Month, Eighteenth Day

---

aaa. *yarō hōkō ni ide sōro*
bbb. *mata jibun nite mo*
ccc. *tayū-moto*

Matazaburō's Employee Ima Yoshiiyo
[3 other persons]
Householder: Rihei
[2 other persons]
Second Year of Genroku, Year of the Snake, Eighth Month, Second Day[77]

It appears from these documents that Shōzen plied his trade in Kazen's teahouse as well as at the home of the actor Matazaburō. Apparently the latter two had an arrangement whereby the actor would provide boys (ostensibly his apprentices) to the teahouse to support his theatrical troupe. The most remarkable points in the documents are the leniency of the judgment, even though all parties violated laws depicted as having existed "from long ago,"[ddd] and the seeming absence of responsibility borne by the prostitute himself, probably because of his age.

Neither Yoshibei's teahouse nor Rihei's theatrical company was closed down as a result of this episode. The regime was usually willing to tolerate such establishments. Yoshibei could argue that his house simply allowed patrons to meet their favorite performers, to drink and dine with them or hire them for private dances and skits. Perhaps Rihei's boys engaged in legitimately theatrical entertainment as well as commercial sex. The circumstances surrounding this intervention by the officials are unclear, but we can assume that this was an unusual case; the authorities seldom significantly impeded the purchase and sale of *nanshoku*.

Many laws dealing with homosexuality reflect a concern with the behavior of the highest-ranking strata in the feudal order: the daimyo and bannermen.[eee] These were supposed to serve as moral examples for society, yet, according to an edict issued during the mid-seventeenth century, "Recently daimyo and bannermen have become overwhelmed by *nanshoku*; they assemble their pages[fff] and have them serve sake. Pursuing pleasure, they compete at law-breaking."[78]

ddd. *maemae yori*
eee. *hatamoto* (direct retainers of the shogun)
fff. *kachi*

The shogunate associated *nanshoku* with extravagance and violence in general. A law[ggg] issued in the ninth month of 1650 forbade officials[hhh] working in the Nishi-maru section of the shogun's
castle from quarrelling, holding meetings in private residences, or
engaging in *nanshoku*. Presumably these three activities were associated with one another.[79] Similarly, a law of the second month
of 1654 prohibited bannermen from a curious set of actions: flying
kites, attiring manservants in beautiful clothes, and employing
footboys[iii] as "objects of *nanshoku*."[80] These were no doubt seen
as related phenomena: the lord pampered his beloved boy with
gorgeous outfits and amused him with such pastimes as kite flying.

These laws seem to reflect the same concerns raised by the
critic in *Denbu monogatari*. The last seems less a piece of moral-
istic legislation than another of the (generally ignored) sumptuary
laws. But urban authorities' greatest concern was the violence
that so often stemmed from homosexual involvements, especially
those between samurai and their servants.

Nanshoku and Violence

In his classic *Genroku jidai* (The Genroku era), Kodama Kōta
notes that handsome valets, pages, and footboys[jjj] in samurai mansions often became "the object of *shudō*" and that homosexual
relations involving such servants, however idealized, were often
associated with brutal violence.[81] According to another modern
historian, samurai manservants were the "frequent cause of
bloody strife" during the Keian era (1648–1651) in particular "as
the result of unnatural vice."[82] A chronological chart in the *Edo
gaku jiten* (Dictionary of Edo studies) notes "many quarrels related to *nanshoku*" in the year 1648.[83] The *Nanshoku ōkagami*
gives many examples, some of them at least quasi-historical. It
seems, indeed, that bloody incidents involving samurai manservants were associated as readily with homosexuality as inner-city

ggg. *hatto*
hhh. *kinshi*
iii. *zōritori*
jjj. *chūgen, komono,* and *zōritori*

shootings are associated with drug trafficking today. A well-known diary of the Genroku era (1688–1704), written by a minor Nagoya official named Asahi Monzaemon, records the murder of a page by two valets. Monzaemon's assumption: "Probably a *nanshoku* affair."[84]

Why was *nanshoku* so closely associated with violence? Clearly homosexual rape was a problem, especially during the seventeenth century in Edo. The *Kiyū shoran* (An amusing miscellany for your perusal), a cyclopedia of manners edited by Kitamura Nobuyo in 1830, reports in its section on *nanchō* ("male favorites") that parents of handsome boys scarcely allowed them out of the house during the early Tokugawa decades for fear that they might be sexually attacked or kidnapped.[85] But even milder harassment could provoke bloodshed if the recipient of unwanted attentions was a sword-wielding samurai.

To be the object of homosexual desire was no insult, but samurai youths were trained to respond to rude advances with swift punishment. The *Hagakure* advises samurai youths to test their blades on unwelcome suitors: "If someone else [besides your 'older brother'] is pressing his attentions on you, you should shake him off abruptly, saying, 'Your overtures are offensive to me'.... If he continues to persist, you should get angry and cut him down on the spot."[86]

The samurai had always been known as proud, arrogant, and sanguinary men; in the mid-sixteenth century the Jesuit Valignano wrote that "no people in the world [are] more punctilius about their honor than the Japanese, for they will not put up with a single insult or even a word spoken in anger."[87] St. Francis Xavier wrote, "Never in my life have I met people who rely so much on their arms."[88] But after the Osaka Campaign of 1614–1615, these features of the warrior personality could no longer be channeled into battle. The Pax Tokugawa produced intense samurai frustration, a feeling compounded by forced urbanization, the revocation of fiefs, and the effort of the regime to transform the warrior class into a stipended officialdom. The unhappiness of the masterless, or unemployed, samurai[kkk] was particularly acute. According-

kkk. *rōnin*

ingly, this century saw virulent urban gang[lll] activity and even an attempt by some disaffected samurai to overthrow the government.[89]

Urban violence involving the samurai tapered off after the late seventeenth century, partly as a result of shogunate efforts to create jobs for unemployed samurai and partly because of a ruthless crackdown on urban gangs during the reign of Tsunayoshi (1680–1709).[90] But throughout most of the century, samurai *nanshoku* was associated with violent incidents. "Whenever this [practice] flourishes," wrote Saikaku, "[men] must lose their lives."[mmm] [91]

The Osaka novelist's samurai works[nnn] contain many tales, including some based on actual events, that clarify this connection. His *Buke giri monogatari* (1688), for example, contains the following story. A samurai manservant named Matsuo Kozen has since age sixteen served a high-ranking official in Kyoto. In his home province of Iwami he had been involved with an "older brother," upon whose advice he initially came to the imperial capital. Still deeply in love with this man, he regularly exchanges letters with him.

Another samurai, named Shigino Uemon, also falls in love with Kozen. He conveys his feelings to the boy in a letter, but Kozen politely writes back that "for good reasons" he cannot requite this love. Infuriated, Uemon confronts the boy, but when informed (of "even the most intimate details") of the prior affair he calms down and agrees to a purely platonic relationship. The two become fast friends.

Thereafter another unsuccessful suitor, one Tamimizu Mohei, notes the close bond developing between Kozen and Uemon. He assumes that the relationship is sexual and is outraged that, having rejected his advances, Kozen has become involved with another samurai. He challenges the boy to a duel, and Kozen accepts. On the appointed evening, as Kozen waits at the designated spot, Uemon happens to pass by. Assuming that Kozen is waiting to

---

lll. Gang members were called *yakko*, *roppōsha*, and *otokodate*. There were both samurai and commoner gangs.

mmm. *Kore sakan no toki wa inochi o sutsubeshi*

nnn. *buke no mono*

tryst with Mohei, Uemon declares that he is "totally disgraced" because the boy has chosen the other suitor over himself. He, too, challenges Kozen to a fight, vowing to punish Mohei as well. The boy, however, explains the situation and, with a mollified Uemon, seeks out the third party at his home.

In the interim, Mohei has been rethinking the whole situation. While Uemon eavesdrops outside Mohei's gate, the samurai tells the boy that he has been reconsidering their duel; if indeed Uemon is only his friend and not his lover, the battle will not be necessary. Uemon and Kozen depart, amused at Mohei's cowardice.[92]

Samurai suitors of this period, it appears, often regarded rejection or infidelity by the object of their homosexual affections as an assault upon their honor, which they were prepared to defend with their lives. *Nanshoku*-related duels and other violent incidents, however, seem to have diminished in the eighteenth century, perhaps because the martial ethos declined, perhaps because the growth of male prostitution provided samurai men with an acceptable alternative to monogamous "brotherhood bond" relationships.

As noted above, the regime understood that commercial sex could provide alternative sexual outlets for such rowdies. Of course, hot-headed gangster types might even quarrel over prostitutes' favors. For example, the bathroom murder of townsman gang[ooo] leader Banzuiin Chōbei by bannerman gang[ppp] chief Mizuno Jurōzaemon in 1657 resulted from their rivalry over a Yoshiwara boy-prostitute's attentions.[93] Because relations with such boys were understood from the outset to be commercial transactions, however, one imagines that they would have produced fewer instances of violence.

The laws I have cited were directed not against homosexual behavior itself nor even against the potential for violence associated

ooo. *machi-yakko*
ppp. *hatamoto yakko*

with *nanshoku* relationships. Rather, they were meant to counter-
act the corrosive effects male prostitutes were thought to wreak
upon the status system. By the late seventeenth century, the growing wealth of the merchant class had come to pose a threat to that
system. Some commoners were dressing more stylishly and living
more lavishly than their "betters," despite the numerous sumptuary laws. This was disturbing enough. The fact that the samurai
and the more respectable commoners were becoming infatuated
with actor-prostitutes was even more alarming. As noted above,
the *Edo meishoki* had referred to the "extremely base" social origins of most actor-prostitutes. Indeed, many prostitutes of both
sexes were drawn from the untouchable communities,[qqq] with
whose members other Japanese had traditionally avoided contact.[94] A work written in 1713 quotes the Confucian scholar Arai
Hakuseki (1656–1725) as complaining that

> the customs of those in an inferior position increasingly shape the
> customs of those above. If one observes the customs prevalent in
> Edo today, the hairstyles and clothes of young men are all modeled
> after those of the actors of Sakai-chō, while female attendants follow
> the lead of the prostitutes of Yoshiwara. When what is improper has
> come to have such power over people, no matter how one preaches
> adherence to what is correct, people will not follow it.[95]

Soon thereafter, the philosopher Ogyū Sorai (who was on most
points opposed to Hakuseki) expressed an identical opinion:

> [T]he manners of male and female prostitutes[rrr] have influenced the
> members of other classes. At present even daimyo and other people
> of high status think nothing of using expressions derived from the
> speech of the courtesans' quarter[sss] and male prostitutes' quarter,[ttt]
> while the wives and daughters of the members of the military class
> think it is no shame to imitate the manners of the courtesans and
> male prostitutes. This is a most obnoxious fashion. Whosoever does
> not join in imitating these people is ridiculed as a boor and the cus-
> toms and manners of the time have become extremely bad.[96]

qqq. *eta* ("the greatly defiled") and *hinin* ("non-humans")
rrr. *yarō* and *yūjo*
sss. *keisei-machi*
ttt. *yarō-machi*

Ogyū goes on to express his dismay that respectable men are even marrying prostitutes.

Such complaints were expressed throughout the period; Buyō Inshi, the author of *Seji kenmonroku* (Record of things seen and heard, 1816), lamented, "Manners are normally something learned from above, but these days it is the manners of the common people that are being transferred to the elite."[97] All those protesting this state of affairs would have approved the shogunate's effort to prohibit overnight visits by prostitutes to client's homes, but they did not all advocate a crackdown on either male or female prostitution as such. On the contrary, Ogyū suggested the further institutionalization of commercial sex.

To discourage intermarriage between prostitutes and more respectable folk, Ogyū proposed that courtesans only be allowed to wed male prostitutes. (Significantly, he assumed that the latter would be interested in such unions.) The children of such couplings—indeed, all offspring of prostitutes—should then, according to Ogyū's view, pursue the same vocation as their mothers. Ogyū advocated the establishment of a prostitute *caste*, thereby condemning all sons born of prostitutes to careers as catamites![98]

Though a creative and original thinker, Ogyū was extremely conservative on most social questions. For example, he deplored the growth of the money economy, the decline in feudal values, and the increasingly impersonal nature of master-servant relations. But he did not question the relatively recent institutionalization of male prostitution; he sought only to regulate it in the interests of the status system. There seems to be no evidence, however, that the shogunate implemented his draconian proposal.

Individual daimyo, meanwhile, were free to issue their own laws in their own domains,[uuu] as long as these did not contravene the laws of the shogunate. The Maeda daimyo of Kanazawa, for example, prohibited all prostitution as well as kabuki drama for most of the Tokugawa period.[99] This decree did not constitute a ban on *nanshoku*, of which some Maeda daimyo were fond. It was indeed so common for feudal lords throughout the country

uuu. *kuni* or *han*

to retain pages as bed partners that the very term "page"[vvv] had, and still has, a distinctly homosexual connotation. The behavior of these servants was regulated by domain laws; like the wives and concubines of the daimyo, they were forbidden to develop outside sexual contacts. Just as a wife's adultery was viewed as treason, unauthorized homosexual liaisons by a favorite page were punishable by death.[100]

Thus, the laws dealing with *nanshoku* reflect two central concerns: the maintenance of order and the preservation of the status system. Notably absent is any substantial argument concerning the "unnaturalness" of *nanshoku* or any grave concern about the inherent moral content of a given sexual act.

vvv. *koshō*

Chapter Five

Nanshoku and the Construction of Gender

> The figure, as it sauntered onto the stage in high spirits,
> did not appear to be that of a woman but of a true-
> hearted man: it was indeed the image of Narihira....
> When she reached the stage, her face ... was indeed
> that of [the famed Chinese woman] Yang Kuei-fei....
> Anyone who would not fall in love with such a beautiful
> figure is more to be feared than a ghost.
>
> Miura Jōshin (1565–1644) on an
> androgynous kabuki performer

Three Distinctive Features of *Nanshoku*

When compared to other homosexual traditions in world history, particularly the Greek and later Mediterranean traditions, *nanshoku* reveals some conspicuous particularities. In male-male relationships (except some involving prostitutes), the insertee role is invariably assigned to the younger partner, regardless of class background. This convention, observed even between partners very close to one another in age, reflects the extreme emphasis upon hierarchy found in Japanese society from ancient times, reinforced by Confucian notions of precedence based upon age.

Only patrons of male prostitutes might assume the inserter role with somewhat older males—but these were usually *wakashū*-role performers seeking to appear and behave like "younger brothers" or cross-dressing actors seeking to imitate women. Thus, although Tokugawa society insisted upon a clear distinction between older/ inserter and younger/insertee, it allowed a certain blurring of gender categories. It celebrated not only the *onnagata*, who was trained to realistically mimic female behavior and appearance, but a range of androgynous performers and prostitute-types as sexual objects. This is a second characteristic feature of Japanese *nanshoku*. The literary and iconographic evidence, depicting the views of "older brothers" or patrons of prostitutes, indicates that some men preferred brawnier, more "masculine" partners, but much more commonly we encounter references to androgynous or feminine-looking insertee partners.[1]

It might be argued that the latter were surrogate females and that, because they always assumed the "passive" role, the gender blending was in fact quite limited. But these individuals acted as the inserter partner *in relationships with women* and, probably, in some relations with other males (such as younger fellow prostitutes). The situation is further complicated by the fact that some female prostitutes were taught to dress and behave like boys, servicing both a male and female clientele.

A third important feature of *nanshoku* pertains to the tolerance for male sexual "passivity." No stigma was attached to the performance of the insertee role; indeed, one's position as "younger brother" of a reputable man might confer considerable status. Because age, rather than social status, defined male-male sex roles, no shame could apply to the receptive partner.

I examined the first of these features earlier. In this chapter, I will discuss the Tokugawa fascination with androgyny, its implications for women's status, and the tolerance for the insertee's role in male-male sex.

The Fascination with Androgyny

The establishment of the Pax Tokugawa and its policy of peasant-warrior separation produced various new social problems: demographic imbalances, gang violence, the weakening of traditional lord-retainer relationships. The new regime also witnessed a decline in the martial ethos and skills of the samurai class. After the Battle of Sekigahara (1600), the sustained period of peace encouraged a slackening of the military lifestyle, and it was widely believed that men were becoming effeminate.[2]

The early eighteenth-century miscellany *Hagakure*, for example, records how a physician, on the basis of extensive research, found that whereas male and female pulses had differed appreciably in his youth, they had gradually become identical. According to the doctor, medical treatments previously appropriate for women now had to be applied to men, "since when one tries to treat men with [the previously effective] men's cures, they don't work. The world is degenerating,[a] men's spirit is declining and they are becoming indistinguishable from women.[b] I've definitively concluded this from [medical] practice."[3] *Yin-yang* principles, the doctor suggested, were no longer useful in treating ailments, as men were rapidly gaining *yin* at the expense of the male principle.

Nearly a century later, the scientist Sugita Genpaku (1733–1817) declared that eight of every ten retainers of the shogunate "look like women and think like merchants."[4] Meanwhile, in the view of contemporary commentators, women were losing traditional virtues such as modesty. The author of *Seji kenmonroku* (Record of things seen and heard, 1816) noted what he regarded as moral deterioration in women's reactions to erotic stage plays. Whereas eighty years before women would blush even to see couples embrace in kabuki plays, "[n]owadays sexual intercourse is plainly shown on the stage, and women in the audience watch on, unblushing, taking it in their stride. It is most immoral."[5] The heroine of Saikaku's *Kōshoku ichidai onna* reflects that whereas young women of eighteen or nineteen once wept bitterly at the prospect of leaving their homes and parents to marry, they now eagerly anticipated the joys of the marriage bed.[6]

Equally objectionable, perhaps, were female interests in such traditionally male pursuits as the viewing of sumo wrestling matches. In Ejima Kiseki's *Seken musume katagi* (Characters of young women in the floating world, 1717), young wives of the Kyoto merchant elite rush off to see the bouts at Matsugahara—something unheard of in former times. Worse still, they prepare

---

a. *yo ga matsu ni nari* (a reference to the Buddhist concept of *mappō*, the degenerate age prior to the end of the world)

b. *otoko no ki otoroe, onna dōzen ni nari sōrō*

picnic lunches and go on outings to observe criminals' beheadings at Awataguchi. And whereas prostitutes used to be the only women who smoked tobacco, "today women who abstain are as few as monks who fast."[7]

This putative feminization of the male and masculinization of the female was not universally condemned. In both samurai and commoner society, indeed, a sexual interest in androgyny (*futanari*, literally "dual form") persisted throughout the Tokugawa period. A poem written before 1644, for example, celebrates the female-role actor Shimada Manosuke for this *futanari* quality:

> *Onna ka to mireba*
> *otoko no Manosuke*
> *futanari taira no*
> *kore mo omokage*

> Looks like it might be a woman
> [But it's] Manosuke, the man
> His face, too, is androgynous
> Equally [male and female][8]

Some dramatic parts, such as those involving female warriors, allowed *onnagata* performers to play upon audiences' appetite for gender blending. Androgyny was not even necessarily thought incompatible with samurai virtues. Saikaku, writing of a daimyo's retainer "famed as one of the most beautiful youths of the time," describes him as "soft and yielding in manner"; he might at first glance be taken for a girl, "but he possessed the stalwart heart of a warrior."[9]

The fascination with gender blending had ancient roots. The phallic cult associated with the indigenous religion involved the worship of a deity named Dōsojin who, though represented as a phallus, was neither male nor female. Dōsojin phalli often bear the images of men and women who may be engaged in sex, exchanging affectionate gestures, or simply positioned side by side.[10] Buddhism, despite its historical misogyny, also reveres various androgynous deities, especially the boddhisattva Kannon, an Indian male deity who became feminized with the transmission of Buddhism through Asia.[11]

The popularity of sexually ambiguous performers in the Tokugawa period had medieval antecedents. From the twelfth through fourteenth centuries, female dancers called *shirabyōshi* "dressed in men's *suikan* overshirts and high caps and wore daggers with silver-decorated hilts and scabbards; their performances were thus called 'male dancing.'"[12] Thereafter, boy actors in noh drama exuded a similar kind of androgynous charm.

But this interest in gender blending seems to have reached a peak in the Tokugawa period. It was most clearly reflected in the popularity of cross-dressing performers, who were admired and patronized as prostitutes by both men and women.[13] Laws against visits of male prostitutes to women's houses refer to a number of prostitute types, including cross-dressers. A humorous poem (*senryū*) of the 1780s runs:

> *okama no*
> *baku-baku o*
> *goke wa kai ni kuru*

> The widow
> hurries off
> to buy a female role actor[14]

The *okama*, as noted previously, often served as the insertee partner in male-male sex.

An anonymous "novel of the floating world" published in Edo in 1755 contains a chapter in which a popular young female-role actor[c] named Minenojō is pursued by both a virgin girl and a widow. The narrator seems to find nothing incongruous in this, nor in the observation that the dimensions of Minenojō's penis "match . . . the young actor's other talents."[15]

Visual erotica, meanwhile, depicts women and female-role actor-prostitutes in some rather novel situations. A Kiyomitsu-school print shows an older woman with a prostitute who has a *harikata* (dildo) protruding from his rectum. With her hand, she guides his penis toward her vagina.[16] In a woodblock print mentioned earlier (Figure 20), a man's mistress has been making love to a cross-dressing actor-prostitute; the master has joined them and is masturbating the actor while copulating with his mistress.

c. *waka-onnagata*

Males, for their part, were excited by various types of androgynous prostitutes. A "sensualist of broad experience" in one of Saikaku's works likes his boys "bold and masculine" and prefers "strong women to ones possessed of a normal feminine nature."[17] In Kanazawa in the 1610s a male theater fan enthused about actresses who "in clothing and deportment are just like young males."[18]

Catering to such tastes, brothels provided courtesans who imitated the appearance of boy-prostitutes. An establishment called Fujiya, in Osaka's Shinmachi, introduced the "boyish courtesan" (*wakashū jorō*) in 1669. They dressed as boys and, according to the *Shikidō ōkagami* (Great mirror of the way of love), appealed to *nanshoku-zuki*.[19] Similarly, a type of female dancer-prostitute, all the rage among Kyoto men (and women) in Saikaku's time, sported from age eleven the shaven forehead of the adult male and imitated male manners and dress: "[T]hey are trained as dancers from early childhood, and learn to imitate the deportment and behavior of men. From age eleven or twelve to age fourteen or fifteen, they are engaged by women customers as drinking companions, then their forelocks are shaved [in the manner of young men], and they are trained to imitate men's voices."[20] Donning men's *hakama* tunics and sporting the two swords of the samurai at their waists, they attracted much attention as they swaggered down the street.

By the 1690s such prostitutes were referred to by the term *kagema-onna*, suggesting that they were viewed as the female counterparts of male female-role actor-prostitutes.[21] It is also significant that ranking courtesans of unambiguous female identity as a rule adopted men's names.[22] Hayashi Razan (1583–1657), the great Confucian savant, noted that male actors in the early kabuki theater "wear women's clothing: the women wear men's clothing, cut their hair and wear it in a man's topknot, have swords at their sides and carry [men's] purses." They were very popular with samurai men.[23] An actress of the early kabuki theater was described as

> gaily dressed, (wearing) a long and short sword worked in gold, [with] a flint-bag and gourd hung from her waist.... The figure, as it sauntered on [to the stage] in high spirits, did not appear to be that of a

woman but of a true-hearted man: it was indeed the image of Narihira.... When she reached the stage, her face ... was indeed that of
Yang Kuei-fei.... Anyone who would not fall in love with such a beautiful figure is more to be feared than a ghost.[24]

Here male and female images allusions are juxtaposed in the description of the actress: Ariwara no Narihira (825–880) was a semi-
legendary Don Juan figure, and Yang Guifei was the fabled beauty
of ancient China. The swords, flint bag, and gourd were items of
male furniture.

Male prostitutes and actors were often valued for their gender
ambiguity. A critique written in 1704 lavishes praise on the kabuki
actor Yoshizawa Ayame (1673–1729), who performed both male
and female roles: "I do not know," exclaims the critic, "*what* is
under his loincloth!"[25] The aesthetic value of this androgyny was
stressed by Chikamatsu Monzaemon (1653–1725), the greatest of
Tokugawa playwrights:

> In recent plays many things have been said by female characters
> which real women could not utter. Such things fall under the heading
> of art; it is because they say what could not have come from a real
> woman's lips that their [female characters'] true emotions are dis-
> closed. If in such cases the author were to model his character on
> the ways of a real woman and conceal her feelings, such realism, far
> from being admired, would permit no pleasure in the work.[26]

In other words, because women in contemporary Japanese society were discouraged from expressing their feelings directly, the
female-role actors had to depart from realism in articulating their
emotions. The *onnagata* also expressed things women might not
commonly feel but that men (and women) in the kabuki audience
might want to hear. The result was a titillating blend of female
sentiment and male assertiveness. In the words of Yoshizawa
Ayame: "[I]f an actress were to appear [on] stage she could not
express ideal feminine beauty, for she could only rely on the exploitation of her physical characteristics, and therefore not express the synthetic ideal. The ideal woman can only be expressed
by a [male] actor."[27]

Thus, popular culture manifested little concern with the maintenance of rigid gender roles.[28] On the contrary, the fascination of
both men and women with the cross-dressing actor, the beautiful

youth, and the mannish female prostitute suggests that sex roles were in flux and that many people were comfortable with this fact. The authorities, however, found the blurring of genders disturbing. Confucian scholars Arai Hakuseki, Ogyū Sorai, and Hayashi Razan sternly disapproved of the androgynous atmosphere of kabuki. At times, the shogunate took measures to clearly delineate gender roles, as when it acted to force kabuki actors to assume a clear male or female role on the stage. But the policy was inconsistent. For example, in requiring the female-role specialist to shave his forehead, the shogunate inadvertently produced an even more ambiguous sexual object.

The Acceptance of Male Sexual Passivity

In a climate so tolerant of gender blending, a wide range of male homosexual behavior could flourish as long as it remained governed by Confucian rules of status and precedence, which had obviously become deeply ingrained. A *nanshoku* relationship involving alternating active and passive roles in anal intercourse would have challenged those rules, so it is perhaps not surprising that evidence of such unions does not exist. The only references I have found are from earlier eras. In the late-Heian-era diary of Fujiwara Yorinaga, the author seems to assume both roles, and a Muromachi-era poem expresses the desire for a relationship in which the poet can both "thrust" and enjoy a young man's thrust.[29]

> *Tanomu wakazō*
> *amari tsurenaya*
> *hikkunde*
> *sashi mo ireba ya*
> *chigaeba ya*

> The young man I counted on
> seemed oh so very chilly
> Grappling with him
> I would like to thrust in my sword
> and die from his thrust![30]

The document seems all the more interesting given the fact that the poet, the Shingon priest Sōchō (1448–1532), was despite his monastic vows married and the father of two children.

The Tokugawa period offers little evidence for such sexual versatility, although, as already noted, men accustomed to assuming the insertee role (kabuki actors) are sometimes depicted as enjoying the inserter role with *women*. It seems to have been widely understood in this society that some men enjoyed anal penetration on purely physical, rather than emotional, grounds. Indeed, the *Shikidō kinpishō* recommends the following technique in its section on masturbation:[d] "You will increase your pleasure tenfold if, while masturbating with your right hand, you insert the middle finger of your left hand into your anus. The reason for this seems to be that your sexual energy[e] collects in the lower part [of your body], and a bit of that energy[f] spills out into the anus."[31] The belief that the anus is a center of "sexual energy" as well as sexual pleasure probably derives from Chinese texts, such as the sixteenth-century *Jindan jiuzheng pian* (Seeking instruction on the golden elixir), and ultimately from Indian yogic literature.[32]

Jokes refer matter-of-factly to the desire of boys and men from various walks of life to perform the insertee role. In one, a *chigo* returns to his temple after a visit home. Having overeaten at his parent's house, he has a stomach upset. "I feel as if my stomach were burning," he tells an older *chigo*. The latter grins and says, "Well, I wish I could have the same burning in *my* stomach. Where is the origin of the fire?"[33] In another, a male matchmaker volunteers to substitute for a wife who does not share her husband's fondness for anal sex:

> A married man was madly in love with a *wakashū*. Every time he came home drunk, he forced his wife to assume the role of the *wakashū*. His wife was disgusted with his actions and finally consulted with the matchmaker who had arranged the marriage.
>
> The matchmaker understood the wife's problem. "Let me substitute for you. I'll disguise myself and wait for him in your bed. If he does such a thing to me, I'll punish him."
>
> That night, the husband came home in a half drunken condition. He immediately crept into bed into the dark room. Pouncing on the matchmaker's bottom, he thrust his tool into the matchmaker's anus.

d. *senzuri*
e. *shingen no ki*
f. *ki*

The husband whispered, "Mmmmm, this is good, much better than usual."

He casually slid his hand under the stomach of the matchmaker. Shocked, he cried out, "No wonder I feel so good. Look at this. My thing has pierced through you all the way and sticks out this far!"[34]

The woman's description of her problem had aroused the matchmaker's desire. He enjoys taking her place, achieving an erection in the process. He hardly seems interested in punishing the husband.

Some *shunga* show the passive partner ejaculating during anal intercourse; an erotic print by Aikawa Shōzan, for example, depicts the passive partner relishing his role.[35] The print is one of a series of fifty-three, corresponding to the fifty-three post-stations along the Tōkaidō highway, and each depicts a (typically hetero) sexual adventure. The print for Fukuroi shows the traveler-artist having sex with a boy alongside the road. The inscription notes that pilgrims offer small bags of pepper to the deity Kumano Sansho Gongen (Kumano Pepper Boddhisattva) at a nearby temple, continuing:

> I have an amusing recollection regarding pepper.
>
> As I was walking along, I met an attractive lad[g] among the *wakashū* making their pilgrimages. He was traveling on a shoestring, of course, so I helped him out a bit as I led him along. Feeling rather obligated to me, he didn't refuse my request for his back door.[h]
>
> Before fucking his ass[i] I pounded some pepper well and, softening it with saliva, inserted it into his asshole. A bit later his anus began to itch unbearably. I daubed saliva on my penis, and when I [entered him], I eased his itch. The sensation got more and more pleasant, and he liked it.[36]

The dialogue captions run as follows. Boy: "I'm getting off on this too. Go ahead and shove it in all the way." Man: "You've got a hard-on too, huh? I can't stand it! Let me kiss you. In return I'll buy you a prostitute tonight!" The print shows the boy with an

g. *kawairashii mono*
h. *uramon no mushin*
i. *shiri o okosu*

erection, and the text clearly states that he is enjoying himself. It also indicates that males who experienced such enjoyment were not considered less apt to savor sexual intercourse with women.

Here the passive partner is a penniless boy, but courtier-aristocrats also seem to have enjoyed this role. *Nenashigusa* notes that even some members of the Kyoto nobility studied kabuki, including the art of the *onnagata*, and the work links this hobby with the desire to be sexually penetrated: "That they themselves found pleasure in this was laughable. They did not differ from the half-wit who said, 'After I die, in my next life I'd like to be a bonito.' When someone nearby asked him why, he answered, 'Because a bonito is delicious.' A bonito is certainly delicious, but how tasty an experience would it be to become a bonito and be eaten by someone else?"[37] The implication is that it is one thing to desire beautiful actors and to enjoy them sexually but quite another to want to become an actor and be enjoyed sexually.

The *Nenashigusa* is written from the viewpoint of one who finds such a craving "laughable," and other references also make fun of men who relish the insertee role. An Okumura print of 1743 depicts the humorist Shikōden as an old man giving a public recitation of the *Tsurezuregusa*. Instead of holding the usual block of wood to punctuate his performance, he suggestively wields a *harikata*. The poem accompanying the portrait reads:

> *Umi kaki wa*
> *daruma no nari ya*
> *ketsu kusare*

> The overripe persimmon
> looks like Daruma
> with a rotting asshole[38]

"Daruma" could mean male prostitute, but the point seems to be that the storyteller indulges not in prostitution but in anal masturbation. The phrase "overripe persimmon" suggests that Shikōden is a bit old for such pastimes.

In Chikamatsu's *Tanba Yosaku* (Yosaku from Tanba, 1708) a very precocious eleven-year-old packhorseman attempts to impress his maturity on one of his customers. "I've never from the start been a *wakashū*," he boasts, "I'm a born *nenja*."[39] At first glance his declaration seems to indicate a contempt for the *wakashū* role, but the point is not that the insertee role is demeaning. The boy is simply claiming a degree of independence that one would not have expected for one his age.

The mocking references to the *wakashū* role are in any case balanced by tales of heroic "younger brothers" who publicly boast of their relationships with their *nenja* and of leading warriors who in their youth proudly served as bedmates to powerful lords. These fighters made no attempt to conceal the nature of their sexual services, nor did they hide behind the polite fiction, so common in ancient Greece, that they only submitted to the "thigh technique" of intercourse. Well-born and indigent youths alike experienced anal penetration and were not despised for it.

This is a principle distinction between Japanese *nanshoku* and ancient Athenian male homosexuality. I have found in Japan no examples of scatological invective demeaning the insertee role such as one finds, for example, in Old Norse literature or Greek drama.[40] In ancient Athens such terms as *euryproktos* ("wide-assed") or *chaunoproktos* ("with gaping asshole") were commonly employed as insults.[41] One does encounter the epithet, "Suck asshole!"[j] in Tokugawa literature, but it seems to have carried a rather different connotation from the Greek barbs (or the contemporary American expression, "Kiss my ass [and thereby humiliate yourself]"). It seems to simply mean, "Eat shit!" and thus hardly suggests a contempt for the insertee role in anal sex.[42]

Women's Roles and the Insertee's Role

The Japanese attitude toward the insertee's role also differed markedly from the attitude found in early modern Europe. Whereas men in some Mediterranean societies men might brag about their affairs with pretty boys, they would draw their swords at any intimation that they themselves might assume the insertee role.[43] In ancient Athens, men who "enjoyed being passive"

j. *ketsu kurae*; "Suck (somebody's? my?) asshole"

(*hēdomenos tōi paschein*) were considered shamefully "soft" and unmanly; the true male, unlike the female, was unable to respond to a male sexual partner with *charis* (grace or kindness).[44] In Japan, by contrast, the *otōtobun* ("older brother") was expected to respond to his lover with *nasake* (kindness or compassion).

Surely such differences in the construction of homosexuality point to corresponding differences in the construction of gender categories. Although male "passivity" might have been considered analogous to female sexual behavior, perhaps it was not despised in Tokugawa Japan because females themselves were better esteemed there than in societies that disparaged the male insertee's role.

Certainly, many Tokugawa-period texts clearly define gender roles in ways highly unfavorable to women. But these texts, belonging to the Confucian or Buddhist traditions, do not necessarily reflect Tokugawa realities. "A man," according to Confucian belief, "is *yang* and noble, a woman is *yin* and base, just as heaven is *yang* and noble, and earth is *yin* and low."[45] The Japanese Confucian reference invariably cited is the *Onna Daigaku* (Great learning for women), attributed to the famous scholar Kaibara Ekken (1630–1714). "Woman," he wrote, "is by her inborn nature of the quality of *yin*, or softness. She lacks wisdom, is noisy, evil, and finds it difficult to follow the way of righteousness."[46] Immoral by nature, women must be bound by the "three subordinations" (*sanjū*): to parents while single, husbands while married, and eldest sons if widowed.[47]

Women, some texts declare, should be shielded from all contact with men outside their immediate family; as a character in one of Chikamatsu's plays declares, a woman should not so much as look at another man while her husband is away—not even a priest, manservant, or brother.[48] The *Hagakure* justifies a man's slaying of his wife for permitting a passing sick stranger to use the toilet in the husband's absence.[49]

One must question how widely such sentiments were acted upon, however. Much Confucian ideology, promulgated *ad nauseum* by the authorities, was blithely disregarded by both samurai and commoners. Kaibara's choice piece of Confucian misogyny repeats the conventional wisdom of the day but may not accurately reflect his own attitudes. He enjoyed "a married life of rare happiness and genuine mutuality" with his learned wife, who by some accounts actually co- or ghostwrote the *Onna Daigaku*.[50]

Buddhism, fundamentally "an overwhelming male-created institution dominated by a patriarchical power," regarded women as particularly sinful and vulnerable to temptation.[51] "Because of the malice in their natures," asserts a Zen monk in one of Ueda Akinari's tales, "females readily turn into vicious demons."[52] Subject to the Six Lusts and Five Limitations, they were inherently inferior to men, a fact confirmed by females' menstruation.[53] In order to attain nirvana, it was believed, they had first to be reborn as men.[54]

However, the indigenous Shinto tradition, which underwent a revival during the Tokugawa period, elevated the feminine. Chief among its pantheon of divinities was Amaterasu no Ōomikami, the Sun Goddess, from whom the imperial line, and indeed all Japanese, were believed to have descended. The most important Shinto scholar of the period, Motoori Norinaga (1730–1801), stressed the fundamental "femininity"[k] of the Japanese spirit and culture, contrasting this to the "masculinity" of Chinese culture: "In general, the real heart of a human being is effeminate and weak like that of a woman or a child. As far as the depth of a man's real heart is concerned, the wisest men do not differ from a woman or a child. The difference between them lies merely in the fact that the former conceal the real heart for shame, whereas the latter do not."[55]

Earlier, the Shinto popularizer Masuho Zankō (1665–1742) had written that "men and women are on the same level with no distinction of high or low, superior or inferior. To think of women as men's slaves or to expect them to follow men in all matters is a delusion based on Chinese manners and is a deviation from our country's Way."[56]

The respect accorded women in Shinto is reflected through

k. *taoyama buri*

much of Japanese history, particularly the ancient period. John Whitney Hall suggests that by the third century A.D. Japanese elite society was "in a state of transition from matriarchy to patriarchy."[57] Early Chinese records report "no distinction between father and son or between men and women" in the early centuries A.D. and refer to a queen-shamaness named Pimiko.[58] Female scribes[l] were apparently important in this early period; the *Kojiki* was dictated by one Hieda no Are, who was probably female.[59] During the seventh and eighth centuries, half of the emperors were female, and although the throne became a male monopoly after 769, women enjoyed a relatively high degree of freedom during the Heian period (794–1185).[60] Homes were commonly passed down from mother to daughter, and uxorilocal marriages were the norm.[61] Most of this period's great literature, including Murasaki Shikibu's *Tale of Genji* (ca. 1000), was penned by women.[62] Such works indicate that Heian women enjoyed a high degree of sexual freedom, served in high posts at court, and functioned as arbiters of taste.

With the development of warrior society, changing patterns of property and inheritance, and the spread of Confucian ideology, women came more fully under the control of fathers, husbands, and sons. Even so, there are records of women's serving as land stewards[m] and, in very exceptional circumstances, achieving fame as warriors.[63] In the early Tokugawa period, samurai women frequently learned martial arts and attended hunts on horseback.[64] Commoner and samurai women alike were often literate; many scholars believed it essential for them to study the Confucian Four Books. They traveled widely, sometimes disguised as men, and left to posterity over one hundred travel diaries.[65] Tokugawa women managed businesses, often on behalf of delinquent husbands. Humorous stories of the time describe "an impulsive and somewhat careless husband as a foil to his more realistic, practical, and dependable wife. It is clear in all these anecdotes that

l. *kataribe*
m. *jitō*

the boss is actually the so-called 'dependent' marital partner."[66]
Ōta Kinjō declared that the world was kept in order by the three
hō: Buppō (Buddhism), teppō (rifles), and nyōbō (wives).[67]

Women might hold guild membership and work alongside men
as carpenters, day laborers, dyers, and miners.[68] Some, skilled in
the martial arts, served the shogunate as special agents.[n] And,
after more than eight hundred years of ineligibility, women were
even again deemed fit to ascend the imperial throne.[69] Western
visitors in the late Tokugawa period found Japanese women to be
the most liberated in Asia: "The position of women in Japan is
apparently unlike that of the sex in all other parts of the East,
and approaches more nearly their European condition. The Japanese women are subjected to no jealous seclusion, hold a fair
position in society, and share in the innocent recreations of their
fathers and husbands. . . . The minds of the women are cultivated
with as much care as those of the men."[70]

W. E. Griffis, writing in the early Meiji period, made the same
observation:

> The student of Asiatic life, on coming to Japan, is cheered and
> pleased on contrasting the position of women in Japan with that in
> other countries. He sees them treated with respect and consideration
> far above that observed in other quarters of the Orient. They are al-
> lowed greater freedom, and hence have more dignity and self-con-
> fidence. The daughters are better educated, and the national annals
> will show as large a number of illustrious women as those of any coun-
> try in Asia.[71]

Three hundred years earlier Jesuit missionaries had also remarked
on women's ability "to go hither and thither as they list." But they
had coupled such references with the observation that adultery
was a capital crime and the suggestion that women were virtuous
primarily to avoid being divorced by their husbands.[72] By the late
Tokugawa period, divorce and remarriage among the common
people and even samurai had become fairly casual procedures.[73]
There is ample literary evidence that women of the commoner
classes proposed marriage and initiated divorce. So the women

n. kunoichi or female ninja

Griffis encountered seem to have enjoyed higher social status than those observed by Westerners three centuries earlier.

Women's *Iro*

Foreign accounts rarely comment on the sexuality of Japanese women, but it is clear that the Japanese of the early modern period expected women to fully enjoy the sexual act. They may even have considered female orgasm a prerequisite for conception.[74] Popular literary and artistic depictions suggest that many women ignored moralists' admonitions to suppress sexual desire. The sexually assertive women ("soy-sauce barrels")[o] who appear in the literature may represent more than a mere stereotype.[75] In Saikaku's fiction, young women "see the man they want and immediately go after him."[76] Apt to develop infatuations with famous kabuki actors, they offer themselves to such performers in marriage or purchase the favors of male prostitutes simply to relieve sexual tension.[77] Laws forbade various types of actors and male prostitutes[p] from entering women's homes, but some *nanshoku* teahouses in Edo serviced widows and ranking women as well as men (although the policy was to refuse admission to nuns).[78] A print from the *Ehon kaichū kagami* (Pocket mirror picture book, 1826) shows chambermaids of the shogunal palace purchasing the services of *kagema* at a male brothel.[79]

Figure 8 shows a woman and an actor in the throes of love. The caption reads:

(*Woman:*)   The main event gave me an excuse for getting out so that I could meet you here. There's no one in the world who means more to me. Your staff is thicker and longer than the statue of the Buddha in the temple across from here. That's why I love you even more.

        Oh! Go deeper and faster. Push, push, until you break the floor boards. Don't be afraid of anyone hearing us down below. The owner of this teahouse won't interfere.

(*Actor:*)   I'm grateful to you, my lady, but you must try to be calmer. They'll hear us below.[80]

o. *shōtaru*
p. *kagema*

The woman's language, of course, may merely reflect male fantasy, but the situation—a woman making an excuse to leave her companions at the theater and tryst with her favorite performer at a nearby teahouse—surely represents contemporary reality.[81]

One well-documented instance of female patronage of actor-prostitutes occurred in 1714. One of the highest-ranking ladies-in-waiting in the shogun's castle, enjoying a rare outing—a temple pilgrimage—cut the visit short in order to attend a kabuki performance with eleven attendants. Afterward the party went by a secret passageway to a residence near the theater, where they trysted with "many actors, young actors, and youths" before returning to the castle. An investigation revealed that the lady, Ejima, had been secretly seeing the extraordinarily handsome and popular actor Ikushima Shingorō for nine years. All involved were severely punished—not because the shogunate was concerned about female patronage of male prostitutes but because Ejima had shirked her duties and engaged in shameless class-mixing.[82]

Even a woman of commoner status could informally engage a male concubine[q] with no connection to the kabuki theater or pleasure quarters. Examples occur in Saikaku's *Kōshoku ichidai otoko* and Suikyōan's *Kōshoku koshiba-gaki* (The little hedge of lust amid the thicket, 1696). In the first work, Yonosuke is employed by a widow's maidservant to avenge the mistress against an unspecified foe. Later, he learns that the enemy (which "makes her want to die") is her olisbos (*harikata*)[r] and that to wreak vengeance upon the tool she requires his services. Unable to pass up the fee that she offers, he accedes to her request.[83]

In the second tale, the protagonist is a virginal maidservant accustomed to masturbating over salacious prints. Using a subterfuge similar to that described in the first story, she hires a samurai and then a *harikata* maker to service her at a teahouse.[84]

Again, although such literature may merely reflect male fan-

---

q. *otoko no keisei; otoko no geisha*
r. also called *suigyū* ("water buffalo," since they were usually made from water buffalo horn) or, more elegantly, *osugata* ("male shape")

tasies and provide a distorted picture of feminine sexuality, it plainly suggests the existence of a fairly large-scale gigolo trade and indicates a surprising degree of female participation in the world of commercial sex—as buyers as well as sellers. And if male prostitutes offered women a sexual outlet outside the oppressive institution of marriage, *female* prostitutes willing to have lesbian sex reduced or eliminated altogether women's sexual dependence upon men. In the Yoshiwara pleasure district of Edo, a section was reserved for lesbian prostitution, and a number of references to this phenomenon appear in Tokugawa literature.[85] Kiseki describes a mannish woman who—along with her husband—purchases the favors of Shimabara beauties (Figure 32), and Saikaku includes a tenure as lesbian concubine among the adventures of his *Kōshoku ichidai onna*.[86] Lesbian relationships, Sasama Yoshihiko suggests, were particularly common in the shogun's seraglio, where men other than the shogun himself were forbidden to enter, but "there were also rare instances in which they occurred among 'people who despised liaisons with men.'"s [87]

The flourishing market in *harikata*—many of them true works of art—gave women yet another sexual outlet. Double-headed *harikata* called *tagaigata* were designed for use by two women.[88] They were sometimes sold under a label with a contrived character consisting of two radicals for "female."[89] These and other masturbatory aids were openly marketed.

Women were often depicted as having an interest in erotic pictures; indeed, the introduction to one of Utamaro's erotic albums, *Ehon warai jōgo* (Laughing drunkards' picture-book, ca. 1790), was supposedly written by the artist's wife. She notes modestly that "the work is highly embarrassing to a lady" but adds, "[T]hink what a happily loving couple we are and now, by this means, with the husband making the designs and the wife coloring them, an intimate union of male and female has come about that harmonizes excellently with the drift of one picture book."[90]

Although it is doubtful that Utamaro's wife actually penned this, consumers of such material apparently would have been titil-

s. *dansei to no seiji o kirau mono*

Fig. 32. A woman, dressed in male clothing and sporting a sword, patronizes a courtesan brothel. The male attendant announces, "The courtesan is waiting." From Ejima Kiseki's *Seken musume katagi* (*Characters of Worldly Young Women*, 1717). Source: Howard Hibbett, *The Floating World in Japanese Fiction* (Tokyo and Rutland, Vt.: Tuttle, 1975), p. 109.

lated by the notion of a husband-wife team cooperating in the production of erotica. Women probably purchased such material, just
as they purchased *harikata* and other sex-toys. In the well-known
play *Chūshingura*, a merchant, attempting to conceal a crate of
weapons from men he believes to be police, attempts to put
them off by claiming that "[t]his box contains personal articles ordered by the wife of a certain daimyo, including pornographic
books. . . . Her name is written on each article, even on the order
for the erotic materials. If you open the box you will be exposing
to public view the name of a great family."[91] The passage suggests
that, although some embarrassment might be associated with such
purchases, women were interested in such material and had the
ability to acquire it.

The Taboo Against Male-Male Fellation

Tokugawa bourgeois society clearly recognized women as vital
participants in society, including its economic life. The association of a man with some role traditionally constructed as "female" (including the "passive" sexual role) would therefore not
have suggested his exclusion from that society—as it would have
in ancient Athens or Renaissance Italy. In Japan, moreover, fairly
aggressive forms of female sexuality—like the purchase of the
services of male prostitutes—were acknowledged and tolerated.
Even if the male insertee was deemed to be performing the "female role," he would have been extended the same tolerance
granted to the sexually aggressive female.

But Tokugawa society preserved one significant gender-blending taboo: as noted in Chapter 3, the Tokugawa period has left
little evidence of homosexual fellation. In this Japan was by no
means unique. Indeed, in most premodern societies, oral sex
seems to have been the exception rather than the rule in male homosexual contacts.[92] Some societies, such as ancient Babylon,
have left no record of any kind of oral sex, and one finds little
reference to either homosexual or heterosexual fellation in ancient Rome.[93] Studies of sexuality in Renaissance England and
eighteenth-century Holland also reveal a lack of interest in oral

sex.[94] One finds such activity between men and women depicted in erotica from pre-Columbian Peru, ancient Greece, and premodern China, but male-male examples seem nonexistent.[95]

Yet why would Tokugawa Japan, a society that tolerated homosexuality and that applauded both heterosexual fellatio and cunnilingus, seemingly recoil from male-male fellatio? What did such a sex act signify that it should have been scrupulously avoided? Why should youths who routinely submitted to anal sex have rejected the idea of "passive" oral sex? Why should men who enjoyed heterosexual fellatio have restrained themselves from requesting this service from male partners?

Comparisons with other societies yield few insights into Tokugawa attitudes. The English and Dutch seem to have avoided oral sex for hygienic reasons.[96] Other societies rejected it in general on ideological grounds. The Roman Artemidorus Daldianus (second century A.D.) denounced heterosexual oral sex, in particular the "wasteful" discharge of semen into a woman's mouth, as "an awful act," "a moral wrong."[97] Heterosexual cunnilingus, meanwhile, was thought to indicate weakness and servility in a man.[98] Thus, the Romans viewed both "active" and "passive" male roles in heterosexual oral sex as repugnant. One assumes that the same disgust was applied to male-male fellatio. Men in ancient Athens engaged in heterosexual fellatio but apparently only with prostitutes, and, like the Romans, they considered cunnilingus unmanly.[99]

The *shunga* clearly attest that the well-bathed Japanese of the Tokugawa era enjoyed heterosexual oral sex and had no ideological problem with heterosexual oral-genital contact. A work by Okada Shogi, published in 1793, refers to sex manuals instructing women "as to tongue and lips, pressure, pace and intensity."[100] *Yin-yang* teachings regarded ejaculation into the woman's mouth as unwise, as it would result in loss of *yang* with no corresponding acquisition of *yin*. (Any slight secretions during foreplay were compensated for by *yin* obtained from female saliva.)[101] The Okada book described the oral attentions of Yoshiwara prostitutes, recommending that younger men (with plentiful *yang*) should be fellated to orgasm but that older men—with diminishing *yang*—should not: "If the guest is elderly, this 'silk trembling' should not continue to the discharge of his vital juices. But of a young man the pleasure should continue to full flood. Elderly guests who have come stored with their carefully hoarded potency for this night, should be caressed, mouthed, but not brought to full flowing too soon unless that is their way to pleasure."[102]

The Chinese seem to have regarded homosexual fellatio no more favorably than the Japanese. Ming and Qing erotica depicts heterosexual fellatio and cunnilingus in a tender, positive light.[103] It also depicts homosexual anal intercourse and mutual masturbation. But it does not show male-male oral sex. The Chinese, however, did not view the practice with disgust, as the Romans did; rather, the idea seems to have produced amusement.[104]

Obviously the Japanese regarded fellatio as a feminine specialty. But even cross-dressing male prostitutes who had adopted a female identity apparently refrained from offering their clients this service. Why did a society so fascinated by androgyny draw the line at male-male oral sex, particularly when it seemed to avoid the risk involved in heterosexual fellatio? *Yin-yang* theory taught that male-male sex involved no exchange of energy; a man who would lose *yang* by ejaculating in a woman's mouth could do so into a male partner's anus *or* mouth without such loss of potency.[105]

One can only advance an hypothesis. Perhaps in reserving for the female the active role in fellatio, Tokugawa men were expressing an anxiety about the results of thorough gender blending in the sexual act. For centuries, homosexual anal sex had been sanctioned or tolerated by elites who saw in it no threat to the patriarchal premises of their society. As we have seen, Tokugawa society did not view even sexual relationships between adult men of comparable status as threats to the social order, as long as such relationships observed the principles of precedence and the active/passive dichotomy.

The problem with male-male fellatio may have been that in this type of sex the active and passive roles are more difficult to determine. The "younger brother" in anal intercourse could heighten his partner's sensation in various ways, but the latter's pleasure was not much dependent upon such considerations. There was no question as to who was the dominant and who was the submissive partner in the act. In the case of oral sex, however, the insertee typically nurtures the inserter's erection through a conscious, sustained effort.[106] The process requires some acclimatization to overcome what has been termed the "gag reflex." In this case the insertee may have greater control over the experience than his partner, raising in the latter's mind the question of who was indeed submissive and who was dominant.

Certainly the inserter could perform in such a way that the roles were unequivocally clear. Athenian vases contain scenes in which men force their organs into the mouths of female prostitutes while otherwise abusing and humiliating them. Such depictions have little in common with Japanese prints showing heterosexual oral sex as tender, mutually gratifying love-play.[107] In these more one-sided encounters, the inserter's self-image would not have suffered from the female's attentions, however aggressive. He could enjoy them with little anxiety about who was in control during the encounter. The female was by definition inferior, and he need not have feared any dishonor even if she dominated the session.

But if another male were to pleasure his penis this way, the inserter might feel some anxiety as to who was indeed the "older brother" in the exchange. Male-male fellatio was too ambiguous an act for men whose sexuality had been molded to fit clear active and passive categories. As a patriarchal, hierarchical class society, Japan had to preserve *some* exclusively heterosexual role, lest the whole basis of the society be undermined. Perhaps a ban on homosexual fellatio was necessary to preserve the fundamental notion of male-female sexual roles.

Lesbian cunnilingus apparently was not thought to threaten that notion; it, as well as mutual dildo-play, is depicted in the *shunga*.

Nanshoku and Heterosexual Romance

Tokugawa society, though hesitant to accept complete symmetry in heterosexual and homosexual acts, readily accepted a great deal of gender-blending behavior. We might therefore expect conventions and expressions of homosexual and heterosexual passion to resonate against one another in this society; indeed, the culture of *nanshoku* significantly influenced the development of male-female romantic love from the seventeenth century.

We have already noted that Tokugawa Japan shared with many other societies a profound mistrust of intense romantic love relationships. To be sure, the love of husband and wife was sanctioned, and love within the family, as long as it was not too demonstrative, was considered natural and proper. But such love was supposed to develop after marriage, to strengthen a bond arranged by the couple's parents. Romantic love between unmarried men and women, like the forms of homosexual passion discussed previously, was seen as a dangerous and unpredictable emotion. This had been the orthodox Buddhist view, and the Confucian scholars who largely dominated Tokugawa intellectual life "condemned love as an irrelevant and possibly disruptive element."[108]

Thus, popular culture, in treating the theme of love, pitted the force of "human feelings" (*ninjō*) against that of "duty" (*giri*). Romantic love in the writings of Saikaku or Chikamatsu is almost invariably tragic; the lovers are caught, like Romeo and Juliet, in an impossible situation and must choose between their obligations to their parents or spouses and their desire to be with their beloved. An element of danger and risk tinged these love affairs and served to equalize the male-female relationship. In such unions, loyalty to the death was expressed in sworn contracts and gestures of painful sacrifice; thus, these ties resembled the *nanshoku* "brotherhood bond" far more than they resembled the typical heterosexual marital relationship.

There is much evidence that by the late seventeenth century heterosexual romance mirrored the "brotherhood bond." For example, the exchange by lovers of repeated written oaths, sewn into clothing or worn in amulet bags[t] next to the skin, was apparently unknown before the Tokugawa era. Early in the period, however, such practices became common among male lovers,

t. *mamori-bukuro*

and thereafter heterosexual couples also adopted them.[109] Meanwhile, men and women exchanged "love pledges" (*shinjū*) in imitation of such pledges exchanged between male lovers.[110] These included, according to Fujimoto Kizan's *Shikidō ōkagami* (The great mirror of the arts of love, 1678), not only written oaths but also tattooing, scarring, and the cutting off of locks of hair, fingernails, and even fingers.[111] Sometimes the severed part would be worn in a bag around the lover's neck.

Fujimoto regarded finger cutting as the supreme pledge of a prostitute's sincerity toward her lover, but elsewhere one encounters reference to even gorier rites. Flesh gauging began as an expression of male-male love, but in 1661 a Yoshiwara female prostitute performed this act to demonstrate her love for a patron. Subsequently the practice became quite common in heterosexual relationships. "It is clear," writes Koike, "that this was derived from *nanshoku*."[u] [112]

Surely women were familiar with much of the literature and folklore of the *nanshoku* tradition. Some must have been familiar with the story of Itami Ukyō and Mokawa Uneme, two young samurai men who committed double suicide in Edo in 1640. Popular accounts of the tragedy appeared soon after it occurred, and later it was treated in *Fūryū Soga kōyō* (1683), Saikaku's *Nanshoku ōkagami* (1687), and *Nanshoku giri monogatari* (Tales of *nanshoku* honor, 1699).[113] This homosexual love-suicide inspired others throughout the period, but these in turn may have encouraged the heterosexual love-suicides that became rampant in the late seventeenth century.[114]

By the Genroku period (1688–1704) the term *shinjū*, or *shinjū-shi* ("*shinjū* death"), had come to refer exclusively to these most radical of love pledges.[115] It is perhaps no accident that the first depiction of a heterosexual *shinjū* was staged in 1683—the year *Fūryū Soga kōyō* appeared in print. *Nanshoku* love-suicides continued until the end of the period and were chronicled alongside heterosexual *shinjū* in such works as *Shinjū ōkagami* (*The Great Mirror of Shinjū*, 1704).[116] Chikamatsu's last love-suicide play,

u. *sore ga nanshoku kara kiteiru koto wa akiraka de aru*

Shinjū yoigōshin (*Shinjū* on the eve of the *kōshin* festival, 1722) depicted as a subplot the love of the pageboy[v] Yamawaki Koshi-chirō and the outlaw[w] Koichibei.[117] But when the shogunate banned the love-suicide theme from the stage in 1723, its edict defined *shinjū* as "men and women perishing together, having been influenced by [theatrical] plots."[118] The ultimate expression of male-male passion had become more closely associated with the romantic effort of heterosexual lovers to escape the oppressive social relations of early modern Japan.

v. *koshō*
w. *yakko*

Conclusions and Speculations

In studying Tokugawa *nanshoku*, we have been able to draw upon an exceptionally rich documentary record. Few other societies, aside from those of Western classical antiquity, have produced such well-documented traditions of male homosexuality.[1] One might argue that the profusion of primary sources simply reflects the sexual openness of a bourgeois society that lionized courtesans, associated cultural refinement with the licensed quarter, and generated some of the world's most sophisticated erotic art. But biographical information, and the manner in which the merits of *nanshoku* and *joshoku* are discussed in popular literature, strongly suggest that in Tokugawa Japan homosexual behavior not only was discussed more matter-of-factly than in most other societies; it also more commonly *occurred*.

Why was this the case? Various factors combined to produce the *nanshoku* tradition, with its specific conventions and taboos. In examining the topic, we have had to consider such disparate factors as Japan's relations with China, religious and philosophical trends, folklore, the status of women, monasticism, feudalism, lord-vassal relationships, and urban demographics. Plainly there was a mix of factors, unique to Japan, which encouraged widespread homosexual behavior, and its specific role-structure. But if we are to hazard a general explanation for the prevalence of *nanshoku* in Tokugawa Japan, we must note that 1) traditions of male-male sexual behavior among the elite (monks and samurai) were well established long before the emergence of the Tokugawa order; 2) although these earlier traditions might be termed "situational," reflecting the absence of women in monasteries and warrior bands, the Tokugawa tradition arose in urban environments where women were always conspicuously present, if often underrepresented; and 3) the existence of prior, elite homosexual traditions may have encouraged male commoners to tolerate, desire, and experience male-male sex—while also maintaining heterosexual relations.

Nanshoku, in short, arose largely to compensate for men's lack of female companionship, but at some point its culture came so to influence the structure of male desire that its vitality no longer required the absence of women. Indeed, it remained a vigorous tradition in Tokugawa cities even as the institution of the female courtesan throve. Tokugawa *nanshoku* was not, generally speaking, an alternative to *joshoku* but its corollary. The *iro* of most Tokugawa men was bisexual.

This eros was specifically constructed to mirror the hierarchical human relations specified in Confucian thought and in feudal society; males were socialized to desire to penetrate younger males and to be penetrated by older males. The only exception to this rule involved the actor who cross-dressed or played the androgynous *wakashū* role. The rule of precedence based on age did not apply in male-female relations, so the actor-prostitute, in his capacity of fictive youth or woman, could assume the insertee role even with a younger man. Thus, Tokugawa *nanshoku* principally reflected notions of power, deference, and service deeply rooted in feudal society, modified by the influence of heterosexual roles.

As we have noted, some scholars have linked traditions of age-structured homosexuality to ancient initiation rites, in which boys were ritualistically inseminated by men, and gender-structured homosexuality to the tradition of the cross-dressing shaman. The most ancient Japanese texts are completely silent on the topic of male-male sex, but it is conceivable that these two traditions met and merged in prehistoric Japan, remaining below the surface prior to the introduction of Buddhist monasticism.

The Japanese language and ancient culture appear to represent a convergence of Southeast Asian and Northeast Asian elements.[2] In the former region, from Melanesia to southern China, age-structured male-male relationships were common; in the latter, the tradition of the cross-dressing shaman prevailed. In simultaneously reflecting a deep sensitivity to the question of age and a fascination with the cross-dressing or androgynous entertainer, Japanese *nanshoku* seems to fuse these primeval paradigms of homosexual behavior.

The most central and fruitful debate among scholars who have studied homosexuality in historical context pits those often termed "essentialists" against "social constructionists." The former maintain that homosexual human beings have always existed, whereas the latter insist that homosexual cultures of the twentieth century have emerged as a result of specific social evolutions.[3]

The two views are not entirely incompatible. Recent medical and biological research lends some support to the possibility that genetic or physiological factors may influence the nature of sexual desire, a thesis favored by essentialists.[4] Yet even if proof for a biological source of difference ultimately emerges—even if we find evidence that 2, or 5, or 10 percent of all people are born with the inclination towards homosexual desire—we will still be confronted with enormous evidence that the willingness and ability of these people to act upon such desire, and the physical expressions it takes, are conditioned by constructs that differ radically between societies. We will still need to account for the fact that in various societies, many among the remaining ninety to ninety-eight percent of human beings experience sexual desire and engage in sexual behavior for reasons that cannot be explained on the basis of the size of their hypothalamus neurons or the freight carried on their X chromosomes.

To understand such realities, we must explore socioeconomic factors. Numerous recent studies have demonstrated that, as David Halperin puts it, "sexual desires are [socially] constructed, mass-produced, and distributed among the various members of human living-groups."[5] To understand how and why such desires alter over time, we need not to produce histories of "sexuality" (conceived of as a natural given, common to all human beings but repressed in various ways by civilized authority) but "to define and refine a new, and radical, historical sociology of psychology."[6]

This work is one contribution toward that historical sociology. I have attempted to identify the "deep, seismic shifts in the structure of underlying social relations" that produced the several homosexual traditions in preindustrial Japan, particularly the bourgeois *nanshoku* tradition of the Tokugawa period.[7] These shifts are the spread of Buddhist monasticism, particularly after the introduction of the Tendai and Shingon sects in the early ninth century; the rise of feudalism and the idealized lord-retainer relationship; and the emergence of a vibrant bourgeois society, subject to feudal authority, inclined to accept its mores and encouraged to develop a culture of hedonism from the early decades of the Tokugawa era.

One must acknowledge the likelihood that throughout Japanese history some men have, for whatever reasons, exclusively experienced and acted upon homosexual desires. The literary references to *onna-girai* provide evidence of such men within the bourgeois tradition, as do the examples of men who wish to desire women but simply cannot. But far more men would have engaged in *nanshoku* because it was pleasurable, convenient, not forbidden nor regarded as immoral, and suggested by the nature of power relationships of the time.

Modern Japan, it may be argued, is less homophobic than most Western societies.[8] Contemporary popular literature, from comic books to novels, reflects the assumption that role-structured homosexual activity is a common male experience.[9] For example, in Ōe Kenzaburō's 1964 novel *Kojinteki na taiken* (A personal matter), a man's female lover casually remarks, "You strike me as the type that younger men tend to fall in love with. Haven't you ever been to bed with such guys?"[10] She raises the issue not because she finds something exceptional in her partner's personality or behavior but because she wants to have anal sex and wonders whether he has ever done this before. Her matter-of-fact and tolerant attitude toward the possibility of a lover's past homosexual experience is not uncommon in today's Japan.[11]

But today's Japan is not the bisexual world of the Tokugawa townspeople.[12] Few Japanese today would echo the declaration of Saikaku's Gengobei: "*Nanshoku, joshoku*—there's no difference." The prevalent view in Japan is that homosexual acts are abnormal and that those inclined to engage in them should at least tactfully conceal their sexual preference from relatives and co-workers. Openly gay people face institutional discrimination; members of one gay and lesbian group, for example, were barred in recent years from overnight stays at a Tokyo youth activities center.[13]

Attitudes toward male-male sex have thus altered dramatically during the past 125 years. The changes are due in large part to the nature of Japan's incorporation into the world system since 1859, when the first treaty ports were opened to foreign trade. A consensus developed within the Japanese ruling elite that Japan must absorb Western learning in order to obtain the respect of Western nations and to reverse the terms of the unequal treaties.

Such "learning" included the hitherto unknown concept of "illegitimacy"; a new conviction that phallic religious images were shameful and deserving of destruction; and homophobia.[14] As early as the mid-eighteenth century, Andō Shōeki (1703–1762) had favorably commented on Dutch sexual mores, including the intolerance of homosexuality.[15] The scholar of "Dutch Learning" (*Rangakusha*), Morishima Nakayoshi, wrote in 1787 that in Holland "*nanshoku* is strictly forbidden, and if someone acts contrary to nature and commits this crime,[a] the active partner[b] is burned, and the youth who takes the passive role[c] is drowned in the sea."[16] By the late nineteenth century Japanese elites had come to share the view that homosexuality (now referred to by the term *dōseiai*, or "same sex love") was "unnatural," and some called for its crim-

a. *hito jinri ni somuku o motte nari, tōji kore o okasu*
b. *okaseshi hito*
c. *okasaretaru shōnen*

inalization. The editors for the progressive newspaper *Yorozu chōhō* ran exposes on the prevalence of homosexual behavior among Tokyo students, and in 1899 the English-language publication *Eastern World* editorialized against the "bestial," "unnatural," "infamous" and "unclean" practices "of the future lawgivers, officials, and teachers of Japan." Male-male sex acts, it argued, "are condemned and punished as crimes in all civilized countries."[17] It called for a provision in the Japanese criminal code comparable to Article 174 of the German code, which punished homosexual acts with up to five years' imprisonment.[18]

Thus, Western cultural influence was a major factor in the decline of the *nanshoku* tradition. But surely this decline also reflects the collapse of the feudal structure that had shaped the development of male homosexuality in Japan. As we have seen, Japan's *nanshoku* tradition was not unique in dignifying both partners in role-structured homosexual relationships; the Chinese tradition also did so. But Japanese society, unlike Chinese society, generally insisted that long-term male-male sexual relationships occur only between an "older brother" and a "younger brother." Such relationships were rooted in, and mirrored, the lord-retainer bond. Even male prostitution developed in ways that reflected feudal values and institutions. With the fall of the feudal order, these values and institutions were for the most part either weakened or eradicated.

To be sure, *nanshoku*—in the sense of role-structured male homosexuality involving "brotherly bonds," finger cutting, and violent rivalries all reminiscent of the Tokugawa era—survived, even flourished, in the schools and military academies of Meiji Japan (1868–1912).[19] The terms *chigo* and *shōnen* were used in this period to refer to male students who received the attentions of older students.[20] A guide to schools in Tokyo published in 1901 warned students to be wary of those offering help in study in exchange for *nanshoku*, and the popular writer Mori Ōgai recorded his own near-rape by classmates in the 1909 novel *Wita Sekusuarisu* (*Vita Sexualis*).[21] But the world of *nanshoku* was now a surreptitious underground occasionally brought to light by investigative journalists or moral reformers. Educators such as Nitobe Inazō regarded "homosexual desires"[d] as primitive and violent urges to be suppressed through spiritual cultivation.[22]

Nanshoku rapidly moved from the center stage of popular culture to its margins. Homosexual desire was no longer celebrated in literature, theater, and art; rather, it was discouraged as one of the "evil customs" of the past, a national embarrassment given attitudes in the modern West.[23] The concept of *nanshoku-zuki* gave way to the German concept of the *urning*—one suffering from a peculiar psychological disorder.[24] Such an environment was less conducive to the generation of male-male sexual desire than that of Tokugawa Japan; males became less likely to experience, and even less likely to act upon, such desire. No transition in sexual attitudes and behavior better illustrates the social-constructionist thesis.

    d. *dōseiteki yokujō*

Appendix

A Boor's Tale
(*Denbu monogatari*)

(Anonymous, between 1636 and 1643)

Around the beginning of July,[a] feeling oppressed by the lingering summer heat, I stepped out of my shabby brushwood hermitage and, inviting several companions, left the village. We walked down to the river, and since no one else was around, bathed our limbs in its clear water, cracking jokes all the while.

"Surely you've all heard about it," someone said. "Lately our friend So-and-so has been going crazy over young men.[b] When night falls, he washes up, and taking pains to look his best, lingers under the eaves over there, near the miscanthus. Or he waits under the verandah of the prayer hall or the temple. He meets a lover and they lie together, speaking intimately. Or he falls in love with someone completely out of reach and, tormented by passion, prays to the gods and buddhas to permit a meeting.[1] He imposes on someone to serve as a go-between, declaring, 'I'd give my life just to meet him!'

"The feelings in his breast weigh almost as heavily as Fuji's lofty peak, and in love-letters he expresses passions profound as the deepest ocean. His love, though unrequited, is boundless as the waters in their unceasing flow.

a. literally, "the beginning of the seventh [lunar] month"
b. *wakashū-gurui to iu koto o shiidashi*

"Then there are the sort of men who, cherishing secret loves and dismayed that their feelings aren't reciprocated, want to cut their arms or slash their thighs.[2] If their love is returned, they swear by 'the endless Matsuyama' that their hearts will never change.[3] They call upon the intertwined branches [to witness their love-oaths] and envy [male lovers who, having committed love-suicides, now rest on the] Island of Double-Graves.

"One man like this will anxiously wait for a partner who never shows up. Another will curse the tolling of the bell [announcing dawn], which reverberates just after his mate finally says, 'Let's go to bed,' or sigh, 'It never rains except when he's planning to visit!' An insatiable lover resents the parting, the heartbreak of the cock's crow at daybreak. He sighs about the brevity of the night, thinking gloomily that even the long autumn nights end too soon. Recalling a song about Muro no Yashima, he yearns for someone to whom he can reveal his 'burning heart.'[4] He wistfully compares his sleeves, still wet with tears, to 'a rock jutting out of the sea at low tide.'[5]

"Citing the song *Shinobu Mountain,* he begs to know the sincerity of the other's feelings, or after a tryst his thoughts grow angry and violent.[6] He sings *Asuka River*, regretting that the sex isn't as good as it used to be, and grieves that life is endless misery and no one understands him.[7]

"There are also men who walk around together, in the gaudiest costumes, holding hands, practically shouting, 'Look at us!' They could care less whether or not people see them expressing their feelings for one another. Some men envy people able to follow both the ways [of homosexual and heterosexual love]. Their violently passionate hearts are agitated like the deep Yoshino River, rapidly flowing with the passing days and months; but they compare their lovers' feelings to a [shallow] salt pan, complaining 'This is the most worthless relationship[c] imaginable!'

"Someone listening to the paddling wings of the snipe at dawn, counting the number of nights his lover hasn't visited, resents the other for coolly taking him for granted. Such men are like generals

c. *chigiri*

counting the nights they have had to campaign in the deep grass.... But other men prepare sake, fish, and sing and play [with their lovers] every night. People tell me about all these cases and urge me, 'At least try a little sex with men[d]!'"

Another member of our party had listened to all of this. "Well now," he declared in a loud voice, "What useless passions such people have! How much better to enjoy the Way of Women, which has delighted people from antiquity!"

[Suddenly we noticed] four or five people running along the dike behind us, so fast that their feet hardly touched the ground. They [had overheard our conversation and] seemed extremely angry. When they got close, we could see that they were boy-lovers[e]; the group included some [youths who still wore] their forelocks.

"How can you say such nasty things about boy-lovers?" one of them demanded. "How absurd! How unpardonable for someone who enjoys the vulgar[f] way [of heterosexual love] to speak like that of our refined and charming way![g] You won't escape one inch from that spot!"

He rolled up his sleeves and drew his great side sword, which measured five *shaku*, eight *sun*.[8] At this point another [in the boy-lover group] hurried to separate these two.[9] "Come, now," he reasoned, "these people are saying foolish things, but shouldn't we be tolerant of one another?"[h] Even so, the boy-lover continued, "Don't try to stop me! And you," [he told my friend], "don't you run off!" The faces of both were flushed as they glared at one another.

"If this is the way it's going to be," I then proposed with some amusement, "why don't we debate the issue? Is the Way of Women truly vulgar, and is the Way of Youths[i] really more refined? Let's see whose logic[j] is superior and be tolerant toward the weaker argument!"

d. *nanshoku*
e. *wakashū-zuki*
f. *iyashii*
g. *warera ga kyasha ni omoshiroki michi*
h. *tagai ni kannin shitamae*
i. *jakudō*
j. *ri*

This proposal met with general agreement, so I sat down on the riverbank, holding a round Shibu fan on my lap, and with great interest and enjoyment listened to what both parties had to say.

The boor fond of women started off. "You said the Way of Women is vulgar and the Way of Youths refined. Well then, why don't you explain that to us? Let's hear it!"

The boy-love advocate made himself comfortable, fanned himself, and replied: "We say the Way of Youths is refined because it's usually preferred by high-ranking samurai and priests. Really, a youth's elegant form, when he's dressed in beautiful clothes, decked out in gold and silver and sporting the great and small swords,[10] is like the willow-tree bending in the wind. You invite him to view cherry-blossoms, or the moon; or you take him along to an incense-guessing party.[11] His charms, even the way he smells, are so intoxicating! And when you see him walking along the road humming a tune–what could be more refined?

"As for women being vulgar: could you walk along sight-seeing, holding a *woman's* hand? If men who delight in courtesans did such things, they'd be denounced as fools or blockheads, incur their masters' disfavor or be disinherited by their parents. They'd have nowhere to go and nothing to do but steal and lose their lives. Their whole household would be disgraced. But boy-lovers don't get treated that way.

"Let's say somebody's mistress makes him a belt from torn padded clothing. It makes him grimace when it chaps and cracks his legs.[12] Or she meets a friendly man and greets him with a flattering smile, not caring what those around might think. You never know who's gotten her pregnant or whose child she bears. You often hear about such idiocy. I absolutely can't understand how someone could enjoy such a vulgar way and censure ours!"

"Well," replied the boor, "if I were a high-ranking samurai like the man you mentioned, I too might enjoy [sex with youths]. But how much comfort will this 'forbidden way'[k] you enjoy so much provide you in the *next* life? Even I'd like to employ five or ten

k. *hidō*

beautifully dressed boys as my attendants. But you are as different from a ranking samurai as heaven is from earth, and your boy-
lover[l] friends are fools.

"Here's my image of a boy-fanatic,[m] a boy-lover.[n] First of all,
he wears a backless, well-starched, hempen tunic, and at his
shoulders and waist he sports colored paper and poem cards. He
wraps himself in a thick cotton loincloth knotted high on the belly.
His face is blacker than the 'old man' noh mask, and his neck and
forehead are grimy. He doesn't cut his nails, and his hair is as reddish and wild as that of an orangutan. Even if he sometimes puts it
up, bundling it with cut straw or used ribbons, lice come crawling
out. His [head is covered] with stinking boils. When he catches a
boy—one with an indescribably strange smell—they lie next to
one another on a mat, sharing a pillow, expressing their inmost
feelings to one another. They say things like, 'If we die, let's go
together,' and, absorbed in their love, don't even look one another in the eye.[13]

"And I hear that such boys are greedy. They don't just expect
sweet words but demand fans and towels and tissue paper. But
while you're fucking them, they knit their eyebrows, and screw
up their mouths in pain—that's real pathos[o] for you! Afterwards
they don't treat you so nice. They suffer from hemorrhoids and
become bow-legged. When their parents inquire, 'Why do you
walk as though you were being stuck with a bamboo cane?' they
can't explain what's ailing them. They just blush with embarrassment. Pitiful! Then, too, they contract incurable diseases, which
even the springs of Arima and Totsukawa can't cure. So they come
to resent their 'older brothers.'[p] Their lovers might apologize afterwards, but the boys get no pleasure out of these encounters.

"I even hear that these days, when the boys and their lovers
write love-oaths[q], including clauses like, 'You may not have other

l. *wakashū-gurui*
m. *waranbe-gurui*
n. *wappa-gurui*
o. *aware*
p. *nenja*
q. *chigiri*

boys,' or 'You may not have women,' the older partner signs with blood squeezed from his finger. Some tough, warlike youths— very rough fellows—[get involved in such relationships]. I think it'd be all right to send this type out on the battlefield.

"Lots of men waste away their lives infatuated with female prostitutes. But recently something called 'youths' kabuki' has appeared, and not only priests but multitudes of common people also enjoy it, spending lots of gold and silver [on the actor-prostitutes] and losing their property in the process. Surely you know about this. It's probably not much different from throwing away your life for a prostitute.[14]

"True, it's said that priests prefer [the love of youths], but this is only because when priests take up their calling, renouncing attachments to this world, they give up any hope of having children. Even so, the very fact that the Way of Women is more attractive than the Way of Youths has recently led even priests to lose themselves in relationships with women. Of course, if priests firmly adhere to the way of Buddha and avoid this tempting Way, they'll probably avoid disaster. But if their desire [for women] is denied by the society around them, what on earth can they do [but turn to boys]? Since priests must avoid the Five Deadly Sins,[15] they lack freedom; they shave their heads, don surplices and priestly robes, and abstain from fish and fowl. So how can they avoid the so-called 'forbidden way'? The proverb says, 'Cattle follow cattle, birds follow birds.' But it would be best for these people to hurry up and follow a way more suitable to human beings!"

The refined one answered angrily: "I still can't understand how you can suggest that the Way of Youths is wrong. It's precisely because of the excellence of this Way that Buddha[r] had Ananda,[16] Confucius had Yan Hui,[17] Su Dongpo[18] had Li Jietui. If the Way of Youths were wrong, would Buddha and Confucius have enjoyed it? Buddha *despised* women; one of his Five Commandments forbids [monks to have sex with them].

"It's said that men infatuated with women are reborn in hell when they die. It's also said that women who die in childbirth

r. *Shaka*

sink into a sea of blood.[19] As the *Ten Kings' Sutra* explains, 'In one day ten thousand people descend into hell.'[20] Seven or eight thousand of these are women, two or three are men. That's why the founders of Japan's Buddhist sects despised women and forbade them to visit the holy mountains and temples. But I've never heard of anyone despising *men*!

"You've heard the expression, 'People are eternally encumbered by their children.'[s] The hermit Ikkaku lost his immortality because of a woman.[21] In our country the hermit Kume glimpsed the leg of the washer-woman and lost his supernatural powers. Why would any man desire such villainous people?"

"You've no grounds to claim that Buddha completely despised women," the boor replied. "Lady Yashodara, his queen, bore their child Rahula. Confucius also had a child named Li Yu, and I've heard Su Dongpo had lots of children. And the reason that temples exclude women is precisely because they're so fascinating! They arouse deep passion in men's hearts, so a scripture says, 'Priests must not go near the imperial court, even briefly. If they do, they will surely be soiled with sexual desire.'[22] If a monk from Mt. Kōya or Miidera[23] could feel the tender graces of an elegant lady, sixteen years of age, with a face like a rose mallow, clothed like a rain-moistened pear blossom—well then, he'd be unable to continue his studies! No matter how resolute the monk! He'd be in danger—and might even demand to return to lay life! That's why Buddha issued his commandment.

"As for your comment about the hermit Kume and the sage of Shiga Temple—they weren't destroyed by women. And anyway, didn't they fall in love of their own free wills? In Japan, Shōtoku Taishi also had his consort[t] Seritsumi. Furthermore, the first rule of humanity and justice is cause and effect.[u] For example, ancestors and parents are the cause, children are the result. Isn't it precisely because there are parents that there are children? If, as you

---

s. *Ko wa sangai no kubikase*, or "Children are bound to us through our three incarnations (past, present, future)." Women are being faulted here for giving birth to these troublesome offspring.

t. *kisaki*

u. *motosue*

said, men in the world all loved youths and no one had children, the world would decline, and neither Buddhism nor Confucianism would be any good for anybody. It would be nice if youths could bear babies, but weren't the Buddha and Confucius, and the buddhas of the three worlds, and you yourself, all born by women?

"Next: let's talk about 'the forbidden way' you're trying to justify as it relates to filial piety. This is the most important thing for children to observe. Do you think parents are happy when, for example, they've taken the trouble to finally arrange a good marriage for a son, and then he tells them, 'I only like youths. Please find a youth for me—I hate women'? Or when he marries in order to please his parents but then greets his bride with, 'I'm a boy-lover'?

"As for myself, I'm a woman-lover. I enjoy casual sex with a prostitute at night and take off the next morning. But when my parents finally choose a woman for my bride, I'll feel happy about it. She and I will behave filially toward my parents and make them happy by having a harmonious relationship. We'll maintain proper contact with near and distant relatives, avoid drinking too much sake, and add to the prosperity of our household. Isn't this the proper way? You can talk about the virtues of the 'forbidden way,' but I've never heard of anyone getting their parents' consent to take in a young *man* as their bride! The whole family would be extremely unhappy!

"Anyway, Confucius didn't despise the family system—on the contrary, he emphasized the need to continue the family line. Buddha established the Law of Easy Life[v] for mothers.[24] Didn't Maudgalyāyana[w] save miserable women who had fallen into hell? [According to Buddhism,] if one child enters the priesthood, the whole family will be reborn in heaven.

"Minamoto no Tameyoshi no Ason was ruined by Kiyomori, but [his filial sons] Yoritomo and Yoshitsune destroyed the Heike.[25] Sanetomo killed Yoritomo's son Yoriie, but [Yoriie's son] Kugyō

v. *ango no nori*
w. Japanese *Mokuren*; one of Buddha's ten disciples

appeared and killed [Sanetomo]. After that, people like the Soga brothers and Kono Michinobu all killed their parents' enemies. Taira Tomonori became the vicarious substitute for Lord Tomomori.[26] All these events occured because sons [were loyal to their parents].

"I can't understand what you mean by calling women 'vulgar.' When Susano-o no Mikoto was about to marry his queen, the shrine in Izumo province was built, and he began to chant, 'I build a many-fenced palace.'[27] Women wrote many of the poems selected [for inclusion in anthologies] by the sage emperors of antiquity, and the *Genji Monogatari, Sagoromo Monogatari, Ise Monogatari, Yamato Monogatari, Eiga Monogatari* and many other works were authored by women.[28] But there are no poems written by youths! Maybe they've written other things—but one searches in vain for their poems. So given all these facts, can we consider the Shining Genji[29], Narihira,[30] and the Sagoromo general[31] 'boors'?"

"Despite your clever speech," the refined one replied, "there is nothing worse than a woman. She is the great enemy who destroys countries and breaks up households. For example, King Zhou Yin was ruined because of Da Ji, King Wang of Zhou destroyed his country because of Bao Shi, Xuan Zong of Tang loved Yang Gueifei and brought disorder to the world by Lu Shan. Yue plundered the world because of Xi Shi, and Wu was also ruined by Yue because of Xi Shi. In our country, retired emperor Shirakawa loved Bifukumon-in, and when he unwisely abdicated [at her bidding], the Hōgen Disturbance immediately broke out.[32]

"In more recent history, [the shogun] Ashikaga Yoshinori was struck by Akamatsu Mitsusuke at the Fukōin Palace solely on account of a woman.[33] Women are, at any rate, heartless and never think of their husbands. Rikiju—was that her name?—tried to have [her husband] Satō Tadanobu attacked.[34] A chaste woman is not supposed to serve two husbands, but the fact is such women, and the women of today as well, will in nine cases out of ten find a new man once their husband dies.

"Since they have to have *some* companion, their relatives give

them to anybody at all, even a man with a collapsed eye and bro-
ken nose. In this fleeting world of empty dreams,[x] why should
[such women have to spend their lives] looking at ugly men?
Youths, in contrast, can freely give their hearts to the person
they desire, and if both parties consent to the relationship,
there's no problem. For example, cherry-blossoms and autumn
leaves are fleeting things, and people love them for precisely that
reason. Women can't be like that. Their skin, once smooth and
young-looking like a peach or plum, becomes like a pear. The
hair turns grey, the face fills with wrinkles like the waves of the
four seas. However much you once loved them, growing old with
them is rather painful.[35]

"Our Way, I argue, is based on sound precedents. There was
once a Chinese emperor who took a youth for his lover, and they
lay down on a brocade cushion. When the emperor was awakened,
the youth was laying upon the emperor's sleeve. The emperor,
hating to interrupt the boy's dreams, took out his knife and cut
the sleeve. The youth, grateful for this [extraordinary considera-
tion], accompanied the emperor to his grave when he died.[36]
This, I've heard, is the origin of the custom of a retainer's committing suicide to follow his lord to the grave[y] in both China and
Japan. And most of those who storm onto the battlefield, warding
off the enemy and accompanying their lords to the end, are the
lords' male sex-partners.[z]

"Mongaku saved the life of Rokudai because he'd fallen in love
with the youth's [beautiful] body.[37] Such loyalty is noble! But I've
never heard of women ruling countries or accompanying their
lords to the end!"

"Even the fact that women ruin countries and wreck families
shows that the Way of Women is very exciting!" replied the boor.
"Having lots of gold and silver would create problems for anybody; you can't say that women are *particularly* apt to throw
countries into turmoil and cause the decline of families. A woman

x. *yumemaboroshi*
y. *oibara*
z. *gomotsu*

has preserved the Empire on more than one occasion. In Tang China the wife of Emperor Gao Zong, mother of Zhong Zong, became [reigning] Empress. When Zhong Zong died, the crown prince was still a child, so the empress ascended the throne, appointed wise officials, removed the corrupt, preserved the country, and loved the people. That's why we call women 'Yao' and 'Shun.'[38]

"In our country too, after the death of Shogun Yoritomo in Kamakura,[39] his widow, the second-degree nun Masako had compassion for the people and governed the country, bringing a long period of peace to the land.[40] Hence she's called the Nun Shogun of Japan. And while people say that women lack military valor, when the sixteenth emperor Chūai died, didn't Empress Jingu succeed him and subdue the Three Kingdoms of Korea?[41] Didn't Yu Shi in China, and in our country both Tomoe of Kiso and Yoshitsune's mistress Shizuka, prove their valor on the battlefield? As you pointed out, Rikijū tried to stab Tadanobu but Aijū saved him.

"There *are*, in fact, examples of women following their lovers to the grave. Recently, when I went on a pilgrimage to Mt. Kōya, I looked at the various stone graves around the temple, and there were several with the inscription, 'These are the remains of Sendai Chūnagon Date Masamune.[42] Next to him are all his attendants.' Deeply moved by this, I went on reading [the tombstone inscriptions]: 'This is Lord So-and-so, this is So-and-so-zaemon.' There were also tombstones of women—proving that women, too, have followed their lords in death.

"Let me also tell you a little story. A long time ago, there was a woman in Settsu province who had two suitors. She was unable to decide between the two, and her parents said, 'Make up your mind about one or the other.' But she didn't do that. Instead, she threw herself into the Ikuta River, taking her own life. And in China there was once an official who received a love letter from a woman. The emperor saw this letter and fell in love with her because of the beauty of the handwriting. Indulging his passion, he then had the woman brought to him, but she didn't return his feelings in the slightest. [In a rage, the emperor] had the official's nose cut off, but even when the woman saw him in his disfigured state [her feelings remained unchanged]. 'How terrible that for my sake you've been mutilated so!' she exclaimed and rejected the emperor even more strongly. Meanwhile the man, preferring to have been killed, threw himself in the water and drowned. The disconsolate woman also drowned herself.

"Ono no Yorikaze lost his life because of a woman. And Ame no Mikado no Uneme, the nun Utsusemi, Kenreimon-in's Yokobue, Senjū of Kamakura, Kosaishō no Tsubone of Michimori, Ichinoniya no Miyasudokoro, Enya Hangan's wife—all these were chaste women whose love [for their husbands] couldn't be destroyed.[43] Yet you say women are unreliable! You need to think again.

"There are some married men who also love boys. But don't they as a result ignore their wives and children, wasting their wealth and property? They turn the keys of their treaure-storehouses over to their boys. And have you heard about men who leave their fortunes to youths instead of their wives and children?

"You made the point that women stay with you as you grow older. Doesn't that just show how reliable they are? Men who want to [maintain their marriages] after death recognize that women's feelings run deep. Your boys, on the other hand, don't really give themselves freely. You treat them affectionately now, but in the end your ardor cools. Eventually they become adults and shave their whole foreheads. However regrettably, the beard begins to appear on the cheeks. Then how undignified the former lovers must feel when they meet one another and remember the past!

"You can't say that youths have never ruined countries. No, I'd say that they're really the greatest enemies of the state. There are daimyo households that have continued for many generations, protected by loyal chancellors.[aa] But then the lord falls in love with a youth and appoints him to high office. When quarrels develop between the youth and the loyal chancellors, the daimyo invariably sides with the youth. When such things come to the shogun's attention, the youth blames his lord [for the conflict], and the daimyo loses his domain. There are lots of recent examples.

aa. *karō*

"If such people, mismanaging the Empire, or their domains, fail to produce descendents, society itself is endangered. Even the lower-ranking people of such household can't help feeling troubled. If they have no offspring, won't their fiefs vanish meaninglessly when they die? Their own fates aside, won't many of their retainers become miserable, masterless samurai?[bb] Everbody knows that when a shogun dies without descendents, the world is thrown into disorder.

"Ours is the country of the gods. After the seven generations of celestial dieties, Izanami and Izanagi had heterosexual intercourse under the Floating Bridge of Heaven, and then, following the Five Generations of Earth Dieties, Emperor Kanmu mastered our country. Since his time, over one hundred emperors have continued his line. Amatsugoya Neno Mikoto's grandson became lord of the country, and after that men like Kiyomori and Minamoto Yoritomo wielded great power as generals. Then came the nine generations of the Hōjō and the thirteen generations of Ashikaga shoguns, beginning with Takauji. [But throughout our history, one finds] no examples of boy-lovers protecting the world or ascending to rule the country. It's precisely because men appoint their sons as heirs that the country and nation are protected.

"Finally, the birds who fly in the sky, and the beasts who run on the land, all exchange the lover's vows of male and female. And since Japan is the land of the gods, all manner of deep blessings will come our way so long as we keep to this Way. So hurry up and renounce your 'forbidden way'!"

The face of the refined one was no longer laughing but had turned red. I watched with great amusement as the two debaters pushed past one another. "It's dusk," [declared the refined one]. "The village gates are probably locked already. We'd all best run along home. Let's leave this for the time being and continue the discussion later."

So we parted, some heading north, some heading south.

bb. *rōnin*

List of Characters

Japanese

aikake	相掛
ainame	合い甞め
aiyoku no meiro	愛欲の迷路
akusho	悪所
amae	甘え
anibun	兄分
arakawa	荒皮
azunai no tsumi	阿豆那比之罪
bidō	美道
bishōnen	美小年
bōkoku	亡国
bōzu	坊主
bugyō	奉行
bumon no hana	武文の花
butai-ko	舞台子
chaya	茶屋
chigiri	契

chigo	稚児
chishi	茅子
chō	町
chōji yu	丁字油
chōnin	町人
chōshin	寵臣
chūgen	中間
danjo yūretsu ron	男女優劣論
denbu	田夫
deyarō	出野郎
Dōsōjin	道相神
eboshi-oya	烏帽子親
eta	穢多
fundoshi	褌
funori	布海苔
futanari	二形，二成、双成
fūzoku shi	風俗史
gandō	玩童
genpuku	元服
giri	義理
gomotsu	御持
hachimaki	鉢巻き
han	藩
harikata	張形
hatamoto	旗本
hatto	法度
heinō bunri	兵農分離
higa	秘画

himitsu no sumata	秘密のすまた
hinin	非人
hito-yado	人宿
hōkan	幇間
ichi chigo ni sannō	一稚児二山王
iemochi	家持
iemori	家守
iki	意気
in-yō	陰陽
in-yō shizen	陰陽自然
iran	違乱
iro	色
iro-ko	色子
ishi	異志
iyashii	卑しい
jakudō	若道
jakudōgata	若道方
jodō	女道
jōin	上淫
joshiki-girai	女色嫌い
joshoku	女色
jusha	儒者
kabuki	歌舞伎
kachi	徒
kage-ko	陰子
kagema	陰間
kain	下淫
kanniku	貫肉

kappa	河童
karisaki	亀頭
kasshiki	喝食
kataribe	語部
kawatsurumi	加波津留実
keikan	渓姦
keisei-machi	形成町
ki	気
kiku	菊
kobanashi	小咄
kōchū o chigiru	口中を契る
kodomo	子供
kodomoya	子供屋
kōgu-uri	香具売
komono	小者
kongō	金剛（近尻・懇尻・金尻）
koshō	小姓
kōshoku	好色
kuchiire	口入れ
kuchi o suu	口を吸う
kuchi-yose	口寄せ
kusemono	癖者
kusoto	糞戸
kyōdai chigiri	兄弟契り
kyōdai keiyaku	兄弟契約
kyōdai musubi	兄弟結
kyōgen	狂言
kyūyū	旧友

machi	町
maegami	前髪
maibito	舞人
makura-e	枕絵
mittsū	密通
miyurushi	見許し
mochi-zuki	餅好き
mura no seigen	斑の誓言
murasaki bōshi	紫帽子
nanchō	男寵
nandō	男道
nanshoku	男色
nanshoku jaya	男色茶屋
nanshoku-zuki	男色好き
nasake	情
nenja	念者
nenyū	念友
nerigi	練木
norito	祝詞
nyake	若気
nyodō	女道
nyodōgata	女道方
ochiru hana	落花
ofuregaki	御触書
okabasho	岡場所
okama	お釜
okasu	犯す
okiya	置屋

oniyake	御若気
onnagata (ōyama)	女方
onna-girai	女嫌い
osugata	男姿
otokodate	男建
otoko no geisha	男芸者
otoko no keisei	男傾城
otōtobun	弟分
oyadama	親玉
renga	連歌
rōnin	浪人
roppōsha	六方者
saibi	採尾
sakari-bana	盛り花
sansuke	三助
seigaiko	制外子
sei seikatsu shi	性生活史
sentō	銭湯
shamisen	三味線
shinjù	心中
shitate	仕立
shudō (or shūdō)	衆道
shudō-zuki	衆道好き
shunga	春画
subari	窄り
suigyū	水牛
sumi-maegami	角前髪
tabiko	旅子

tagaigata	互形
taikomochi	太鼓持
tanin no chigo	他人之稚児
taoyama buri	手弱女振
tayū	太夫
tobiko	飛子
tsubomeru hana	窄める花
tsutomego	努め子
tsūwasan	通和散
uchikowashi	打ち壊し
uiana	うい穴
ukiyo	浮き世
uramon tsūkō	裏門通行
waka	和歌
wakage	若気
wakamono-yado	若者宿
wakashū	若衆
wakashū-gurui	若衆狂い
wakashū-zuki	若衆好き
yakko	奴
yakusha hyōbanki	役者評判記
yarō	野郎
yarō-atama	野郎頭
yarō-machi	野郎町
yaro-zuki	野郎好き
yo no hito	世の人
yo no soshiri	世の誹り
yoru no tomo	夜の友

yowa-yowa   弱々

yuigon   遺言

yūjo   遊女

yūjo jaya   遊女茶屋

yuna   湯女

zōritori   草履取

Chinese

dan   旦

Hanlin feng   翰林風

jijian   鷄姦

longyang   龍陽

nanse   男色

qixiong-qidi   契兄契弟

xianggong tangji   相公

yin-yang   陰陽

Korean

chajewi   子弟衛

hwarang   花郎

midong   美童

namsadang   男寺團

namsaek   男色

yongyang   龍陽

Notes

Introduction

1. On the connections between Athenian democracy and the specific construction of male homosexuality in ancient Athens, see David M. Halperin, *One Hundred Years of Homosexuality and Other Essays on Greek Love* (New York: Routledge, 1990), esp. p. 88f; Kenneth J. Dover, *Greek Homosexuality* (Cambridge, Ma.: Harvard University Press, 1978), p. 19f.

2. Paul Gordon Schalow has translated a key work by the Tokugawa-era writer Ihara Saikaku and published several articles on the *nanshoku* theme in Tokugawa literature. See his *The Great Mirror of Male Love* (Stanford: Stanford University Press, 1990); " Male Love in Early Modern Japan: A Literary Depiction of the 'Youth,'" in Martin Duberman et al., eds., *Hidden from History* (New York: New American Library, 1989); "Kūkai and the Tradition of Male Love in Japanese Buddhism," in Jose Ignacio Cabezon, ed., *Buddhism, Sexuality, and Gender* (New York: State University of New York Press, 1992), pp. 215–230. The standard monograph on male homosexuality in premodern Japan is Iwata Jun'ichi's *Honchō nanshoku kō* (Studies in homosexuality in Japan) (Tokyo: n.p., 1930–1933; Tokyo: Kogawa shoten, 1974). The book includes little material on the Tokugawa period. Part of it has been translated into English in Watanabe Tsuneo and Iwata Jun'ichi, *The Love of the Samurai: A Thousand Years of Japanese Homosexuality* (London: Gay Men's Press, 1987). Watanabe's contribution to this work deals in part with the Tokugawa period but is of limited usefulness.

3. A few years ago, at a cocktail party at an Ivy League university, I happened to casually remark that I was working on a book about Toku-

gawa *nanshoku*. Within a week I received a call from a colleague mentioning a "scandal." This colleague had, upon hearing about my remark from a well-known Japan scholar present at the party, exclaimed in amazement, "But he's *married!*" In the mid-eighties another colleague responded to my pensive comment, "Someone ought to write a book about Tokugawa homosexuality ..." with: "It would be the end of your career!"

4. This was revised and published as Gary Leupp, *Servants, Shophands, and Laborers in the Cities of Tokugawa Japan* (Princeton, N.J.: Princeton University Press, 1992).

5. Leupp, *Servants*, pp. 198-199.

6. On the male brothels, see Takekoshi Yosaburō, *The Economic Aspects of the History of the Civilization of Japan* (London: Allen and Unwin, 1930), vol. 2, p. 357; Nishiyama Matsunosuke et al., *Edo gaku jiten* (Tokyo: Kōbundō, 1984), pp. 556-558; Kodama Kōta, *Genroku jidai* (Tokyo: Chūō kōronsha, 1966), p. 398; Tanaka Kōgai, *Edo jidai no danjo kankei* (Osaka: Keimeisha, 1926), p. 152f. On literary works, see Iwata Jun'ichi's bibliography, *Nanshoku bunken shoshi* (Tokyo: Kogawa shoten, 1973), pp. 38-165; on the shoguns' homosexual relationships, see Saiki Kazuma, "Tokugawa shōgun seibo narabi saisho kō," in Nihon rekishi gakkai, eds., *Rekishi to jinbutsu* (Tokyo: Yoshikawa kōbunkan, 1964).

7. Schalow, "Male Love in Early Modern Japan," p. 119f; Watanabe and Iwata, *Love of the Samurai*, pp. 118-119. Watanabe writes, "It is probable that the spread of *shudō* offered suitable conditions for the development of that bisexuality which, as Freud says, is proper to human nature."

8. On the history of this term and its relationship to the earlier concept of "sexual inversion," see Halperin, *One Hundred Years*, p. 15.

9. David F. Greenberg discusses ancient cult prostitution in *The Construction of Homosexuality* (Chicago: University of Chicago Press, 1988), p. 94f. On the pirates, see B. R. Burg, *Sodomy and the Pirate Tradition: English Sea Rovers in the Seventeenth-Century Caribbean* (New York: New York University Press, 1984), p. 107f.

10. Sigmund Freud, *Three Contributions to the Theory of Sex* (New York: E. P. Dutton, 1962), p. 10.

11. Ibid., p. 8.

12. Ibid., p. 10; Robert A. Nye, *Masculinity and Male Codes of Honor in Modern France* (New York: Oxford University Press, 1993), p. 118; Wilhelm Reich, *Sex-Pol: Essays 1929-1934*, ed. Lee Baxandall (New York: Vintage Books, 1972), p. 297.

13. Jeffrey Weeks, "Preface to the 1978 Edition," in Guy Hocquen-ghem, *Homosexual Desire* (Durham, N.C. and London: Duke University Press, 1993), pp. 26–34.

14. Maurice Godelier, "The Origins of Male Domination," *New Left Review* 127 (1981), p. 17.

15. Karl Marx and Friedrich Engels, *The German Ideology: Parts I & III* (New York: International Publishers, 1967), pp. 14–15.

16. The concept of "ideology," as used by Marx and Engels, refers to distortions of thought that stem from, and reflect, social contradictions, especially class conflict. See Tom Bottomore, ed., *A Dictionary of Marxist Thought* (Cambridge, Ma.: Harvard University Press, 1973), pp. 219–223.

17. Halperin, *One Hundred Years*, p. 40.

18. Translated by Alfred H. Marks as *Forbidden Colours* (London: Penguin Books, 1971).

19. Masuda Koh, editor-in-chief, *Kenkyusha's New Japanese-English Dictionary*, 4th Edition (Tokyo: Kenkyusha, 1974), p. 184. This is the entry for *danshoku*, the more contemporary reading of *nanshoku*. The modern term *dōsei-ai*, meanwhile, is rendered "homosexual love; homosexuality; homoerot(ic)ism; unnatural love; (between women) lesbianism; lesbian love [vice]; sapphism" (p. 221).

20. Andrew Nathaniel Nelson, *The Modern Reader's Japanese-English Character Dictionary*, 2nd Revised Edition (Tokyo and Rutland, Vt.: Tuttle, 1974), p. 621.

21. The term simply means "love of boys." I recognize, however, that the dominant culture uses this term disparagingly.

22. *Kenkyusha's New Japanese-English Dictionary* equates *shudō* with pederasty; see p. 1614.

23. "Bugger" comes from the Middle Latin *Bulgarus*, or "Bulgarian"; see John Boswell, *Christianity, Social Tolerance, and Homosexuality: Gay People in Western Europe from the Beginning of the Christian Era to the Fourteenth Century* (Chicago and London: University of Chicago Press, 1980), p. 284. I hope I will not irritate readers in sometimes using the verb "to bugger" (as in, "Raijin, the god of thunder, is shown being buggered by the illness-preventing god") when alternative phraseology strikes me as flat or awkward.

Chapter 1

1. *Nanse* ("male eros" or "male eroticism") came to be used as a euphemism for male-male sex in China during the Northern Qi dynasty (550–577 A.D.). See Bret Hinsch, *Passions of the Cut Sleeve: The Male*

Homosexual Tradition in China (Berkeley: University of California Press, 1990), p. 57.

2. Boswell, *Christianity, Social Tolerance, and Homosexuality*, p. 52.

3. G. S. Rousseau, "The Pursuit of Homosexuality in the Eighteenth Century: 'Utterly Confused Category' and/or Rich Repository?" in R. P. Maccubin, ed., *"'Tis Nature's Fault": Unauthorized Sexuality During the Enlightenment* (Cambridge, U.K.: Cambridge University Press, 1987), p. 71. I am indebted to Howard Solomon for this and the previous reference.

4. Alan Bray, *Homosexuality in Renaissance England* (London: Gay Men's Press, 1982), pp. 280–282.

5. Ibid., pp. 52, 75.

6. Dover, *Greek Homosexuality*, p. 34.

7. Classical Chinese learning and culture was valued by most Japanese scholars even after the last native Chinese dynasty, the Ming, fell in 1644. Indeed, they presented the appropriation of this culture as one indicator of Japan's greatness. See Marius B. Jansen, *China in the Tokugawa World* (Cambridge, Ma.: Harvard University Press, 1992), p. 79f.

8. If the Japanese believed that homosexuality flourished in these highly civilized societies, they apparently thought it was not practiced among the more primitive society of the Ainu in Hokkaido. "The Japanese say there is no sodomy in Ezo," reported Jesuit missionary Jeromino de Angelis, who visited the northern island in 1618. See Michael Cooper, comp., *They Came to Japan: An Anthology of European Reports on Japan,* 1543–1640 (Berkeley: University of California Press, 1965), p. 290

9. Burton Watson, trans., *Han Fei Tzu: Basic Writings* (New York: Columbia University Press, 1964), p. 78.

10. Warren J. Blumenfield and Diana Raymond, *Looking at Gay and Lesbian Life* (New York: Philosophical Library, 1988), p. 103.

11. Robert H. Van Gulik, *Sexual Life in Ancient China* (New York: 1974), p. 48

12. Burton Watson, *Records of the Grand Historian of China* (New York: Columbia University Press, 1964), vol. II, p. 462.

13. Van Gulik, *Sexual Life*, p. 63.

14. Watson, *Records of the Grand Historian*, II, p. 462.

15. Van Gulik, *Sexual Life*, pp. 192–193.

16. Ibid., p. 92; Laurence Bresler, *The Origins of Popular Travel and Travel Literature in Japan* (unpublished Ph.D. dissertation, Columbia University, 1975), p. 305; Jean-Jacques Matignon, "Deux mots sur la

pédérastie en Chine," *Archives d'anthropologie criminelle* (Paris) 14 (1899), p. 38.

17. Frederic Wakeman, Jr., *The Great Enterprise: The Manchu Reconstruction of Imperial Order in Seventeenth-Century China* (Berkeley, Ca.: University of California Press, 1975), vol. I, p. 95; Jonathan D. Spence, *The Memory Palace of Matteo Ricci* (New York: Viking, 1984), p. 227; Arthur Waley, *Yuan Mei, Eighteenth Century Chinese Poet* (Stanford: Stanford University Press, 1956), p. 27.

18. Mitamura Taisuke, *Chinese Eunuchs: The Structure of Intimate Politics* (Tokyo and Rutland, Vt.: Tuttle, 1970), pp. 64–65; Spence, *Memory Palace*, p. 227; Hinsch, *Passions*, p. 127f.

19. Spence, *Memory Palace*, p. 226; Van Gulick, *Sexual Life*, p. 163; Jacques Gernet, *Daily Life in China on the Eve of the Mongol Invasions, 1250–1276* (Stanford, Ca.: Stanford University Press, 1962), pp. 98–99.

20. Gernet, *Daily Life*, pp. 98–99.

21. Ibid.; Van Gulick, *Sexual Life*, p. 163; Wakeman, *Great Enterprise*, p. 95; Vivian Ng, "Ideology and Sexuality: Rape Laws in Qing China," *Journal of Asian Studies* 46, 1 (February 1987), pp. 57–80.

22. Van Gulik, *Sexual Life*, p. 163; Gernet, *Daily Life*, p. 98.

23. Spence, *Memory Palace*, p. 226; Colin P. Mackerras, *The Rise of the Peking Opera, 1770–1870: Social Aspects of the Theatre in Manchu China* (London: Oxford University Press, 1972), p. 45.

24. John Byron, *Portrait of a Chinese Paradise: Erotica and Sexual Customs of the Late Qing Period* (London: Quartet Books, 1987), p. 37.

25. Ibid., p. 36.

26. Ng, "Ideology and Sexuality," pp. 67–68. For the etymology of *jijian*, see Hinsch, *Passions*, pp. 88–89.

27. Lawrence E. Gichner, *Erotic Aspects of Chinese Culture* (Washington, D.C.: n.p., 1967), p. 76; Sir John Barrow, *Travels in China* (London: T. Cadell and Davies, 1804); Arlo Karlen, *Sexuality and Homosexuality: A New View* (New York: W. W. Norton, 1971), p. 230; Byron, pp. 35–36; Jonathan D. Spence, *Emperor of China: Self-Portrait of K'ang-hsi* (New York: Knopf, 1974), pp. 125–127.

28. Vern L. Bullough, *Sexual Variance in Society and History* (New York: John Wiley and Sons, 1976), p. 305.

29. Spence *Memory Palace*, p. 220.

30. Mackerras, *Peking Opera*, pp. 87–88.

31. Ibid., pp. 149–150.

32. Yang Hsien-yi and Gladys Yang, trans., *The Scholars* (Peking: Foreign Languages Press, 1957), pp. 378–381.

33. Keith McMahon, *Causality and Containment in Seventeenth-Century Chinese Fiction* (Leiden: E. J. Brill, 1988), p. 75f.

34. Van Gulick, *Sexual Life*, p. 63.

35. Hinsch, *Passions*, p. 8.

36. For a fictional example, see MacMahon, *Causality and Containment*, pp. 74−76.

37. Ayukai Fusanoshin, *Zakkai* (Seoul: Chikazawa shuppan, 1932), vol. 4, p. 36; see also William E. Henthorn, *A History of Korea* (New York: Free Press, 1971), p. 45.

38. Richard Rutt, "The Flower Boys of Silla (Hwarang): Notes on the Sources," *Transactions of the Korean Branch of the Asiatic Society of Japan* 38 (1961), p. 61.

39. Peter Lee, *Lives of Eminent Korean Monks* (Cambridge, Ma.: Harvard University Press, 1969), p. 70.

40. Rutt, "Flower Boys," p. 57.

41. Ibid., p. 58.

42. Ibid., p. 56f; John Stevens, *Lust for Enlightenment: Buddhism and Sex* (Boston: Shambala Publications, 1990), pp. 139−140.

43. Quoted in Watanabe and Iwata, *Love of the Samurai*, p. 88.

44. On Vietnam, see Jean-Noül Bergmann, *La sexualite à travers le monde: études sur la péninsule Indochinoise* (Paris: Le Tréfle d'Or, 1966).

45. Rutt, "Flower Boys," pp. 57−58.

46. Compare Anne Carson, writing on ancient Greek thought: "Male homosexual activity seems not to have been regarded as drying and debilitating for men to the same degree as relations with a woman." See "Putting Her in her Place: Women, Dirt, and Desire," in David M. Halperin, John J. Winkler, and Froma I. Zeitlin, eds., *Before Sexuality: The Construction of Erotic Experience in the Ancient Greek World* (Princeton, N.J.: Princeton University Press, 1990), p. 143, note 21.

47. Van Gulik, *Sexual Life*, pp. 48, 62.

48. The Tantric sects are special cases. The Japanese Tachikawa sect, founded in the early twelfth century as an offshoot of Shingon, preached that "the Way of Man and Woman, of *yin* and *yang*, is the secret art of becoming a Buddha in this life." It was denounced as heretical by monks of the Shingon headquarters on Mount Kōya in 1335 and suppressed by the Muromachi *bakufu*. See Tsunoda Ryūsaku et al., (New York: Columbia University Press, 1958), vol. 1, pp. 156, 163−165.

The Tachikawa sect celebrated heterosexual pleasure but denounced homosexuality as sterile and counterproductive. Indeed, its emergence might be seen as a reaction not to the tradition of sexual denial in Buddhism but to the rampant homosexuality in medieval monasteries. See Stevens, *Lust for Enlightenment*, p. 82.

49. *Sutanipata: The Group of Discourses*, IV.9, Magandiya # 835; quoted in Mary Jo Weaver, "Pornography and the Religious Imagination," in Susan Gobar and Joan Huff, eds., *For Adult Users Only: The Dilemma of Violent Pornography* (Bloomington and Indianapolis: Indiana University Press, 1989), p. 74.

50. In Tibetan monasteries in recent times, homosexuality was indeed viewed favorably as an indication that monks had conquered their desire for women. See Stevens, *Lust for Enlightenment*, pp. 139–140.

51. The *Vinaya* ("discipline," or "precepts") were, according to tradition, first recorded at a council in Rājagriha soon after Buddha's death (478 B.C.?). Most scholars date the texts from a later period; in any case, they antedate the *sūtras* and thus probably more accurately reflect original Buddhist moral teachings.

52. T. W. Rhys Davids and Hermann Oldenberg, eds., *Vinaya Texts*, vol. IV of F. Max Muller, ed., *Sacred Books of the East* (New York: Charles Scribner's Sons, 1899), p. 205. A *dukkata* offense is one that stems from craving or desire.

53. Daigan and Alicia Matsunaga, *The Buddhist Concept of Hell* (New York: Philosophical Library, 1972), p. 112.

54. Minakami Tsutomu, whose own childhood was spent in part in a Zen monastery in Japan, notes the continued prevalence of homosexual activity in such institutions in the twentieth century. See "Ikkyū," *Umi* (April 1974), pp. 41–42.

55. On Korea, see Howard S. Levy, *Korean Sex Jokes in Traditional Times* (Washington, D.C.: The Warm-Soft Village Press, 1972), pp. 208–209.

56. Rutt, "Flower Boys," p. 59.

57. Brett Hinsch suggests that from the sixth century on, Buddhist moral tracts (*shan shu*) modeled on Indian predecessors hostile to homosexuality profoundly influenced believers' views on male-male sex. See Hinsch, *Passions*, pp. 96–97.

58. Iwata, *Honchō nanshoku*, pp. 2–3.

59. W. G. Aston, trans., *Nihongi: Chronicles of Japan from Earliest Times to A.D. 697* (Tokyo and Rutland, Vt.: Tuttle, 1972), p. 238

60. Watanabe and Iwata, *Love of the Samurai*, p. 33.

61. See Ōno Susumu et al., eds., *Iwanami kogo jiten* (Tokyo: Iwanami, 1974), p. 37.

62. The recently excavated Fujinoki tomb in Nara Prefecture yielded a coffin containing two adult, aristocratic males. They died some time in

the sixth century. See *Japan Pictorial Quarterly Magazine* 16, 1 (1993), p. 6.

63. Quoted in Negishi Kennosuke, *Kodaijin no sei seikatsu* (Tokyo: Kindai bungeisha, 1983), p. 66.

64. Shinmura Izuru, ed., *Kōjien* (Tokyo: Iwanami shoten, 1969), p. 998.

65. Book 4, poems 680–682. This translation comes from Ian Hideo Levy, *The Ten Thousand Leaves* (Princeton, N.J.: Princeton University Press, 1981), p. 308. See also p. 339 (Book 4, poems 786–8), and Iwata Jun'ichi's remarks on these poems in *Honchō nanshoku kō*, pp. 1–10.

66. Helen Craig McCullough, trans., *The Tales of Ise: Lyrical Episodes from Tenth-Century Japan* (Stanford, Ca.: Stanford University Press, 1968), pp. 101–102. This is tale number 46.

67. Pamela Doe, *A Warbler's Song in the Dusk: The Life and Works of Ōtomo Yamamochi (718–785)* (Berkeley, Ca.: University of California Press, 1982), p. 136.

68. Edward C. Seidensticker, trans., *The Gossamer Years: A Diary of a Noblewoman of Heian Japan* (Tokyo and Rutland, Vt.: Tuttle, 1964), p. 48 and p. 173, note 61.

69. In the mid-tenth century work *Utsuho monogatari*, courtiers excitedly compete to retain handsome, talented boys in their service. See Uraki Zirō (Jirō), *The Tale of the Cavern* (Tokyo: Shinozaki Shorin, 1984), p. 487f.

70. Edward C. Seidensticker, trans., *The Tale of Genji* (New York: Alfred A. Knopf, 1976), p. 48; compare Arthur Waley, trans., *The Tale of Genji* (New York: Anchor, 1955), p. 57.

71. Ivan Morris, in claiming an absence of evidence for male homosexuality in the Heian period, seems to have been unaware of such references. See *The World of the Shining Prince: Court Life in Ancient Japan* (Oxford and New York: Oxford University Press, 1964), p. 232.

72. Tōno Haruyuki, "Nikki ni miru Fujiwara Michinaga no nanshoku kankei," *Hisutoria* 84 (September 1979), p. 17.

73. Fujiwara Yorinaga, *Daiki*, 3 vols. (Kyoto: Rinsen shoten, 1966), vol. 1, p. 63; see the gloss in *Kōza Nihon fūzoku shi*, supplemental vol. 3, *Sei fūzoku*, Book 3: *Shakai hen* (Tokyo: Yūzankaku, 1963), part 3, p. 337.

74. Iwata, *Honchō nanshoku*, pp. 21–26.

75. Tōno, "Nikki ni miru," p. 17.

76. David Asher Sitkin, *An Edo Satire: Hiraga Gennai's Nenashigusa* (unpublished master's thesis, University of Hawaii, 1977), p. 115, note 113.

77. There are many such references in the *Utsuho monogatari*. For

references in *Genji*, see Seidensticker, pp. 24, 136; in *Torikaebaya*, see Rosette F. Willig, trans., *The Changelings: A Classical Japanese Court Tale* (Stanford, Ca.: Stanford University Press, 1983), pp. 25, 30, 83.

78. See Willig, *Changelings*, esp. pp. 82–85.

79. Earl Miner, Odagiri Hiroko, and Robert E. Morrell, *The Princeton Companion to Classical Japanese Classical Literature* (Princeton, N.J.: Princeton University Press, 1985), p. 250.

80. Koike Togorō, *Kōshoku monogatari* (Tokyo: Kamakura insatsu, 1963), p. 180.

81. For Hebrew law, see Leviticus 18:22 and 20:13; for Persian Zoroastrian law, see *Vendidad* I, 12 and VIII, 27; for Hindu law, see *The Laws of Manu*, XI, 175.

82. Donald L. Philippi, trans., *Kojiki* (Princeton, N.J. and Tokyo: Princeton University Press and University of Tokyo Press, 1969), p. 259 (Book 2, Chapter 93).

83. Lise Manniche, *Sexual Life in Ancient Egypt* (New York: Routledge and Kegan Paul, 1987); Greenberg, *The Construction of Homosexuality*, pp. 96–97, 165; Bernard Sergent, *La homosexualité dans la mythologie grecque* (Paris: Payot, 1984); Thorkil Vanggaard, *Phallos: A Symbol and Its History in the Male World* (New York: International Universities Press, 1973), p. 77; Benjamin Walker, *The Hindu World: An Encyclopedic Survey of Hinduism* (New York: Praeger, 1968), vol. 2, p. 343.

84. Kozo Yamamura, "The Decline of the Ritsu-Ryō System: Hypotheses on Economic and Institutional Change," *Journal of Japanese Studies* 1, 1 (1974), p. 17.

85. For data on monastic populations, see Martin Collcutt, *Five Mountains: The Rinzai Zen Monastic Institution in Medieval Japan* (Cambridge, Ma.: Council on East Asian Studies, Harvard University, 1981), pp. 10–11.

86. Tsunoda Ryūsaku Tsunoda et al., eds., *Sources of Japanese Tradition* (New York: Columbia University Press, 1958), vol. 1, p. 114.

87. On the Laios myth, see Plato's *Laws*, 835b–842a and Dover, *Greek Homosexuality*, pp. 199–200.

88. Schalow, *Great Mirror*, p. 7.

89. The text is dated 1598 and attributed to Mitsuo Sadatomo. The actual authorship and date are unclear. See Sasama, p. 78.

90. Jingū Shichō, *Koji ruien* (Tokyo: Hyōgensha, 1927–1930), vol. 46, p. 923.

91. Sasama Yoshihiko, *Kōshoku engo jiten* (Tokyo: Yūzankaku, 1989), p. 108.

92. Donald Keene, trans., *Major Plays of Chikamatsu* (New York: Columbia University Press, 1961), p. 132; Chikamatsu zenshū kankō-kai, eds., *Chikamatsu zenshū*, vol. 5 (Tokyo: Iwanami shoten, 1985), p. 687.

93. An Edo-period humorous poem (*senryū*) has the great sage recommending *tsūwasan*, a lubricant used in anal sex: *Taishi ryū nite fude-buto ni tsūwasan* ("The Sage's teaching, expressed in bold strokes, [is nothing other than:] *tsūwasan*)"; Sasama, *Kōshoku engo*, p. 285.

94. Karlen, *Sexuality and Homosexuality*, p. 229; Barrow, *Travels in China*, p. 101. Apparently the source for these references is Abbe Renaudot, trans., "An Account of the Travels of Two Mohammedans through India and China in the Ninth Century," in John Pinkerton, ed., *A Collection of the Best and Most Interesting Voyages and Travels in All Parts of the World*, vol. 7 (London: Kimber and Conrad, 1811). Also see Spence, *Memory Palace*, p. 227; Ng, "Ideology and Sexuality," p. 68.

95. Wakeman, *Great Enterprise*, vol. 1, p. 93, note 23.

96. However, if pederasty flourished in Chinese Zen monasteries, one would expect to find references to it in the writings of Chinese monks or Japanese visitors to Chinese monasteries. The Japanese monk Dōgen, who visited China from 1223 to 1227, quoted his Zen mentor, Ju-ching (1163–1228), as warning monks about contact with "eunuchs, hermaphrodites and the like." But Dōgen says nothing about sex between monks. See Takashi James Kodera, *Dōgen's Formative Years in China: An Historical Study and Annotation of the Hōkyō-ki* (Boulder, Colo.: Prajna Press, 1980), p. 120. I thank Bret Hinsch for this reference.

97. Heinrich Dumoulin, however, repeats the report of widespread homosexuality in Tang China in *A History of Zen Buddhism* (New York: 1963). The only contemporary reference I have come across mentions a male prostitute who "indiscriminately associated with Buddhist and Taoist monks" (Hinsch, *Passion*, p. 88).

98. Hanayama Shōyū, ed., *Ōjōyōshū* (Tokyo: Tokuma shoten, 1972), p. 52. (The editor, in his commentary, liberally interprets this section as a blanket prohibition of male and female homosexuality and sado-masochism; see p. 53).

99. Genshin's work is based in part upon the Chinese sutra *Zhengfa nianchu jing* (Jp. *Shōbōnenkyō*). See A. K. Reischauer, trans., "Genshin's Ojo Yoshu: Collected Essays on Rebirth into Paradise," *Transactions of the Asiatic Society of Japan*, 2nd series, 7 (1930), p. 33.

100. Quoted in Watarai Keisuke, *Kyō no hanamachi* (Tokyo: Tairiku shobō, 1977), p. 243. See also Schalow, "Kūkai," p. 216.

101. The reasons for the decline in direct Sino-Japanese contact after a final official mission of the Japanese court to China in 838 are unclear. The decline of the Tang court, Buddhist persecutions in China, a lessening of Japanese aristocrats' need to derive inspiration from China, and even a depletion of timber for shipbuilding may all have been factors.

102. One such notion is that some women—with certain physical abnormalities—can attain religious enlightenment without being reborn as men. For an early ninth-century reference to this belief, see Kyoko Motomochi Nakamura, trans., *Miraculous Stories from the Japanese Buddhist Tradition: The Nihon ryōiki of the Monk Kyōkai* (Cambridge, Ma.: Harvard University Press, 1973), pp. 246–248.

103. John C. Pelzel, "Human Nature in the Japanese Myths," in Albert M. Craig and Donald H. Shively, eds., *Personality in Japanese History* (Berkeley: University of California Press, 1970), p. 52.

104. Michael Czaja, *Gods of Myth and Stone: Phallicism in Japanese Folk Religion* (Tokyo and New York: Weatherhill, 1974), pp. 44–45.

105. Higuchi Kiyoyuki, *Nihon josei no seikatsu shi* (Tokyo: Kōdansha, 1977), p. 56.

106. Teruoka Yasutaka et al., eds., *Ihara Saikaku shū* (Tokyo: Shōgakukan, 1971–1972), vol. 2, p. 315 (hereafter cited as *ISS*); Schalow, *Great Mirror*, p. 51.

107. Koike, *Kōshoku*, p. 210.

108. Ibid., p. 184; Ōmura Shage, ed., *Nanshoku yamaji no tsuyu* (Tokyo, 1978), pp. 31–35.

109. Paul Gordon Schalow, "The Invention of a Literary Tradition of Male Love: Kitamura Kigin's *Iwatsutsuji*," *Monumenta Nipponica* 48, 1 (Spring 1993), p. 8.

110. On daimyos' being influenced by the fashions of male prostitutes and actors, see J. R. McEwan, trans., *The Political Writings of Ogyū Sorai* (Cambridge: Cambridge University Press, 1962), p. 55; for original text, see *Seidan*, in Takimoto Seiichi, ed., *Nihon keizai taiten* (Tokyo: Shishi shuppansha and Keimeisha, 1928–1930), vol. 9, p. 28.

111. Passage from *Bunbyō gaiki* (Unofficial account of the reign of King Bun, ca. 1740), cited in Kate Wildman Nakai, *Shogunal Politics: Arai Hakuseki and the Premises of Tokugawa Rule* (Cambridge, Ma. and London: Council on East Asian Studies, Harvard University, 1988), p. 49.

112. See, for example, the excerpts from Tanba no Yasuyori's *Ishinbō* (Quintessence of medicine, 984) in Michel Beurdeley et al., *Erotic Art of Japan: The Pillow Poem* (Hong Kong: Leon Amiel, n.d.), pp. 35–36.

113. Van Gulik, *Sexual Life*, pp. 194–196.

114. H. D. Harootunian, *Things Seen and Unseen: Discourse and*

Ideology in Tokugawa Nativism (Chicago: University of Chicago Press, 1988), pp. 299-301.

115. Koike, *Kōshoku*, p. 184.

116. Translated as "The Scarlet Princess of Edo," in James R. Brandon, *Kabuki: Five Classic Plays* (Cambridge, Ma.: Harvard University Press, 1975).

117. *ISS*, vol. 1, p. 417.

118. Schalow, "Literary Tradition of Male Love," p. 10

119. For more examples, see Jinbō Kazuya et al., eds., *Kanazōshishū Ukiyō-zōshishū* (Tokyo: Shōgakukan, 1971), pp. 162; Keene, *Major Plays of Chikamatsu*, pp. 153, 445.

120. Koike, *Kōshoku*, p. 182.

121. Maeda Isamu, *Edogo no jiten* (Tokyo: Kōdansha, 1979), p. 617; Donald Jenkins, *Ukiyo-e Prints and Paintings: The Primitive Period, 1680–1745: An Exhibition in the Memory of Margaret O. Gentles, November 6–December 26, 1971* (Chicago: Art Institute of Chicago, 1971), p. 102.

122. For insight into the court's mistrust of the Nara monastic establishments, see Ross Bender, "The Hachiman Cult and the Dōkyō Incident," *Monumenta Nipponica* 34, 2, pp. 125–153.

123. Saichō, the founder of the Tendai sect and author of the regulations requiring Tendai monks to spend twelve years in isolation on Mount Hiei, referred even to an enlightened female glorified in the *Lotus Sutra* as "an animal, obviously as a result of bad karma. She is female and clearly has faculties which are not good." See Paul Groner, "The *Lotus Sutra* and Saichō's Interpretation of the Realization of Buddhahood with This Very Body," in George J. Tanabe and Willa Jane Tanabe, eds., *The Lotus Sutra in Japanese Culture* (Honolulu: University of Hawaii Press, 1989), p. 61.

124. Ōtō Tokihiko, "Chigo," in *Kōdansha Encyclopedia of Japan* (Tokyo: Kodansha, 1983), vol. 1, p. 274; "Chigo," in *Dictionnaire historique du Japon* (Tokyo: Librairie Kinokuniya, 1975), fasc. III, Lettre C, p. 23.

125. Miyao, Shigeo, "Kobanashi ni arawareta sei fūzoku," *Sei fūzoku shi*, vol. 3: *Shakai hen* (Tokyo: Yūzankaku, 1959), pp. 241–245.

126. Margaret H. Childs, "*Chigo Monogatari*: Love Stories or Buddhist Sermons?" *Monumenta Nipponica* 35, 2 (1980), p. 127.

127. For example, no. 495 in the *Kokin wakashū*. Perhaps the following poem recorded in the Buddhist work *Nihon ryōiki* (ca. 820) refers to a sexual relationship; it expresses the sorrow of the Hossō priest Shingon at the death of his beloved disciple Gyōgi:

Did you not promise me that we would die together?
But alas, you are gone,
Leaving me behind.
Are you a crow, to be such a great liar?

The crow signifies an adulterous wife. See Kyoko, *Miraculous Stories*, p. 161.

128. D. E. Mills, *A Collection of Tales from Uji: A Study and Translation of Uji Shui Monogatari* (Cambridge: Cambridge University Press, 1970), pp. 148–150.

129. Takeuchi Rizō, comp., *Kamakura ibun* (Tokyo: Tōkyōdō shuppan, 1971), vol. 7, p. 3069 (item 5190). I am indebted to Professor Taira Masayuki for this reference.

130. Collcutt, *Five Mountains*, p. 247; Tsuji Mannosuke, *Nihon bukkyō shi. Chūsei hen no go* (Tokyo: Iwanami shoten, 1951), p. 335.

131. Tsuji, *Nihon bukkyōshi*, p. 336.

132. Dōmoto Masaki, "'Chigo no sōshi': Honbun shōkai," *Yasō* (Tokyo) 15 (April 1985; reprint, November 1989), special edition on *Shōnen*, pp. 167–188; Philip Rawson, *Erotic Art of the East: The Sexual Theme in Oriental Painting and Sculpture* (London: Weidnfeld and Nicolson, 1973), pp. 294, 307.

133. Tsuji, *Nihon bukkyōshi*, pp. 336–337.

134. Iwata, *Honchō nanshoku*, p. 140f; Childs, "Love Stories or Buddhist Sermons?"; idem., *Rethinking Sorrow: Revelatory Tales of Late Medieval Japan* (Ann Arbor: University of Michigan Press, 1991), pp. 31–52.

135. Thomas Blenman Hare, *Zeami's Style: The Noh Plays of Zeami Motokiyo* (Stanford, Ca.: Stanford University Press, 1986), pp. 228–229; Watanabe and Iwata, *Love of the Samurai*, p. 76

136. For example, see the synopsis of the play *Rōmusha* (*Old Warriors*) in Don Kenny, *A Guide to Kyogen* (Tokyo: Hinoki Shoten, 1968), pp. 221–222.

137. Katō Shūichi, *A History of Japanese Literature: The First Thousand Years* (Tokyo: Kodansha, 1979), p. 283.

138. Nishio Minoru, ed., *Hōjōki Tsurezuregusa* (Tokyo: Iwanami shoten, 1983), pp. 124, 126–127, 133–134, 163. For an English translation, see Donald Keene, trans., *Essays in Idleness: The Tsurezuregusa of Kenkō* (New York: Columbia University Press, 1967), pp. 39, 39–40, 47–50, and 76–77 (Chapters 43, 44, 54, and 90).

139. Donald Keene, "The Comic Tradition in Renga," in John Whitney Hall and Toyoda Takeshi, eds., *Japan in the Muromachi Age* (Berkeley, Ca.: University of California Press, 1977), pp. 274–275; James H. Sanford, *Zen-Man Ikkyū* (Chico, Ca.: Scholars Press, 1981), p. 33.

140. Watanabe and Iwata, *Love of the Samurai*, p. 110.

141. On Jōha, see Donald Keene, "Jōha, a Sixteenth-Century Poet of Linked Verse," in George Elison and Bardwell L. Smith, eds., *Warlords, Artists and Commoners: Japan in the Sixteenth Century* (Honolulu: University Press of Hawaii, 1981), p. 123.

142. Quoted in Stevens, *Lust for Enlightenment*, p. 97.

143. Spence, *Memory Palace*, pp. 224–225.

144. Cooper, *They Came to Japan*, p. 46.

145. Charles H. Boxer, *The Christian Century in Japan, 1549–1650* (Berkeley, Ca.: University of California Press, 1967), p. 69.

146. Valignano listed as the four great defects of the Japanese: 1) "their great dissipation in the sin that does not bear mentioning," 2) disloyalty, 3) dissimulation, and 4) cruelty. See Cooper, *They Came to Japan*, pp. 46, 49.

147. George Elison, *Deus Destroyed: The Image of Christianity in Early Modern Japan* (Cambridge, Ma.: Harvard University Press, 1973), p. 41.

148. François Caron and Joost Shouten, *A True Description of the Mighty Kingdoms of Japan and Siam, London, 1663* (London: Argonaut Press, 1935), p. 43. See also Karlen, *Sexuality and Homosexuality*, p. 231.

149. Englebert Kaempfer, *The History of Japan Together with a Description of the Kingdom of Siam, 1690–92*, trans. J. G. Scheuchzer (Glasgow: James MacLehose and Sons, 1906), vol. 3, p. 53.

150. Takahatake Takamichi, *Young Man Shinran: A Reappraisal of Shinran's Life* (Ontario: Wilfrid Laurier University Press, 1987), p. 20.

151. The first character suggests both desire and concern; the second means "person."

152. The term is written with the characters for "youth" and "spirit"; the word also comes to mean "anus."

153. Iwata, *Nanshoku bunken*, 1973), p. 314.

154. Apparently the first known appearance of this vocabulary in a published work occurs in the *Shikidō jitsugo kyō* (*True Sutra of the Way of Sex*, 1678).

155. Michel Foucault, *The Use of Pleasure: Volume Two of the History of Sexuality* (New York: Vintage, 1985), p. 96; idem., *The Care of the Self* (New York: Pantheon, 1986), p. 193f.

156. Dover, *Greek Homosexuality*, pp. 100–106.

157. This was also the characteristic homosexual act among the Azande of the Sudan. See E. E. Evans-Pritchard, "Sexual Inversion Among the Azande," *American Anthropologist* 62 (1970), pp. 1428–

1435. For references to the practice in China, see Hinsch, *Passions*, pp. 111–112; in Renaissance Italy, Guido Ruggiero, *The Boundaries of Eros: Sex Crime and Sexuality in Renaissance Venice* (New York: Oxford University Press, 1985), p. 114.

158. A jocular anecdote in the *Tsurezuregusa* suggests that a relationship could go on for some time without the boy even seeing his partner's face; Keene, *Essays in Idleness*, pp. 76–77.

159. The Ninnaji was a Shingon temple, founded in 886, located northeast of Kyoto.

160. Anal sex is not the sole homosexual act represented in this scroll. One section shows a priest performing analingus on a boy, who in turn fellates him. But such depictions are extremely rare. See Dōmoto, "Chigo no sōshi," p. 187.

161. Andrew H. Dykstra, *Laughing Stories of Old Japan* (Honolulu: Kanji Press, 1987), p. 51.

162. James Murdoch, *A History of Japan* (Kobe and London: K. Paul, Trench, Trubner and Co., 1926), vol. 1, pp. 603–604; see also Tsuji, *Nihon bukkyō*, p. 335.

163. Helen Craig McCullough, trans., *Yoshitsune: A Fifteenth-Century Japanese Chronicle* (Stanford, Ca.: Stanford University Press, 1966), pp. 80, 84, 242.

164. Ibid., p. 242.

165. Warriors preferred somewhat older partners—boys in their mid-teens—but they preserved the tradition of age-structured, contractual, and exclusive relationships.

166. William Wayne Farris, *Heavenly Warriors: The Evolution of Japan's Military, 500–1300* (Cambridge, Ma.: Council on East Asian Studies, 1992), p. 335f.

167. Stephen Turnbull, *Samurai Warlords: The Book of the Daimyo* (London: Blandford Press, 1989), p. 52.

168. See references in Jan Bremmer, "An Enigmatic Indo-European Rite: Paederasty," *Arethusa* 13, 2 (1980), p. 279.

169. Greenberg, *The Construction of Homosexuality*, p. 242f.

170. For interesting comparative discussions of Japanese and European feudalism, see Marc Bloch, *Feudal Society*, vol. 2: *Social Classes and Political Organization* (Chicago: University of Chicago Press, 1985), p. 446f; John W. Hall, "Feudalism in Japan—A Reassessment," in Hall and Marius B. Jansen, eds., *Studies in the Institutional History of Early Modern Japan* (Princeton, N.J.: Princeton University Press, 1968), pp. 15–54.

171. Hitomi Tonomura, "Women and Inheritance in Japan's Early

Warrior Society," *Comparative Studies in Society and History* 32, 3 (July 1990).

172. Greenberg, *The Construction of Homosexuality*, p. 257.

173. Ibid., pp. 257–258.

174. Turnbull, *Samurai Warlords*, pp. 110–114.

175. I must disagree with Nitobe's contention that "the separation of the sexes" in premodern Japan, having "denied to affection the natural channel [sic] open to it," thus produced numerous "Japanese versions of the story of Damon and Pythias or Achilles and Patroclos"; *Bushido, the Soul of Japan* (Tokyo and Rutland, Vt.: Charles E. Tuttle, 1969), p. 156. One looks in vain through the military sagas for references to egalitarian homosexuality.

176. This text, incidentally, reports a legend reminiscent of the Kūkai story. It alludes to one Hoshino no Ryōtetsu, the "originator of *shudō* in (Hizen) province (*gokuni shudō no gansō*)," who "individually trained many disciples" and thus spread his knowledge and this practice.

177. See Farris, *Heavenly Warriors*, and Karl F. Friday, *Hired Swords: The Rise of Private Warrior Power in Early Japan* (Stanford, Ca.: Stanford University Press, 1992)

178. Cooper, *They Came to Japan*, p. 46

179. Joyce Ackroyd, "Women in Feudal Japan," *Transactions of the Asiatic Society of Japan* (1959), p. 46.

180. Turnbull, *Samurai Warlords*, p. 31f.

181. Minamoto Ryōen, *Giri to ninjō* (Tokyo: Chūō kōronsha, 1967), p. 27.

182. This incident may, in fact, have had a homosexual element. Some accounts suggest that the quarrel originated when the Akō daimyo refused to give his young retainer Ōishi Chikara to the courtier Kira Yoshitake as a "beloved boy" (*chōdō*). See Nishigori Takeo, *Yūjo to gaishō: Kyōto o chūshin toshite baishun shi* (Tokyo: Keibunkan, 1964), p. 84.

183. See the translation of the main version of the puppet play Chūshingura—Donald Keene, *Chūshingura: The Treasury of Loyal Retainers* (New York: Columbia University Press, 1971).

184. Ibid., p. 71.

185. Compare C. S. Lewis's observation concerning the twelfth-century French epic *Song of Roland*, as paraphrased by Vern Bullough: "The deepest signs of affection in the poem ... appear in the love of man for man, the mutual love of warriors who die together against odds, and the affection between the vassal and lord or within the church, between two clergy, usually an older and younger." See *The Subordinate Sex* (Urbana: University of Illinois Press, 1973), p. 165.

186. Doi Takeo, *The Anatomy of Dependence* (Tokyo and New York: Kodansha, 1973), p. 125.

187. Ibid., p. 114.

188. For instance, the relationship between the warrior Tsunemasa and the abbot of Ninnaji in the thirteenth-century war romance *Genpei seisuiki* seems to have been on this type; Iwata, *Nanshoku bunken*, p. 13. The reference is to Book 31; see also Book 28.

189. Collcutt, *Five Mountains*, p. 226.

190. Koike, *Kōshoku*, p. 226.

191. Fukuda Kazuhiko, *Mihō ukiyoe* (Tokyo: KK Bestsellers, 1988), pp. 14–17.

192. Koike, *Kōshoku*, p. 184.

193. On the Ashikaga, see Iwata, *Honchō nanshoku*, p. 103f; Koike, *Kōshoku*, p. 184f; Watanabe and Iwata, *Love of the Samurai*, pp. 75–76 (on Yoshimitsu and Zeami and other actors); and Donald Keene, *Nō: The Classical Theatre of Japan* (Tokyo: Kodansha International, 1966), p. 39.

194. On the Tokugawa, see Nishikiori, *Yūjo to gaishō*, pp. 83–84; Naramoto, vol. 1, p. 46; and Nakai, *Shogunal Politics*, pp. 50–51. On Iemitsu, see Kita Sōichirō, *Edo no geisha* (Tokyo: Chūō kōronsha, 1989), pp. 25–26, and Caron, *Mighty Kingdoms*, p. 24; on Tsunayoshi, see Donald Shively, "Tokugawa Tsunayoshi, the Genroku Shogun," in *Personality in Japanese History*, ed. Albert Craig and Donald Shively (Berkeley: University of California Press, 1970), and Kita, *Edo no geisha*, p. 26; and on Ieshige and Ieharu, see John Whitney Hall, "Forerunner of the Modern Statesman: Tanuma Okitsugu," in Murakami Hyoe and Thomas J. Harper, eds., *Great Historical Figures of Japan* (Tokyo: Japan Culture Institute, 1978), pp. 211–212.

195. Nishiyama Matsunosuke, "Shudō fūzoku ni tsuite," in *Sei fūzoku shi*, vol. 3: *Shakai hen* (Tokyo: Yūzankaku, 1959), pp. 339–340; Sakamoto Tarō, supervising ed., *Fūzoku jiten* (Tokyo: Tōkyōdō, 1960), p. 549.

196. Paul Schalow, "Japan," in *Encyclopedia of Homosexuality* (New York and London: Garland, 1990), vol. 1, p. 635.

197. On Hidetsugu, see Iwata, *Honchō nanshoku*, p. 314, and Nishiyama, "Shudō fūzoku ni tsuite," p. 340.

198. Iwata, *Honchō nanshoku*, p. 242.

199. Sugita Kōzō, "Miyamoto Musashi," in idem., *Genroku no wakaru hon* (Tokyo: Kosaidō shuppan, 1975); for modern depictions, see Ian Buruma, *Behind the Mask* (New York: Meridian, 1984), p. 139.

200. Koike, *Kōshoku*, p. 245.

201. Noguchi Takehiko, *Edo wakamono kō* (Tokyo: Sanseidō, 1986), p. 52.

202. Nishikiori, *Yūjo to gaishō*, pp. 83–84.

203. Watanabe and Iwata, *Love of the Samurai*, pp. 49–50; Iwata, *Honchō nanshoku*, pp. 108–109.

204. Koike, *Kōshoku*, pp. 184–185.

205. Henry D. Smith, "Consorts and Courtesans: The Women of Shogun," in idem., ed., *Learning from Shogun: Japanese History and Western Fantasy* (Santa Barbara, Ca.: Program in Asian Studies, University of California, Santa Barbara, 1980), p. 111.

206. Nishiyama, "Shudō fūzoku ni tsuite," p. 342.

207. Kita, *Edo no geisha*, p. 26.

208. Shively, "Tokugawa Tsunayoshi," p. 100; Hall, "Modern Statesman," pp. 211–212.

209. Greenberg, *The Construction of Homosexuality*, p. 25f.

210. See Gilbert H. Herdt, ed., *Guardians of the Flutes: Idioms of Masculinity* (New York: Columbia University Press, 1981), esp. 217f.

211. Walter L. Williams, *The Spirit and the Flesh: Sexual Diversity in American Indian Culture* (Boston: Beacon, 1986).

212. Bremmer, "Indo-European Rite," p. 284–287.

213. Ibid., p. 288; Hamish Henderson, "The Women of the Glen: Some Thoughts on Highland History," in Robert O'Driscoll, *The Celtic Consciousness* (New York: Braziller, 1981), pp. 257–258.

214. Evans-Pritchard, "Sexual Inversion," pp. 1428–1434.

215. Greenberg, *The Construction of Homosexuality*, p. 126.

216. Serena Nanda, "The Hijras of India: Cultural and Individual Dimensions of an Institutionalized Third Gender Role," in Evelyn Blackwood, ed., *The Many Faces of Homosexuality: Anthropological Approaches to Homosexual Behavior* (New York: Harrington Park Press, 1986), p. 35f.

217. B. R. Burg argues that some Caribbean pirates of the seventeenth century went to sea partly in anticipation of opportunities for homosexual contact. See *Sodomy and the Pirate Tradition: English Sea Rovers in the Seventeenth-Century Caribbean* (New York: New York University Press, 1984), p. 139f.

Chapter 2

1. By "cities" I mean castle-towns or population centers of 10,000 or more.

2. For a fuller discussion, see Leupp, *Servants*, pp. 9–11.

3. For Tokugawa policy, see T. G. Tsukahira, *Feudal Control in Toku-*

gawa Japan: The Sankin-Kotai System (Cambridge, Ma.: Harvard University Press, 1966).

4. Japan's population ca. 1600 is variously estimated at between 12 and 18 million. Those of samurai status (including women) are thought to have been about 7 percent of the population.

5. John Whitney Hall, "The Castle Town and Japan's Modern Urbanization," in Hall and Marius Jansen, eds. *Studies in the Institutional History of Early Modern Japan* (Princeton, N.J.: Princeton University Press, 1968), p. 176; also Gilbert Rozman, *Urban Networks in Ch'ing China and Tokugawa Japan* (Princeton, N.J.: Princeton University Press, 1973), p. 6.

6. See Hall, "Castle Town," pp. 169–188, for additional data.

7. The character of urban populations varied widely, however. The samurai probably made up less than 10 percent of the population in Osaka, whereas in Kagoshima they constituted well over 50 percent.

8. Nishiyama, "Shudō fūzoku ni tsuite," p. 344.

9. Ejima Kiseki, *Nihon meicho zenshū*, 31 vols. (Tokyo: Nihon meicho zenshū kankōkai, 1926–1929), vol. 9, p. 619.

10. Jinbō et al., *Kanazōshishū Ukiyozōshishū*, p. 127.

11. Nishiyama et al., *Edo gaku jiten* p. 698; Yazaki Takeo, *Social Change and the City in Japan: From the Earliest Times through the Industrial Revolution* (Tokyo: Japan Publications, 1978), p. 141. For sex ratios of other Tokugawa-period cities, see my article, "Population Registers and Household Records as Sources for the Study of Urban Women in Tokugawa Japan," *Gest Library Journal* (Princeton University) 5, 2 (Winter 1992), p. 51.

12. Boswell, *Christianity, Social Tolerance, and Homosexuality*, pp. 127, 208; also William Monter, "Sodomy and Heresy in Early Modern Switzerland," in S. J. Licata and R. B. Petersen, eds., *Historical Perspectives on Homosexuality* (New York: Haworth Press, 1984), pp. 40–53.

13. Mary Elizabeth Perry, "The 'Nefarious Sin' in Early Modern Seville," in Kent Gerard and Gert Hekma, *The Pursuit of Sodomy: Male Homosexuality in Renaissance and Enlightenment Europe* (New York and London: Harrington Park Press, 1989), p. 67f; also Dirk Jaap Noordam, "Sodomy in the Dutch Republic, 1600–1725," in Gerard and Hekma, p. 207f.

14. Greenberg, *The Construction of Homosexuality*, p. 330, and Bray, *Homosexuality in Renaissance England*, p. 43 and p. 81f.

15. Bray, *Homosexuality in Renaissance England*, especially p. 80f; Randolph Trumbach, "London's Sodomites: Homosexual Behavior and Western Culture in the Eighteenth Century," *Journal of Social His-*

tory 11 (1977), p. 9f; Michel Rey, "Parisian Homosexuals Create a Lifestyle, 1700–1750: The Police Archives," in Robert Purks Maccubbin, *'Tis Nature's Fault: Unauthorized Sexuality during the Enlightenment* (New York: Cambridge University Press, 1987); Rey, "Police et sodomie à Paris au XVIIIe siècle," *Revue d'histoire moderne et contemporaine* 29 (1982), pp. 113–124; and Arend H. Huusen, Jr., "Sodomy in the Dutch Republic during the Eighteenth Century," in Maccubbin.

16. Watanabe Tsuneo refers to a "15th-century book of travels" that records "the universal fashion for homosexuality in the provinces." See *Love of the Samurai*, p. 79.

17. Bray, *Homosexuality in Renaissance England*, p. 35f; Lawrence Stone, *The Family, Sex, and Marriage in England 1500–1800*, abridged edition (London: Peregrine, 1979), pp. 337–338.

18. Bray, *Homosexuality in Renaissance England*, p. 81f.

19. Saikaku's story appears in *Kōshoku gonin onna* and is included in *ISS*, vol. 1, p. 392. Here a manservant in Edo openly attempts to fondle the boyfriend of his mistress's daughter. English translation by William Theodore de Bary, trans., *Five Women Who Loved Love* (Rutland, Vt. and Tokyo: Tuttle, 1956), pp. 178–179.

20. Shikitei Sanba's *Ukiyoburo* (Bathhouse of the floating world, 1809) suggests that the male baths had a homoerotic atmosphere. See *Ukiyoburo*, ed. Nakamura Michio (Tokyo: Iwanami shoten, 1985), p. 97.

21. Sasama, *Kōshoku engo*, p. 188.

22. Greenberg, *The Construction of Homosexuality*, p. 347f; see also the provocative discussion of "Capitalism, the Family, and the Anus," in Hocquenghem, *Homosexual Desire*, pp. 93–112.

23. Kobayashi Yoshimasa, *Nihon shihonshugi no seisei to sono kiban* (Tokyo: Nihon hyōronsha, 1949), p. 23.

24. Trumbach, "London's Sodomites," p. 19; Michel Rey, "Police et sodomie," p. 135.

25. Harada Tomohiko, *Hisabetsu buraku no rekishi* (Tokyo: Asahi shinbunsha, 1975), p. 105.

26. On street performers, see Jacob Raz, *Audience and Actors: A Study of Their Interaction in the Japanese Traditional Theater* (Leiden: E. J. Brill, 1983), pp. 38, 84, 150.

27. Cited in Jingū, *Koji ruien*, vol. 46, p. 923. *Dengaku* ("field music") and *sarugaku* ("monkey music") were types of performance originating in peasant society.

28. Ibid., p. 923.

29. For an English translation see Edward Putzgar, "Inu makura: The Dog Pillow," *Harvard Journal of Asiatic Studies* 28 (1968), pp.

98–113. I believe Putzgar's translation is misleading at points, however. He renders *dai chigo no musha*, for example, as "overaged samurai-dressed male prostitute" (p. 111), but this phrase probably refers to a daimyo's beloved retainer. See Asakura Haruhiko, ed., *Kanazōshi shūsei*, vol. 5 (Tokyo: Tōkyōdō, 1983), p. 167, for Japanese original.

30. Leupp, *Servants*, pp. 16–25.

31. Ibid., p. 41f.

32. Nishiyama (1959), p. 344.

33. Haga Noboru, *Edo no asobi* (Tokyo: Kashiwa shobō, 1981), p. 243.

34. Koike, *Kōshoku*, p. 210. Shinto shrine land was typically owned by Buddhist monasteries.

35. Nishiyama et al., *Edo gaku jiten*, pp. 556–558; Kodama, *Genroku jidai*, p. 398; Tanaka, *Edo jidai*, p. 78.

36. Most are listed in Koike, *Kōshoku*, p. 211. Others are referred to in various literary works. Of course, this list is by no means exhaustive, and male prostitution may also have flourished elsewhere. Conspicuously absent from the list is any castle-town in Kyushu. Satsuma men, however, had a reputation as *nanshoku-zuki*; see *ISS*, I, p. 405, and Watanabe Kazuo, *Seso iromegane* (Tokyo and Osaka: Shinbun jidaisha, 1963), p. 266. And the *Hagakure*, written by a samurai in the Kyushu province of Hizen, refers to local *yarō kagema*; see Yamamoto Jōchō, *Hagakure zenshū*, ed. Nakamura Toitsu (Tokyo: Gogatsu shobō, 1978), p. 69.

37. Kaempfer, *History of Japan*, vol. 3, p. 53.

38. Oliver Statler, *Japanese Inn* (New York: Arena Books, 1961), p. 160; Ihara Saikaku, *Budō denrai ki*, ed. Asō Isoji and Fuji Akio (Tokyo: Meiji shoin, 1978), pp. 124–132.

39. Iwata, *Honchō nanshoku*, pp. 206–207; 210–211.

40. *ISS*, vol. 1, pp. 126–127. See also p. 143, where Saikaku describes Edo-based effeminate boy-prostitutes who, posing as perfume-sellers, travel about the country.

41. Miyamoto Mataji, *Keihan to Edo* (Tokyo: Aogaerubō, 1978), p. 195.

42. Mackerras, *Peking Opera*, p. 149f.

43. Miyamoto, *Keihan*, pp. 194–195.

44. Koike, *Kōshoku*, p. 211; Tanaka, *Edo jidai*, p. 175.

45. Nakano Eizō, *Kōshoku bungei hon jiten* (Tokyo: Yūzankaku, 1988), pp. 18–19; See also Tanaka, *Edo jidai*, p. 173.

46. Ivan Morris, "Appendix III: The Hierarchy of Courtesans," in Ihara Saikaku, *The Life of an Amorous Woman and Other Writings* (New York: UNESCO, 1963), pp. 285–288; see also idem., "The Hierarchy of

Lust in Seventeenth-Century Japan," in Maurice Schneps and Alvin D. Coox, eds., *The Japanese Image* (Tokyo and Philadelphia: Orient/West, 1965).

47. Paul Gordon Schalow, "The Great Mirror of Male Love," by *Ihara Saikaku* (unpublished dissertation, Harvard University, 1985), vol. 2, p. 98–99.

48. Nishikiori, *Yūjo to gaishō*, p. 88. See also Ono Takeo, *Edo bukka jiten* (Tokyo: Tenbōsha, 1983), p. 431

49. Morris, trans., *Amorous Woman*, p. 287.

50. Nishiyama et al., *Edo gaku jiten*, p. 557. Also see *ISS*, vol. 2, p. 467, for Saikaku's comments on the rising fees of male prostitutes. For English translation, see Schalow, *Great Mirror*, pp. 189–190.

51. Ono, *Edo bukka*, p. 431.

52. Kitajima Masamoto, "Buke no hōkōnin," in Shinji Yoshimoto, ed., *Edo jidai bushi no seikatsu*, second edition (Tokyo: Yūzankaku, 1984), p. 141.

53. Ono, *Edo bukka*, p. 435.

54. Donald Shively, "The Social Environment of Tokugawa *Kabuki*," in James R. Brandon, William P. Malm, and Donald Shively, ed., *Studies in Kabuki: Its Acting, Music, and Historical Context* (Honolulu: University Press of Hawaii, 1978), p. 36.

55. See illustrations in ibid., pp. 30–33 (Plates 6–9).

56. Schalow, *Great Mirror*, p. 197.

57. Ibid.

58. Fukuda Kazuhiko, *Nikuhitsu fūzoku emaki* (Tokyo: KK Bestsellers, 1988), pp. 58–59; discussion on pp. 173–174.

59. These include the *Shikionron* (1644) and *Kosogurigusa* (1653). For a discussion of this literature, see Nakano, *Kōshoku bungei*, p. 60f

60. Nakano, *Kōshoku bungei*, pp. 17–19; Nishiyama et al., *Edo gaku jiten*, p. 557.

61. Ōsaka-shi shi hensangakari, *Ōsaka-shi shi* (Osaka: Seibundō, 1911–1914), vol. 2, p. 572.

62. Maeda, *Edogo no jiten*, p. 1020.

63. The Eight Sects were the Six Nara Sects (Sanron, Jōjitsu, Hossō, Kusha, Kegon, and Ritsu), introduced in the seventh and eighth centuries, plus the Tendai and Shingon sects, introduced in the early ninth century. Of the former, only Hossō, Kegon, and Ritsu developed as independent institutions. Curiously, this group of eight omits not only the Jōdo and Jōdo Shin sects, which permitted priestly marriage, but also Zen, whose priests were often associated with homosexuality. At any rate, the point of the expression quoted seems to be that clergy of *all* the Buddhist sects patronized male brothels.

64. *ISS*, vol. 1, p. 127; vol. 2, pp. 481–482, 582.

65. In one *kobanashi*, a country bumpkin, having sex with a *wakashū* for the first time, wonders whether or not they will have to "report this to the landlord." (According to the law, tenants were obliged to report injuries involving any loss of blood to their landlords.) For this and other examples, see Mutō Sadao, ed., *Edo kobanashi jiten* (Tokyo: Tō-kyōdō, 1955), pp. 26, 99, 180, 288.

66. Nishiyama et al., *Edo gaku jiten*, p. 557.

67. Quoted in Rawson, *Erotic Art of the East*, p. 103.

68. Leupp, *Servants*, pp. 62–63; Hayami Akira, "Tokugawa kōki jinkō hendō no chiiteki tokusei," *Mita gakkai zasshi* 64–68 (1971), pp, 67–80.

69. Nishiyama et al., *Edo gaku jiten*, p. 698.

70. Samurai status was hereditary and passed along to daughters. The latter retained the status as long as they married samurai men and maintained the appropriate samurai lifestyle.

71. A Tenpō-era edict issued by an Edo city commissioner even banned portraits of actors and courtesans: "To make woodblock prints of kabuki actors, courtesans, and geisha is detrimental to public morals. Henceforth the publication of new works [of this kind] as well as the sale of previously procured works is strictly forbidden." The edict urged artists to "select designs that are based on loyalty and filial piety and which serve to educate women and children." See Akai Tatsurō, "The Common People and Painting," in Nakane Chie and Ōishi Shinzaburō, eds., *Tokugawa Japan: The Social and Economic Antecedents of Modern Japan* (Tokyo: University of Tokyo Press, 1990), p. 183.

72. Jinnai Hidenobu, "The Spatial Structure of Edo," in Nakane and Ōishi, *Tokugawa Japan*, p. 137.

73. Ōsaka-shi shi hensangakari, *Ōsaka-shi shi*, vol. 2, p. 572.

74. Yazaki, *Social Change*, p. 143.

75. Again there is a parallel with female prostitution. In the Genroku period, female spinners, weavers, and textile saleswomen typically doubled as prostitutes. See Yasukuni Ryōichi, "Kinsei Kyōto no shōmin josei," in Joseishi Sōgō Kenkyūkai, eds., *Nihon josei seikatsushi*, vol. 3: *Kinsei* (Tokyo: Tōkyō daigaku shūppankai, 1990), pp. 90–91.

76. Donald Jenkins, "Ukiyoe," *Kodansha Encyclopedia*, vol. 8, p. 138.

77. Richard Lane, "Shunga," *Kodansha Encyclopedia*, vol. 7, p. 187.

78. Capt. Frank Brinkley, quoted in Lawrence E. Gichner, *Erotic Aspects of Japanese Culture* (New York: n.p., 1963), p. 48. Compare Sir George Aston on Saikaku in *A History of Japanese Literature* (1899; reprint, Rutland, Vt. and Tokyo: Tuttle, 1972), p. 269.

79. One should note that the genitalia in such pictures are often fantastically exaggerated. Even so, the Japanese artists seem to have possessed a remarkably sophisticated understanding of human anatomy, especially when compared with their Indian or Chinese counterparts who produced erotica.

80. For one example, see Hanasaka Kazuo, *Edo no deai chaya* (Tokyo: Kinsei fūzoku kenkyūkai, 1972), p. 99.

81. Ōmura, *Nanshoku yamaji*, p. 51.

82. Iwata, *Honchō nanshoku*, pp. 307f; Kenneth P. Kirkwood, *Rennaisance in Japan: A Cultural Survey of the Seventeenth Century* (Rutland, Vt., and Tokyo: Tuttle, 1970), p. 297; Schalow, *Great Mirror*, p. 25.

83. Kobayashi Takashi, *Ukiyoe* (Tokyo: Kodansha International, 1982), p. 35. Kobayashi sees the appearance of this work as an indication of a new, distinctly Edoite urban culture, adding that its publication "so soon after the great fire was certainly a symbolic occurence."

84. Iwata, *Honchō bunken*.

85. Koike, *Kōshoku*, p. 264; Imoto Nōichi, *Bashō: Sono jinsei to geijutsu* (Tokyo: Kōdansha, 1968), pp. 76–77, 177.

86. Bashō wrote that he was "fascinated with the ways of homosexual love." See *Narrow Road to the Interior*, trans. Sam Hamill (Boston and London: Shambala, 1991), p. xv.

87. Koike, *Kōshoku*, pp. 191–192.

88. For comparable Western literature, see S. C. Campbell, *Only Begotten Sonnets* (London: Bell and Hyman, 1978), pp. 159–160.

89. Nakano, *Kōshoku bungei*, pp. 61–62.

90. Schalow, "Saikaku on 'Manly Love,'" p. 6.

91. *ISS*, vol. 2, pp. 309–597; English translation in Schalow, *Great Mirror*.

92. Partially translated by William Scott Wilson as *Hagakure: The Book of the Samurai* (Tokyo: Kodansha, 1979). Ivan Morris has called this work "the most important samurai treatise ever written."

93. *Nenashigusa* has been translated into English by David Asher Sitkin as *An Edo Satire*. The title, connoting both "rootless grass" and "unfounded rumors," is untranslatable.

94. Hubert Maes, *Hiraga Gennai et son temps* (Paris: École François d'extrême-Orient, 1970), p. 91. I have not found the original text but have translated this passage from Maes' French.

95. Hiraga Gennai, *Hiraga Gennai shū*, ed. Miura Satoshi (Tokyo: Yūhōdō, 1915), p. 162.

96. Ibid., p. 163.

97. My wife, who hails from Sapporo, was cautioned some thirty

years ago by an aunt about swimming in the Japan Sea off Hokkaidō after the summer Obon festival. At this time, she was told, one risks encountering *kappa*, who like to thrust their hands into swimmers' anuses, plucking out *oshiritama* ("ass-jewels"). The modern-minded aunt was only joking to her six-year-old niece, but her warning indicates how well this folklore has survived.

98. Hiraga, *Hiraga Gennai*, pp. 206–207.

99. Sitkin, *An Edo Satire*, p. 18.

100. Ibid., p. 1.

101. Takada Mamoru, "Haishi bishōnen roku: Bakin no dōji kami shinkō," *Yasō* 15 (April 1985; reprint November 1989), special edition, *Shōnen*, pp. 66–79.

102. Quoted in Bray, *Homosexuality in Renaissance England*, p. 35. See also Kristina Straub, *Sexual Suspects: Eighteenth-Century Players and Sexual Ideology* (Princeton, N.J.: Princeton University Press, 1992), especially p. 47f.

103. For a lengthy discussion, see Shively, "Social Environment," p. 231f.

104. Earl Jackson, Jr., "Kabuki Narratives of Male Homoerotic Desire in Saikaku and Mishima," *Theatre Journal* 41, 4 (1989), p. 461.

105. The term *kabuki* itself may have had homoerotic connotations. Derived from the verb *kabuku* ("to be inclined"), it could also suggest "to be eccentric." From the late sixteenth century, the term *kabuki-mono* was being used to refer to gamblers and members of gangs of troublemaking samurai whose appearance and argot were considered strange. It has been suggested that a second meaning of *kabuku* ("to bend forward") constituted "an obvious, and essential [homo]sexual innuendo." See Jackson, "Kabuki Narratives," p. 464, note 26.

106. Natalie Davis, "Women on Top," in idem., *Society and Culture in Early Modern France* (Stanford, Ca.: Stanford University Press, 1975), p. 135.

107. Shively, "Bakufu versus Kabuki," in John W. Hall and Marius B. Jansen, eds., *Studies in the Institutional History of Early Modern Japan* (Princeton, N.J.: Princeton University Press, 1968), p. 237.

108. Watarai Keisuke, *Kyō no hanamachi* (Tokyo: Tairiku shobō, 1977), p. 244.

109. Charles J. Dunn and Torigoe Bunzō, trans. and ed., *The Actor's Analects: Yakusha Rongō* (New York: Columbia University Press, 1969), p. 43.

110. Ibid., pp. 41–43.

111. Shively, "Bakufu versus Kabuki," p. 237.

112. Boswell, *Christianity, Social Tolerance, and Homosexuality*, pp. 3–4.

Chapter 3

1. *ISS*, vol. I, p. 445.

2. Quoted in Derek Massarella, *A World Elsewhere: Europe's Encounter with Japan in the Sixteenth and Seventeenth Centuries* (New Haven, Ct.: Yale University Press, 1990), p. 239

3. Edward Putzgar, "The Dog Pillow," p. 101.

4. Brandon, trans., *Kabuki: Five Classic Plays*, pp. 117–118.

5. Chinese humor also equates the smell of feces with "boys' aroma." See Levy, *Chinese Sex Jokes*, p. 257.

6. *ISS*, vol. 1, pp. 355–356.

7. *ISS*, vol. 1, p. 103.

8. Other descriptions of bisexual behavior may be found in Saikaku's *Nippon Eitaigura*, section 5, story 3, and section 5, story 5. See Fujimura Tsukuru and Higashi Akimasa, eds., *Ihara Saikaku shū*, vol. 3 (Tokyo: Asahi shinbunsha, 1977), pp. 127–132, 136–139. For English translation, see G. W. Sargent, trans., *The Japanese Family Storehouse, or the Millionaire's Gospel Modernized* (Cambridge: Cambridge University Press, 1959), p. 118 and 124. In the first of these stories, a young heir patronizes both the boy-prostitutes of Niōdō village and the courtesans of Nara and Kyoto; in the second, a husband provokes his wife to leave him after retaining a concubine and attempting to procure boy-lovers.

9. *ISS*, vol. 2, pp. 504–507.

10. Jinbō Kazuya et al., eds., *Kanazōshishū Ukiyozōshishū* (Tokyo: Shōgakukan, 1971), p. 139.

11. My interpretation here follows that of Mishima Yukio. The passage is ambiguous, however; William Scott Wilson thinks the "ways" refer to those of the samurai and of *shudō*. See Kathryn Sparling, trans., *Yukio Mishima on Hagakure: The Samurai Ethic and Modern Japan* (Tokyo and Rutland, Vt.: Tuttle, 1976), p. 142; Wilson, *Book of the Samurai*, pp. 59, 171; and Mukoh Takao, *The Hagakure: A Code to the Way of the Samurai* (Tokyo: Hokuseido Press, 1980), p. 76.

12. *ISS*, vol. 1, p. 400.

13. Keene, trans., *Major Plays of Chikamatsu*, p. 140. I have substituted "younger brother" for Keene's "minion"; *Chikamatsu zenshū kankōkai*, vol. 5, p. 701.

14. Jinbo et al., *Kanazōshishū*, p. 128.

15. *ISS*, vol. 1, p. 419. *Check*

16. Brandon, trans., *Five Classic Plays*, pp. 245–349.

17. Fukuda Kazuhiko, *Ehon ukiyoe sen* (Tokyo: Kawade shobō, 1990), pp. 57, 166

18. See the print attributed to Bukiyo Matabei in Theodore Bowie, "Erotic Aspects of Japanese Art," in Theodore Bowie et al., *Studies in Erotic Art* (New York and London: Basic Books, 1970), illus. 93.

19. In the first of these, the youth copulating with a woman resists anal penetration by a man; in the second, an Utamaro print, he submits readily enough to being buggered by a monk. In the caption, the woman complains to the monk of the youth's inadequacy; the cleric obligingly masturbates her as the youth withdraws his penis.

20. Jinbō et al., eds., *Kanazōshishū*, p. 124.

21. Koike, *Kōshoku*, p. 210.

22. Maes, *Hiraga Gennai*, p. 91.

23. One finds examples of this type in the literature of comparably developed class societies. In the Ming work *Julin waishi*, translated by Yang Hsien-yi and Gladys Yang as *The Scholars*, a character who is "grieving and pining away" for lack of a male lover declares that were it not for the fact that he was born of a woman, he would "kill all the women in the world! … Have you ever met a woman you could respect? I assure you, they affect me so painfully, I can smell a woman three rooms away!" (pp. 377–378).

In early modern England, the term "woman-hater" seems to have referred to men who despised women and indulged in homosexual activity. See illustrations from the anonymous work *The Woman-Hater's Lamentation* (London: 1707) in Bray, *Homosexuality in Renaissance England*, pp. 83, 94–95.

24. *ISS*, vol. 2, p. 455; Schalow, *Great Mirror*, pp. 180–183.

25. Schalow, *Great Mirror*, p. 139; *ISS*, vol. 2, p. 410.

26. Howard Hibbett, *Ejima Kiseki and the Hachimonjaya: A Study in Eighteenth-Century Japanese Fiction* (unpublished Ph.D. dissertation, Harvard University, 1950), p. 137.

27. Hibbett, *Floating World*, pp. 145–151.

28. *ISS*, vol. 2, p. 593. *check my translation*

29. Sitkin, *An Edo Satire*, p. 67.

30. Hiraga adds that in the less cultured Edo, women are mannish. From their "crimson lips," he notes, issue such pleasantries as "Go ta hell, you jailbird!"

31. Nishiyama et al., *Edo gaku jiten*, pp. 556–557.

32. V. Golovnin, *Memoirs of a Captivity in Japan, during the Years*

1811, 1812, and 1813, with Observations on the Country and the People, 2nd edition (London: H. Colburn and Co., 1824), vol. 3, pp. 25–26.

33. Statler, *Japanese Inn*, pp. 158–159.

34. Jinbo et al., *Kanazōshishū*, p. 128.

35. According to a third-century Chinese account, "When the lowly meet men of importance on the road, they stop and withdraw to the roadside. In conveying messages to them or addressing them, they either squat or kneel, with both hands on the ground. This is the way they show respect." See Tsunoda et al., *Japanese Tradition*, vol. 1, p. 5.

36. Ibid., p. 356.

37. Koike, *Kōshoku*, p. 181.

38. Schalow, "Kūkai," pp. 219–220.

39. Fukuda, *Nikuhitsu*, p. 56; Gichner, *Japanese Culture*, p. 42.

40. Fukuda, *Nikuhitsu*, p. 56; Sasama, *Kōshoku engo jiten*, p. 150.

41. The word is synonymous with a Buddhist term meaning "extremely hard" or "unbreakable" and is sometimes written with these characters as well. See Iwata, *Honchō nanshoku*, p. 339.

42. The "o" in *okama* is an honorific prefix.

43. Koike, *Kōshoku*, pp. 191–192.

44. Jippensha Ikku, *Tōkaidōchū hizakurige*, ed. Asō Isoji (Tokyo: Iwanami shoten, 1985), vol. 1, p. 105; Thomas Satchell, trans., *Hizakurige or Shanks' Mare: Japan's Great Comic Novel of Travel and Ribaldry by Ikku Jippensha* (Tokyo and Rutland, Vt.: Tuttle, 1960), p. 45. The fee of four *shu* (or about fifteen *monme*) for a Yoshichō *kagema* seems low when compared to the prices circa 1770 given in Chapter 2. No doubt this is the fee for the lowest-quality male prostitute in the ward.

45. Shinmura, *Kōjien*, p. 1202; Matsumura Akira, ed., *Daijirin* (Tokyo: Sanseidō, 1988), p. 1851. Sometimes an honorific "o" was attached to this word (*onyake, oniyake*); see *Nihon kokugo daijiten* (Tokyo: Shōgakukan, 1973), vol. 3, p. 703; Miyatake Gaikotsu, *Waisetsu haigo jii waisetsu fūzokushi* (Tokyo: 1976), p. 40.

46. Miyatake, *Waisetsu haigo*, p. 34.

47. Ibid., pp. 35–36.

48. *ISS*, vol. 2, p. 537; Schalow, *Great Mirror*, p. 252.

49. Miyatake, *Waisetsu haigo*, p. 102.

50. Fukuda, *Nikuhitsu fūzoku*, p. 56.

51. Kazuo, *Edo no deai chaya*, p. 105; Gichner, *Japanese Culture*, pp. 61, 67; Nishiyama, "Shudō fūzoku ni tsuite," pp. 344–345.

52. Sasama, *Kōmshoku engo jiten*, p. 285.

53. Ibid.

54. Suzuki Katsutada, *Senryū zappai kara mita Edo shomin fūzoku*

(Tokyo: Yūzankaku, 1978), p. 182; Sasama Yoshihiko, *Kōshoku engo jiten* (Tokyo: Yūzankaku, 1989), p. 285.

55. Nishiyama, "Shudō fūzoku ni tsuite," p. 348.

56. Dykstra, *Laughing Stories*, p. 68.

57. In Fukuda, *Ehon ukiyoe sen*, pp. 138–139, there is a Tokugawa-period painting in which a man copulates with a women while being buggered by a man, who is himself being anally penetrated by a *third* man.

58. Fukuda, *Nikuhitsu*, p. 181.

59. The *Kōbō daishi ikkan no sho* recommends that an acolyte be seduced by stroking his penis and massaging his chest. See Schalow, "Kūkai," p. 218.

60. The *Kama sutra* refers noncommitally to "a congress in the anus" popular in "the Southern countries," adding, "An ingenious person should multiply the kinds of congress ... according to the usage of each country" in order to win "love, friendship, and respect in the hearts of women." See Sir Richard Burton and F. F. Arbuthnot, trans., *The Kama Sutra of Vatsyayana* (New York: Allen & Unwin, 1963), p. 109.

61. Arthur N. Gilbert, "Conceptions of Homosexuality and Sodomy in Western History," in Salvatore J. Licata and Robert P. Petersen, eds., *Historical Perspectives on Homosexuality* (New York: Haworth Press, 1981), p. 65; see also Gilbert, "Buggery and the British Navy, 1700–1861," *Journal of Social History* 10 (1976), pp. 88–89.

62. Sandor Ferenczi, "The Nosology of Male Homosexuality (Homo-Erotism)," in idem., *First Contributions to Psychoanalysis* (London: Hogarth Press, 1952), p. 317.

63. Quoted in Hocquenghem, *Homosexual Desire*, p. 96

64. Freud, *Three Contributions*, p. 48, note 17.

65. Nishimiya Kazutami, ed., *Kojiki* (Tokyo: Shinchōsha, 1979), p. 176; see also Donald L. Philippi, trans., *Norito: A Translation of the Ancient Japanese Ritual Prayers* (Princeton: Princeton University Press, 1990), p. 46.

66. Since Susano-o is depicted as a willful child, his behavior might be likened to that of Freud's infant, who for purposes of pleasure improperly voids his bowels at the wrong time and place. See Sigmund Freud, "Character and Anal Erotism," in *Collected Papers*, vol. 2 (New York: Basic Books, 1959), pp. 45–50.

67. Philippi, trans., *Kojiki*, p. 57.

68. Cited in ibid., p. 57.

69. Ibid., p. 87

70. Beurdeley et al., *Erotic Art of Japan*, pp. 17, 19.

71. William R. LaFleur, "Hungry Ghosts and Hungry People: Soma-

ticity and Rationality in Medieval Japan," in Michel Feher, ed., *Fragments for a History of the Human Body*, Part One (New York: Urzone, 1989), pp. 271–303. See especially the street scene of defecators, p. 279, and the *gaki* in the cesspool, p. 281.

72. Ibid., p. 282.

73. This point will be obvious to any student of Tokugawa literature, so I will just cite a couple of examples. *Kobanashi* make fun of men who withdraw from boy-partners defiled by feces; see Mutō, *Edo kobanashi jiten*, p. 426, 445, and Dykstra, *Laughing Stories*, p. 68. Shikitei Sanba's *Ukiyoburo* (1809) begins with an introduction referring to people farting in the public bath, concluding that the author, having feasted on sweet potatoes, has now "farted forth" the humorous work. See Robert Leutner, *Shikitei Sanba and the Comic Tradition in Edo Fiction* (Cambridge, Ma.: Council on East Asian Studies, Harvard University, 1985), pp. 137–139.

74. Tanizaki Junichirō, *The Makioka Sisters*, trans. Edward G. Seidensticker (New York: Perigee, 1957), p. 530.

75. The continuing existence of such images and attitudes suggests that we cannot easily dismiss as wartime propaganda anthropologist Weston La Barre's references to the Japanese "love of scatological obscenity and anal sexuality." However, his explanation of this phenomenon (the supposedly early and drastic toilet-training process) does not correspond to contemporary reality. See La Barre, "Some Observations on Character Structure in the Orient," *Psychiatry: Journal of Biology and the Pathology of Interpersonal Relations* 8, 3 (August 1945), pp. 319–342.

76. See, for example, William Hinton's discussion of night soil as "black gold" in a Chinese village in 1948, in *Fanshen: A Documentary of Revolution in a Chinese Village* (New York: Vintage Books, 1966), pp. 428–430. Here the peasants eagerly collected human waste for fertilizer. Peasants in nineteenth-century France, however, regarded the use of human feces for this purpose as an abomination and refused to eat vegetables grown with such fertilizer. See Emile Zola's 1887 novel, *La Terre* (Chartres, France: Alphonse-Marré, 1987).

77. Cooper, *They Came to Japan*, p. 222. Here what Freud depicts as the subconscious association of feces with money acquires a practical character.

78. *ISS*, vol. 2, p. 536, note 7.

79. Miyatake, *Waisetsu haigo*, p. 21.

80. Gichner, *Chinese Culture*, p. 96.

81. Phyllis and Eberhard Kronhausen, *The Complete Book of Erotic*

Art, 2 vols. (New York: Bell, 1987), vol. 1, p. 311. See caption over illustration 398.

82. *ISS*, vol. 1, p. 245.

83. Also see the Miyakawa Chōshun scroll in Watanabe and Iwata, *Love of the Samurai*, p. 142.

84. The scene from Utamaro's satirical series *Michiyuki koi no futozao* (1801–1803) is meant to be comical, but the humor requires some explanation. The scene depicts Shirai Gonpachi, a member of the Edo gang led by the famed *otokodate* Banzuiin Chōbei; his lover, the Yoshiwara courtesan Kourosaki; and Banzuiin Chōbei himself.

Gonpachi, a character popularized in various theatrical works, was based on Hirai Gonpachi, a young samurai from Tottori crucified in 1679. Having fallen in love with Komurosaki, Gonpachi financed his visits to the brothel quarter by committing street robberies. The severity of his sentence resulted from the fact that he murdered many of his victims. After Gonpachi's death, Komurosaki (at least, according to legend) committed suicide and was thereafter popularly regarded as a paragon of womanly faithfulness.

The true Chōbei died in 1657 and has no historical connection with Gonpachi or the courtesan, but in the dramatic treatments he is Gonpachi's valiant friend and patron. He attempts to reform the youth but is obliged to expel him from his home as his crimes multiply. Even so, he arranges the burial of Gonpachi's body after the execution.

Thus, the jarring effect of depicting the three in this *ménage*. In the captions, Komurasaki complains of pain as Chōbei buggers her, but he responds that he holds the couple's fate in his hands and that they owe him their service. See Fukuda Kazuhiko, *Fūzoku ehon ukiyoe* (Tokyo: Kawade shobō, 1991), p. 75

85. Koike, *Kōshoku*, pp. 185–186; *ISS*, vol. 2, p. 491.

86. *ISS*, vol. 2, p. 374; Schalow, *Great Mirror*, p. 106.

87. Gichner suggests that the term *ainame* ("mutual licking") applied to reciprocal homosexual fellation as well as to heterosexual activity, but this seems to be pure conjecture (*Japanese Culture*, p. 68).

88. Dōmoto, "Chigo no sōshi," p. 187.

89. On this practice among men in traditional Polynesia, see Williams, *The Spirit and the Flesh*, p. 256; in ancient India, see Burton and Arbuthnot, *Kamasutra*, pp. 116–119; in New Guinea, Herdt, *Guardians of the Flutes*, passim.

90. For depictions of heterosexual kissing, see the work by Keisai Eizen in Fukuda, *Ehon ukiyoe sen*, vol. 1, p. 122; by Utagawa Kunikari in the same work, p. 138; and by Suzuki Harunobu in the same work,

p. 96, among innumerable examples. Male-male kissing is shown in Illustration 27; in Ōmura, *Nanshoku Yamaji no tsuyu*; and in most compilations of Japanese erotic art.

Men are shown stroking youths' genitals in Illustrations 18 and 19; for depictions of men masturbating female partners, see Fukuda's works (for example, the Nishikawa Sukenobu print in *Ehon ukiyoe sen*, p. 29). For depictions of heterosexual anal sex, see, for example, the work by Torii Kiyonaga in Inoue Shōichi, "Eshi kara gaka e," part 3, *Asahi gakkan* 4, 3 (1992), p. 189; by Bukiyo Matabei in Bowie et al., "Erotic Aspects," illustration no. 93; by Utagawa Kunisada in Yasuda Yoshinari, *Hatago no onna* (Tokyo: Futami shobō, 1990), pp. 48–49. Two women employing a double *harikata* are depicted in Yasuda, *Yotogi no onna* (Tokyo: Futami shobō, 1900), pp. 144–145.

91. A section of the *Shikidō* (1834) poses and answers the question: "Which orgasm is more pleasurable, that derived from a wet dream, masturbation, anal sex or vaginal intercourse?" Nowhere does the work even raise the possibility of ejaculation in a male or female partner's mouth. See Fukuda, *Shikidō kinpishō*, vol. 2, pp. 62–63.

Elsewhere in the same work, reference is made to one Kashiwagi, a transsexual prostitute in Kyoto's Gion renowned for his/her "three holes" (*mitsu ana*): the male and female genital openings and the anus. The author makes no reference to Kashiwagi's mouth. Fukuda, ibid., p. 110.

92. Compare the situation in modern gay communities, in the West as well as in Japan, where relationships between adult men of comparable ages are more common. Accordingly, homosexual pornography seems as likely to celebrate the adult macho male as the beautiful youth as the object of desire. See Michael Pollak, "Male Homosexuality or Happiness in the Ghetto," in Philippe Ariès and Andre Bejin, eds., *Western Sexuality: Practice and Precept in Past and Present Times* (Oxford and New York: Blackwell, 1986), pp. 53–54.

93. Cecilia Segawa Seigle, *Yoshiwara: The Glittering World of the Japanese Courtesan* (Honolulu: University of Hawaii Press, 1993), pp. 85–86.

94. Schalow, "Literary Tradition of Male Love," p. 31.

95. Koike, *Kōshoku*, p. 186.

96. Compare Straton, *Anthologia Palatinus*, XII, 4: "The bloom of a twelve-year-old boy is desirable, but at thirteen he is much more delightful. Sweeter still is the flower of love that blossoms at fourteen, and its charm increases at fifteen. Sixteen is the divine age." Quoted in Reay Tannahill, *Sex in History* (New York: Stein and Day, 1980), pp. 85–86.

97. Caryl Ann Callahan, trans., *Tales of Samurai Honor by Ihara Saikaku* (Tokyo: Monumenta Nipponica, 1981), p. 142.

98. Howard A. Link et al., *Primitive Ukiyoe from the James A. Michener Collection in the Honolulu Academy of Art* (Honolulu: University Press of Hawaii, 1980), p. 235.

99. See appendix to Iwata, *Honchō nanshoku*, p. 327f.

100. Dover, *Greek Homosexuality*, p. 86

101. David W. Plath, "Gempuku," *Kodansha Encyclopedia of Japan*, vol. 3, p. 7.

102. Schalow, *Great Mirror*, pp. 28–29.

103. Koike, *Kōshoku*, p. 264; Iwata, *Honchō nanshoku*, p. 257.

104. Suzuki, *Senryū zappai*, p. 181.

105. Jippensha, *Tōkaidōchū*, vol. 1, pp. 32–33; Satchell, trans., *Hizakurige*, pp. 369–370. Satchell appears to have entirely overlooked the homosexual content of this passage.

106. Jan Bremmer, "Indo-European Rite," p. 282.

107. Plath, "Gempuku," p. 7; Richard Varna, "The Organized Peasant: The *Wakamonoguchi* in the Edo Period," *Monumenta Nipponica* 32 (1977), p. 4.

108. Shinmura, *Kōjien*, p. 2369; David Plath, "Life Cycle," *Kodansha Encyclopedia*, vol. 5, p. 4.

109. Jacques Gernet, *La civilisation chinoise* (Paris: Librairie Armand Colin, 1928), p. 198.

110. Might not the obscure statement in the *Kojiki* (Book One, Chapter 23)—"The inside is hollow-hollow; the outside is narrow-narrow"—which according to Orikuchi Shinobu was a formula imparted to youths at initiation ceremonies in order to explain the nature of female sex organs, have rather been a word of comfort to boys being subjected to anal sex? It may have expressed the sense that, once the adult's penis had penetrated past the narrow spincter, the boy's pain would subside. See Philippi, *Kojiki*, p. 99, including note 11.

111. Frederick Victor Dickens, trans., *The Story of a Hida Craftsman (Hida no Takumi Monogatari)* (London and Glasgow: Gowans and Gray, 1912), pp. 42, 119.

112. Yamamoto, *Hagakure*, p. 69.

113. *ISS*, vol. 2, pp. 333, 369.

114. Ibid., p. 473.

115. Ibid., p. 367; Schalow, *Great Mirror*, p. 98.

116. Bremmer, "Indo-European Rite," p. 282.

117. *ISS*, vol. 2, p. 340. This passage is quoted approvingly in Yama-

moto, *Hagakure*, p. 69. My translation differs from that of Schalow in *Great Mirror*, p. 76.

118. Schalow, *Great Mirror*, p. 119; *ISS*, vol. 2, p. 385.

119. K. J. Dover, "Classical Greek Attitudes to Sexual Behaviour," *Arethusa* 6 (1973), pp. 66–67. Another scholar's suggestion that the *erastes-eromenos* relationship filled a void left by the lack of significant father-son relationships seems less applicable to the Japanese case. See George Devereux, "Greek Pseudo-Homosexuality and the 'Greek Miracle,'" *Symbolae Osloenses* 42 (1968), p. 78. In the cities of Tokugawa Japan, men seem to have enjoyed close ties with their children. See Kathleen S. Uno, "The Household Division of Labor," in Gail Lee Bernstein, ed., *Recreating Japanese Women, 1600–1945* (Berkeley, Ca.: University of California Press, 1991), pp. 31–33.

120. Halperin, *One Hundred Years*, p. 93.

121. Watanabe and Iwata, *Love of the Samuurai*, p. 113.

122. Yasuda Yoshinari, ed., *Ukiyo no onna* (Tokyo: Futami shobō, 1989), pp. 36–37.

123. Donald Keene, trans., *Death in Midsummer and Other Stories* (New York: New Directions, 1966), pp. 139–161.

124. Matsudaira Susumu, "Hiiki Renchū (Theatre Fan Clubs) in Osaka in the Early Nineteenth Century," *Modern Asian Studies* 18, 4 (October 1984); Gunji Masakatsu, "Kabuki and Its Social Background," in Nakane and ōishi, *Tokugawa Japan*, pp. 198–200.

125. Shively, "Bakufu versus Kabuki," p. 241.

126. Gunji, "Kabuki," p. 194.

127. Shively, "Bakufu versus Kabuki," p. 240.

128. Bresler, *Origins of Popular Travel*, p. 304.

129. Ibid.; Shively, "Bakufu versus Kabuki," p. 240.

130. Raz, *Audience and Actors*, p. 151.

131. Wilson, *Book of the Samurai*, p. 304; Yamamoto, *Hagakure*, p. 288.

132. Morris, *Shining Prince*, p. 215.

133. Bresler, *Origins of Popular Travel*, p. 306.

134. Shively, "Bakufu versus Kabuki," p. 238.

135. Bresler, *Origins of Popular Travel*, p. 306.

136. Shively, "Bakufu versus Kabuki," p. 239.

137. Ibid., p. 238

138. *ISS*, vol. 2, pp. 491–492; Schalow, *Great Mirror*, pp. 214–215.

139. Ōsaka-shi shi hensangakari, *Ōsaka-shi shi*, vol. 1, p. 566.

140. *ISS*, vol. 3, pp. 610–611.

141. On fan dealers, see Ejima Tsutomu, "Ogi-uri," in *Ejima Tsutomu chōsaku*, vols. 9, 11 (Tokyo: Chūō kōronsha, 1978).

142. Miyamoto Mataji, *Ōsaka no fūzoku* (Tokyo: Mainichi hōsō, 1973), p. 304; Stephen and Ethel Longstreet, *Yoshiwara: The Pleasure Quarter of Old Tokyo* (Tokyo and Rutland, Vt.: Tuttle, 1970), p. 95.

143. Hibbett, *Floating World*, pp. 117–124; 139–144.

144. Nishiyama, "Shudō fūzoku ni tsuite," p. 349.

145. Imaizumi Atsuo, ed., *Kyōto no rekishi*, vol. 5: *Kinsei no tenkai* (Tokyo: Gakugei shorin, 1972), p. 479.

146. Nishiyama, "Shudō fūzoku ni tsuite," p. 348.

147. Gunji, "Kabuki," p. 194.

148. Schalow, *Great Mirror*, p. 250; *ISS*, vol. 2, p. 536.

149. Dentō geijitsu no kai, *Kabuki*, vol. 4: *Dentō to gendai* (Tokyo: Gakugei shorin, 1969), pp. 107–108.

150. Akai, "The Common People and Painting," pp. 189–190.

151. Lamberto C. Nery, "The Covert Subculture of Male Homosexual Prostitutes in Metro Manila," *Philippine Journal of Psychology* 12 (1979), pp. 27–32; Mervyn Harris, *The Dilly Boys: The Game of Male Prostitution in Piccadilly* (London: New Perspectives, 1973), p. 71; Toby Marotta, *Adolescent Male Prostitution, Pornography, and Other Forms of Sexual Exploitation* (San Francisco: Urban and Rural Systems Associates, 1982), pp. 11–12.

152. Sitkin, *An Edo Satire*, pp. 94–95.

153. Charles Grosbois, *Shunga: Images du printemps* (Geneva: Nagel, 1964), p. 141.

154. *ISS*, vol. 2, p. 537; Schalow, *Great Mirror*, pp. 251–252.

155. Kita, *Edo no geisha*, p. 26.

156. Ibid.; Shively, "Tokugawa Tsunayoshi," p. 98.

157. Shively, "Tokugawa Tsunayoshi," p. 99, note 27.

158. Henri I. Marrou, "Pederasty in Classical Education," in *A History of Education in Antiquity*, trans. George Lamb (New York: Sheed and Ward, 1956), pp. 50–62.

159. For a depiction of a similar lesbian tryst with study books in the background, see the Keisei Eisen print in Fukuda Kazuhiko, *Neya no himitsu o oshiemasu* (Tokyo: KK Bestsellers, 1990), pp. 22–23.

160. Donald Keene, *Travelers of a Hundred Ages* (New York: Henry Holt and Co., 1989), p. 301.

161. Foucault, *The Use of Pleasure*, p. 215.

162. Eva Keuls, *The Reign of the Phallus: Sexual Politics in Ancient Athens* (New York: Harper and Row, 1985), p. 276. See also Thomas Laqueur, *Making Sex: Body and Gender from the Greeks to Freud* (Cambridge, Ma.: Harvard University Press, 1990), p. 53.

163. Trumbach, "London's Sodomites," p. 2.

164. *ISS*, vol. 1, p. 128.

165. Adachi Naoro, *Yūjo fūzoku sugata saiken* (Tokyo: Tōkyōdō, 1962), p. 229.

166. Suzuki, *Senryū zappai*, p. 182.

167. *ISS*, vol. 2, pp. 323–325.

168. Carole A. Ryavec, "Daimyo in an Age of Strife: Takeda Shingen," in Murakami and Harper, *Historical Figures*, p. 153. Takeda Shingen died at age fifty-two.

169. *ISS*, vol. 2, pp. 452–456.

170. Ueda Akinari, *Ueda Akinari shū*, ed. Nakamura Yukihiko (Tokyo: Iwanami, 1959), pp. 50–51.

171. Among the translations are Leon Zolbrod, *Ugetsu Monogatari: Tales of Moonlight and Rain* (Tokyo and Rutland, Vt.: Tuttle, 1977), pp. 109–120; Kengi Hamada, *Tales of Moonlight and Rain: Japanese Gothic Tales* (New York and London: Columbia University Press, 1972); and others by Lofcadio Hearn, Sasaki Takamasa, Dale Sanders, and Lewis Allen.

172. In the *Symposium*, Pausanius regards casual sex with boys as evil and improper, asserting that "pure enthusiasts" of homosexual behavior "love not boys, but intelligent [young men] whose reason is beginning to be developed, much about the time as their beards begin to grow. And in choosing to be their companions, they mean to be faithful to them, and pass their whole life in company with them." "Hasty attachments" are "dishonorable"; "both the lover and the beloved" should endure "contests and trials" before consummating the relationships. See B. Jowett, trans., *Plato: Five Great Dialogues* (Roselyn, NY: Walter J. Black, 1942), pp. 170, 173.

173. Yamamoto, *Hagakure*, p. 69; Wilson, *Book of the Samurai*, p. 58.

174. Ueda, *Ueda Akinari*, p. 50.

175. *ISS*, vol. 2, pp. 452–456.

176. Ibid., p. 580.

177. Ibid., p. 581; Schalow, *Great Mirror*, p. 292.

178. See Iwata, *Honchō nanshoku*, pp. 226–227.

179. A Muromachi-period example has already been cited. In the *Chigo no sōshi*, one acolyte's servant—the son of his wet nurse—trysts with the boy. See Dōmoto, "Chigo no sōshi," pp. 170–173.

180. Bresler, *Origins of Popular Travel*, pp. 244–246.

181. On this, one of the earliest Edo-period *kanazōshi* dealing with *nanshoku*, see Nakano, *Kōshoku bungei*, p. 164–165.

182. James Michener, *Japanese Prints: From the Early Masters to the Modern* (Rutland, Vt. and Tokyo: Tuttle, 1959), p. 50.

183. Koike, *Kōshoku*, p. 265.

184. Ibid., 266–267. The assumption of Iemitsu's pain is, of course, Koike's own.

185. By "status inferiors," I mean men inferior to others within a given class; samurai vassals, for example, were inferior to their lords. I realize that youth, too, is a status category.

Chapter 4

1. In China, the character pronounced *iro* in Japanese, in its literal meaning of "color," appears to have originally alluded to the erotically stimulating effect upon men (and women?) of women's cosmetics.

2. Nishikiori, *Yūjo to gaishō*, pp. 83–84.

3. Kanai Madoka, *Kinsei daimyō ryō no kenkyū: Shinano Matsumoto han chūshin toshite* (Tokyo: Meicho shuppan, 1981), p. 372.

4. Quoted in George Elison, "The Cross and the Sword: Patterns in Momoyama History," in Elison and Bardwell L. Smith, *Warlords, Artists, and Commoners: Japan in the Sixteenth Century* (Honolulu: University of Hawaii Press, 1981), p. 73.

5. Cited in Nakano, *Kōshoku bungei*, pp. 17–18.

6. Ibid., p. 17.

7. Ibid., p. 18.

8. Hiraga, *Hiraga Gennai*, pp. 161, 172.

9. Ishikawa Masamochi, *Ishikawa Masamochi shū*, ed. Tsukamoto Tetsuzō (Tokyo: Yūhōdō bunko, 1918), p. 172.

10. Ibid., p. 246; Dickens, trans., *Hida Craftsman*, pp. 42, 119.

11. *ISS*, vol. 1, p. 416.

12. Koike, p. 264.

13. *ISS*, vol. 2, p. 379.

14. *ISS*, vol. 2, pp. 327–328.

15. Ibid., p. 406.

16. Zolbrod, trans., *Tales of Moonlight and Rain*, p. 112; Ueda, *Ueda Akinari*, pp. 50–51.

17. Iwata, *Honchō nanshoku*, pp. 226–229.

18. Kaempfer, *The History of Japan*, vol. 3, p. 53.

19. Schalow, "Invention of a Literary Tradition," p. 10.

20. Jinbō et al., *Kanazōshishū*, p. 125.

21. Hiraga, *Hiraga Gennai*, p. 162.

22. H. D. Harootunian, *Things Seen and Unseen: Discourse and Ideology in Tokugawa Nativism* (Chicago: University of Chicago Press, 1988), p. 301.

23. Ibid., p. 300.

24. Dover, *Greek Homosexuality*, pp. 165–170; see also Keuls, *Reign of the Phallus*, pp. 298–299.

25. Dover, *Greek Homosexuality*, pp. 169–170.

26. As will be noted in Chapter 5, some Tokugawa scholars believed that sexual *ki* tended to spill out into males' anuses during masturbation.

27. Ueda, *Ueda Akinari*, p. 126; *ISS*, vol. 1, p. 532; vol. 2, p. 423. This association with sexual identity and karma seems to date back to the Heian period; see Willig, trans., *The Changelings*, p. 9.

28. Jinbō et al., *Kanazōshishū*, p. 133.

29. Masako (1157–1225) was the politically powerful wife of the first Kamakura shogun, Minamoto Yoritomo.

30. Jinbō et al., *Kanazōshishū*, p. 139.

31. Ueda, *Ueda Akinari*, p. 288.

32. Jinbō et al., *Kanazōshishū*, p. 129.

33. Hiraga, *Hiraga Gennai*, p. 162.

34. Fukuda Kazuhiko, ed., *Shikidō kinpishō*, vol. 2 (Tokyo: KK Bestsellers, 1991), p. 52.

35. Ibid., pp. 48–49.

36. Suzuki, *Senryū zappai*, p. 183; *Kōshoku akai karasu bōshi* (Erotic red crow hat, 1695) cited in Hayashi Yoshikazu, *Enbon Edo bungaku shi* (Tokyo: Kawade bunko, 1991), p. 45. I am indebted to Gregory M. Pflugfelder for the latter reference.

37. Zolbrod, trans., *Tales of Moonlight and Rain*, pp. 186–188. For the original, see *Ueda Akinari*, p. 124.

38. Zolbrod, trans., *Tales of Moonlight and Rain*, p. 189; *Ueda Akinari*, p. 126. I have changed Zolbrod's translation of *aiyoku* from "lust and covetousness" to the more literal "love and lust."

39. Shively, "Bakufu versus Kabuki," pp. 237, 243.

40. In Asakura Haruhiko, ed., *Nanshoku monogatari kanazōshi* (Tokyo: Koten bunko, 1966), p. 171.

41. Takada Mamoru, "Haishi bishōnen roku," p. 71.

42. Ibid., pp. 66–77.

43. Quoted in Shively, "Bakufu versus Kabuki," p. 236.

44. For the rise of official homophobia in China, see Vivian Ng, "Ideology and Sexuality: Rape Laws in Qing China," *Journal of Asian Studies* 46, 1 (February 1987), p. 68.

45. Tsuda Hideo, comp., *Zusetsu Ōsaka-fu no rekishi* (*Zusetsu Nihon no rekishi*, vol. 27) (Tokyo: Kawade shobō shinsha, 1990), p. 229; Nakano, *Kōshoku bungei*, pp. 55–57.

46. Jinnai, "Spatial Structure of Edo," pp. 132–136.

47. Ibid., p. 133.

48. Ishii Ryōsuke, ed., *Kinsei hōsei shiryō sōsho* (Tokyo: Sōbunsha, 1959), vol. 1, pt. 1. I am indebted to Gregory M. Pflugfelder for this reference, which occurs in his unpublished manuscript "Male-Male Sexual Behavior in Tokugawa Legal Discourse" (1990), p. 6.

49. Endō Motoo, *Kinsei seikaku shi nenpyō* (Tokyo: Yūzankaku, 1982), p. 19; Peter Grilli, *Furo: The Japanese Bath* (Tokyo: Kodansha International, 1985), pp. 76–77.

50. Nishiyama, "Shudō fūzoku ni tsuite," p. 344.

51. Takayanagi Shinzō and Ishii Ryōsuke, eds., *Kanpō ofuregaki shūsei* (Tokyo: Iwanami, 1976), pp. 1238–1253.

52. Gunji, "Kabuki," p. 205.

53. Ronald Dore, *Education in Tokugawa Japan* (Berkeley: University of California Press, 1975), p. 48. See also Tao Demin, "Tominaga Nakamoto no ongaku kan," *Tōhōgaku* (Tokyo) 77, p. 95f.

54. Gunji, "Kabuki," p. 198; idem., *Kabuki*, trans. John Bester (Tokyo: Kodansha International, 1969), pp. 48–49.

55. See, for example, the 1740 Okumura Masanobu print in Kobayashi, *Ukiyoe*, p. 13.

56. Akai, "Common People," pp. 189–190.

57. Watanabe and Iwata, *Love of the Samurai*, pp. 76–79, p. 121.

58. Donald Shively, "Tokugawa Tsunayoshi"; Naramoto, et al., *Yomeru nenpyō*, vol. 1, p. 81; Keene, *Nō*, p. 49.

59. Keene, *Nō*, p. 46. Public performances of noh were only occasionally staged for the benefit of commoners, but this art form apparently had many bourgeois enthusiasts. The great painter Ogata Kōrin (1658–1716), for example, born to a rich merchant family in Kyoto, was a passionate fan. See Yamane Yūzō, "Ogata Kōrin and the Art of the Genroku Era," *Acta Asiatica* 15 (1968), pp. 69–86.

60. In the course of the seventeenth century, the pleasure quarters of the great cities seem to have evolved from "aristocratic salons" patronized by nobles, samurai, and wealthy merchants to more popular centers of entertainment catering to such clients as self-employed tradesmen and servants (Akai, "Common People," p. 180).

61. Chikamatsu Monzaemon, *Chikamatsu jōruri shū*, ed. Shigetomo Ki; *Nihon koten bungaku taikei*, vol. 1 (Tokyo: Iwanami, 1976), p. 360.

62. Shively, "Bakufu versus Kabuki," p. 242. For original text, see Kikuchi Shunsuke, ed., *Tokugawa kinreikō* (Tokyo: Yoshikawa kōbunken, 1931), vol. 1, p. 88.

63. Golovnin, *Memoirs of a Captivity in Japan*, vol. 3, pp. 25–26.

64. Herbert Marcuse, *One-Dimensional Man* (Boston: Beacon Press, 1964), p. 74f.

65. Ibid., p. 75.

66. Ibid., p. 76.

67. See also Shively, "Bakufu versus Kabuki," p. 241; Keene, *World Within Walls*, p. 161.

68. Iwata Kōtarō, "Uchikowashi no minshū sekai," in Takahashi Yasuo and Yoshida Nobuyuki, eds., *Nihon toshi shi nyūmon*, vol. 2, *Machi* (Tokyo: Tōkyō daigaku shuppankai, 1990), p. 79f.

69. Yoshida Nobuyuki, "Edo machi taisho kanekashitsuke ni tsuite," *Shigaku zasshi*, vol. 86, no. 1 (January 1977), p. 33f.

70. Gregory M. Pflugfelder, "Male-Male Sexual Bahavior in Tokugawa Legal Discourse" (unpublished manuscript, 1990), pp. 2–3.

71. Ibid., pp. 3–4, 11.

72. Endō, *Kinsei*, p. 70; Naramoto, ed., *Yomeru nenpyō*, vol. 1, p. 44.

73. Takayanagi and Ishii, eds., *Kanpō ofuregaki*, p. 1307 (Zatsu no bu, no. 2885).

74. Ikeda Shōichirō, *Edo jidai yōgō kōshō jiten* (Tokyo: Shin jinbutsu ōraisha, 1984), p. 213.

75. Compare George A. DeVos, *Socialization for Achievement: Essays on the Cultural Psychology of the Japanese* (Berkeley: University of California Press, 1973), p. 270: "Neither in pre-World War II criminal law nor in the postwar criminal code did Japan prohibit homosexual intercourse. However, overt homosexual soliciting is sometimes classified by the police as 'obscene' or as a form of prostitution and therefore *fore* subject to arrest."

76. Shively has counted twenty edicts banning such visits. See "Bakufu versus Kabuki," p. 246.

77. Haga, *Edo no asobi*, pp. 240–241.

78. Endō *Kinsei*, p. 75.

79. Naramoto, ed., *Yomeru nenpyō*, vol. 5: *Edo hen*, p. 44.

80. Ibid., p. 50

81. Kodama, *Genroku jidai*, p. 78.

82. Takekoshi, *Economic Aspects*, vol. 2, p. 196.

83. Nishiyama et al., eds., *Edo gaku jiten*, p. 775.

84. Kaga Jushirō, *Genroku kakyū bushi no seikatsu* (Tokyo: Yūzankaku, 1970), p. 193. See also p. 41.

85. Kitamura Nobuyo, *Kiyū shoran*, in *Nihon zuihitsu taisei*, 2nd series (Tokyo: Nihon zuihitsu taisei kankōkai, 1929), vol. 2, pp. 398–406.

86. Wilson, trans., *Book of the Samurai*, p. 69; compare Mukoh Takao, trans., *Hagakure*, p. 76.

87. Cooper, *They Came to Japan*, p. 42

88. Ibid., p. 41

89. This episode was known as the Rōnin Plot of 1651. See George Sansom, *A History of Japan*, 1615–1867 (Stanford, Ca.: Stanford University Press, 1963), p. 59

90. Minami Kazuo, *Edokko no sekai* (Tokyo: Kōdansha, 1980), p. 180.

91. *ISS*, vol. 2, p. 320. *check my trans.*

92. Callahan, trans., *Tales of Samurai Honor*, pp. 142–145.

93. Tamura Eitarō, *Yakuza no seikatsu* (Tokyo: Yūzankaku, 1981), p. 173.

94. Raz, *Audience and Actors*, p. 150; Charles Dunn, *Everyday Life in Traditional Japan* (Tokyo and Rutland, Vt.: Tuttle, 1972), pp. 137–143.

95. Quoted in Nakai, *Shogunal Politics*, p. 51. I have altered the translation slightly by adding English equivalents to Japanese terms.

96. J. R. McEwan, trans., *Political Writings*, p. 55. I have altered the translation slightly by adding English equivalents to Japanese terms.

97. Quoted in Akai, "Common People," p. 190.

98. McEwan, *Political Writings*, p. 73.

99. James McClain, *Kanazawa: A Seventeenth-Century Japanese Castle Town* (New Haven: Yale University Press, 1981), p. 113.

100. Schalow, *"Great Mirror"* (dissertation), vol. 2, p. 321, note 14.

Chapter 5

1. *ISS*, vol. 2, p. 593.

2. In Tokugawa depictions of heterosexual lovers, it is often difficult to distinguish the male and female. See Okumura Masanobu's "Pair of Lovers," in Beurdeley et al., *Erotic Art of Japan*, p. 123, or the bathhouse scene by Kiyonaga in Bowie et al., *Studies in Erotic Art*, illus. 72.

3. Yamamoto, *Hagakure zenshū*, p. 29.

4. Dore, *Education in Tokugawa Japan*, p. 193.

5. Quoted in Donald Keene, *World Within Walls* (New York: Grove Press, 1976), p. 458.

6. *ISS*, vol. 1, pp. 531–532.

7. Hibbett, *Floating World*, p. 105

8. Suzuki Katsutada, *Senryū zappai kara mita Edo shomin fūzoku* (Tokyo: Yūzankaku, 1978), p. 181.

9. Callahan, trans., *Tales of Samurai Honor*, pp. 96–97.

10. Czaja, *Gods of Myth and Stone*, p. 30.

11. Diana Paul, *Women in Buddhism: Images of the Feminine in the Mahayana Tradition*, 2nd edition (Berkeley, Ca.: University of California Press, 1985), p. 247f; E. Dale Saunders, *Buddhism in Japan, With an Outline of Its Origins in India* (Philadelphia: University of Pennsylvania Press, 1964), p. 174. Saunders also notes that the popular boddhisattva Jizō, one Tokugawa-period *nanshoku* icon, "has a number of feminine traits, and in previous existences is said to have been a women."

12. Kitagawa Hiroshi and Bruce T. Tsuchida, trans., *The Tale of the Heike* (Tokyo: University of Tokyo Press, 1975), vol. 1, p. 21.

13. Nakano, *Kōshoku bungei*, p. 55.

14. Suzuki, *Senryū zappai*, p. 182.

15. Beurdeley et al., *Erotic Art of Japan*, p. 200.

16. Kronhausen, *The Complete Book of Erotic Art*, vol. 1, illustration no. 373.

17. *ISS*, vol. 2, p. 438; Schalow, *Great Mirror*, p. 166.

18. McClain, *Kanazawa*, p. 64.

19. Nakano, *Kōshoku bungei*, pp. 54, 56.

20. *ISS*, vol. 1, p. 191.

21. Nakano, *Kōshoku bungei*, pp. 57–58.

22. *ISS*, vol. 1, p. 191; Hamada, trans., *Life of an Amorous Man*, p. 112.

23. Shively, "Bakufu versus Kabuki," p. 232

24. Ibid., p. 233.

25. Matte LaDerriere, "Yoshizawa Ayame (1673–1729) and the Art of Female Impersonation in Genroku Japan," in Gordon Daniels, ed., *Europe Interprets Japan* (London: Paul Norbury, 1984), p. 235.

26. Donald Keene, comp., *An Anthology of Japanese Literature* (New York: Grove, 1955), p. 388.

27. Quoted in Earle Ernst, *The Kabuki Theatre* (Honolulu: University Press of Hawaii, 1974), p. 195.

28. Earl Jackson argues that the *onnagata* himself supports hegemonic conceptions of masculinity, and criticizes kabuki for requiring "detailed mimicry of specific stereotypes of women." The all-male noh drama in contrast "does not seem as pernicious as Kabuki, in that its representation of female figures are highly symbolic and abstract...." "Kabuki Narratives of Male Homoerotic Desire in Saikaku and Mishima," *Theatre Journal*, vol. 4, no. 4 (1989), pp. 461. In my view, although it is to be regretted that the Tokugawa regime banned women from the stage, the *onnagata* role created by popular culture in response to the ban was pernicious not so much toward women as toward the accepted neo-Confucian construction of gender.

29. Tōno, "Nikki ni miru Fujiwara Yorinaga," pp. 15–29; idem., "Yorinaga to Takasue," *Izumi* (Osaka) 14 (July 1990), pp. 4–6.

30. Donald Keene, "Comic Tradition," p. 275.

31. Fukuda, *Shikidō kinpishō*, p. 62.

32. Douglas Wile, *Art of the Bedchamber: The Chinese Sexual Yoga Classics, Including Women's Solo Meditation Texts* (New York: State University of New York Press, 1992), especially p. 170f.

33. Dykstra, *Laughing Stories*, pp. 27–28.

34. Ibid., p. 56

35. See Yasuda Yoshinari, *Hatago no onna* (Tokyo: Futami shobō, 1990), pp. 152–153.

36. Ibid.

37. Sitkin, *An Edo Satire*, p. 67.

38. Jenkins, *Ukiyoe Prints and Paintings*, p. 102.

39. Chikamatsu, *Chikamatsu jōruri shū*, vol. 1, p. 98.

40. Thorkil Vanggaard, *Phallos*, pp. 76–81.

41. Keuls, *Reign of the Phallus*, pp. 291–293.

42. Jippensha, *Tōkaidōchū hizakurige*, vol. 1., pp. 76–77.

43. James M. Saslow, *Ganymede in the Renaissance: Homosexuality in Art and Society* (New Haven, Ct.: Yale University Press, 1986), p. 82f.

44. Foucault, *The Care of the Self*, p. 206.

45. Matsumoto Shigeru, *Motoori Norinaga, 1730–1801* (Cambridge, Ma.: Harvard University Press, 1970), p. 52.

46. Quoted in Joyce Ackroyd, "Women in Feudal Japan," *Transactions of the Asiatic Society of Japan* (1959), p. 55.

47. Blake Morgan Young, *Ueda Akinari* (Vancouver: University of British Columbia, 1982), p. 59.

48. The play is *Horikawa nami no tsuzumi*, translated by Keene in *Major Plays of Chikamatsu*. See p. 79.

49. Yamamoto, *Hagakure*, pp. 445–446.

50. Tsunoda et al., eds., *Sources of Japanese Tradition*, vol. 1, p. 365.

51. Paul, *Women in Buddhism*, p. xix.

52. Zolbrod, trans., *Tales of Moonlight and Rain*, p. 189.

53. The Six Lusts in Buddhism are self-adornment, form, ablution, softness, carriage, and voice. Though not exclusive to women, they are more blatant in women than in men. The Five Limitations of women, listed in the *Buddhāvatamsaka sūtra* (Japanese, *Kegon-kyō*), are the inability to become Lord of Heaven, an Indra, Mitra, the Wheel-Turning King, or Buddhas.

54. Takemi Momoko, "'Menstruation Sutra' Belief in Japan," *Japanese Journal of Religious Studies* 10, 2–3 (1983), p. 233.

55. Matsumoto, *Motoori*, p. 49 (quoted from Motoori's *Shibun yōryō*).

56. Peter Nosco, "Masuho Zankō, a Shinto Popularizer," in idem., *Confucianism and Tokugawa Culture* (Princeton: Princeton University Press, 1984), p. 180.

57. John Whitney Hall, *Japan from Prehistory to Modern Times* (New York: Dell, 1971), p. 26.

58. Tsunoda et al., *Sources of Japanese Tradition*, vol. 1, pp. 5–6.

59. Philippi, trans., *Kojiki*, p. 11.

60. E. Patricia Tsurumi, "The Male Present versus the Female Past: Historians and Japan's Ancient Female Emperors," *Bulletin of Concerned Asian Scholars* 14, 4 (1983), pp. 71–75.

61. William McCullough, "Japanese Marriage Institutions in the Heian Period," *Harvard Journal of Asiatic Studies* 27 (1967), pp. 103–167.

62. Among the works by Heian women authors available in translation are *Kagerō nikki* (954–974), *Ochikubo monogatari* (ca. 980), *Murasaki Shikibu nikki* (ca. 1010), Sei Shonagon's *Makura no sōshi* (early eleventh century), and *Izumi Shikibu nikki* (early eleventh century).

63. Hitomi Tonomura, "Women and Inheritance in Japan's Early Warrior Society," *Comparative Studies in Society and History* 32, 3 (July 1990), pp. 592–623. On the twelfth-century female warrior Tomoe, see Hiroshi and Tsuchida, trans., *Tale of the Heike*, vol. 2, p. 512.

64. Dore, *Education in Tokugawa Japan*, p. 65.

65. For some examples see Keene, *Travellors*, pp. 329–338, 374–380.

66. DeVos, *Socialization for Achievement*, p. 38

67. Dore, *Education in Tokugawa Japan*, p. 65.

68. Wakita Haruko, ed., *Nihon joseishi*, vol. 3: *Kinsei* (Tokyo: Tōkyō daigaku shuppankai, 1982), p. 92f; Leupp, *Servants*, pp. 138–139.

69. Empress Meishō (r. 1630–1645) and Empress Go-Sakuramochi (r. 1763–1770).

70. Philipp Franz von Siebold et al., *Manners and Customs of the Japanese in the Nineteenth Century* (Tokyo and Rutland, Vt.: Tuttle, 1973), pp. 122–123.

71. W. E. Griffis, *The Mikado's Empire* (New York: Harper and Brothers, 1877; New York: Harper and Brothers, 1987), vol. 2, pp. 551–552.

72. Cooper, *They Came to Japan*, p. 62.

73. Harada Tomohiko et al., eds., *Zuroku kinsei josei seikatsushi nyūmon jiten* (Tokyo: Kashiwa shobō, 1991), p. 36.

74. Peasant women maintained this up into the early twentieth century. See Robert J. Smith and Ella Lury Wiswell, *The Women of Suye Mura* (Chicago: University of Chicago Press, 1982), pp. 63–64.

75. Miyatake, *Waisetsu haigo*, p. 58.

76. De Bary, trans., *Five Women*, p. 262.

77. Shively, "Bakufu versus Kabuki," p. 236.

78. Endō, *Kinsei seikatsu*, p. 133.

79. Hayashi Yoshikazu, *Jidai fūzoku kōshō jiten* (Tokyo: Kawade shobō, 1977), p. 608; see also Nishikiori, *Yūjo to gaishō*, p. 87.

80. Beurdeley et al., *Erotic Art of Japan*, pp. 248–249.

81. Nagai Kafu's novel *Udekurabe* (1918) illustrates how some women, even in more modern times, did not hesitate to invite kabuki actors to intimate trysts. The geisha Kimiryū, seeing the performance of female-impersonator Segawa Isshi, is so smitten with desire that she sends him a message through an intermediary while the performance is still underway. Observing her from the stage, he finds her agreeable and therefore sends back word that he will meet her in a house of assignation that evening. See Nagai Kafu, *Geisha in Rivalry*, trans. Kurt Meissner with Ralph Friedrich (Tokyo and Rutland, Vt.: Tuttle, 1963), pp. 164–165.

82. Shively, "Bakufu versus Kabuki," p. 254.

83. *ISS*, vol. 1, 187–190.

84. Fukuzawa Yukichi, attacking the sexual double standard, seems to have justified women's dalliances with actors: "Men find their escape in the gay quarters. It should be the same with women." See Kiyooka Eiichi, trans., *Fukuzawa Yukichi on Japanese Women: Selected Works* (Tokyo: University of Tokyo Press, 1988), pp. 125–126.

85. See Asō Isoji and Fuji Akio, eds., *Taiyaku Saikaku zenshū*, vol. 16: *Saikaku zoku tsurezure Saikaku nagori no tomo* (Tokyo: Meiji shoin, 1977), p. 31, p. 36 note 16; Teruoka Yasutaka, trans., *Gendaigo yaku Saikaku zenshū*, vol. 11: *Saikaku okimiyage Saikaku zoku tsurezure Saikaku nagori no tomo* (Tokyo: Shōgakukan, 1977), p. 142.

86. Hibbett, *Floating World*, p. 107; *ISS*, vol. 1, pp. 434–435.

87. Sasama, *Kōshoku engo*, p. 489. Celia Segawa Seigle, however, asserts that "there is no evidence of, nor reference to, lesbianism" among the prostitutes of Edo's Yoshiwara district. See her *Yoshiwara: The Glittering World of the Japanese Courtesan*, p. 156.

88. See Beurdeley et al., *Erotic Art of Japan*, p. 189.

89. Sasama, *Kōshoku engo*, p. 264.

90. Jack Ronald Hillier, *Utamaro: Colour Prints and Paintings* (New York: Dutton, 1979), p. 101.

91. Keene, trans., *Chūshingura*, p. 158.

92. The *Kama Sutra of Vatsyayana* describes the fellatio techniques of prostitute eunuchs, adding that manservants sometimes serviced their masters this way, and oral sex between male friends of respectable status was also not unknown (Burton and Arbuthnot, trans., *Kama Sutra*, pp. 124–126; cited in Bullough, *Sexual Variance*, pp. 261–262).

93. There are, however, Hindu temple sculptures depicting hetero-sexual fellatio. See Kronhausen, *Erotic Art*, vol. 1, p. 88 and p. 238, illus. 274; and Fukuda, *Sekai no ukiyoe*, p. 106, illus. 186, p. 108, illus. 192, and p. 152, illus 290.

94. Burg, *Pirate Tradition*, pp. 136–37; Stone, *Family, Sex and Marriage*, p. 305; Theo van der Meer, "The Persecutions of Sodomites in Eighteenth-Century Amsterdam: Changing Perceptions of Sodomy," in Gerard and Hekma, *Pursuit of Sodomy*, p. 291.

95. On China, see Hinsch, *Passions*, p. 111

96. Burg, *Pirate Tradition*, pp. 135–37

97. Foucault, *Care of the Self*, p. 23

98. Paul Veyne, ed., *A History of Private Life*, vol. 1: *From Pagan Rome to Byzantium* (Cambridge, Ma.: Harvard University Press, 1987), p. 204.

99. Paul Veyne, "Homosexuality in Ancient Rome," in Philippe Ariès and Andre Bejin, *Western Sexuality: Practice and Precept in Past and Present Times* (Oxford and New York: Basil Blackwell, 1985), p. 33

100. Quoted in Longstreet, *Yoshiwara*, p. 78.

101. Bullough, *Sexual Variance*, p. 297.

102. Quoted in Longstreet, *Yoshiwara*, p. 78. I cannot vouch for this translation.

103. Kronhausen, *Erotic Art*, vol. 1, pp. 248–249, illus. 289–290; vol. 2, p. 191, 209, 215, illus. 271, 291, 297.

104. Hinsch, *Passions*, p. 111.

105. In East Asia, however, *yin-yang* notions seem to rule out any gain for the insertee in male-male exchanges.

106. The *Kama Sutra* describes the fellatio techniques of *hijra* as involving eight separate stages: "casual," nibbling the sides, external pinching, internal pinching, the kiss, "browsing," sucking the mango, and devouring. See Alain Danielou, trans., *The Complete Kama Sutra* (Rochester, Vt.: Park Street Press, 1994), pp. 185–187.

107. Keuls, *Reign of the Phallus*, p. 18of.

108. Stevens, *Lust for Enlightenment*, p. 22f; Keene, *World Within Walls*, p. 161.

109. Koike, *Kōshoku*, p. 198.

110. Schalow, *Great Mirror*, p. 28.

111. Saikaku also mentions the practice of burning one's thigh with a hot tobacco pipe to prove one's love (Schalow, *Great Mirror*, p. 276).

112. Koike, *Kōshoku*, p. 198.

113. Schalow, *"Great Mirror"* (dissertation), vol. 2, p. 77.

114. The *Mokuzu monogatari*, written soon after the Itami-Mokawa affair, refers to the many male lovers interred together on the "Island of Double Graves."

115. Keene, *World Within Walls*, p. 253.

116. Iwata, *Nanshoku bunken*, p. 91.

117. Ibid., p. 113.

118. Takayanagi and Ishii, *Ofuregaki kanpō shūsei*, p. 994, edict no. 2022.

Conclusions and Speculations

1. Bret Hinsch notes that male homosexuality "inspired few writings relative to other topics" in China, contrasting this paucity with the "enormous literature" on homosexuality in Japan and ancient Greece. See *Passions of the Cut Sleeve*, p. 6.

2. Even the English-language literature on this subject is massive, but see, for example, Egami Namio, "The Formation of the People and the Origin of the State in Japan," *Memoirs of the Tōyō*, Bunko 23 (1964); Ono Susumu, *The Origin of the Japanese Language* (Tokyo: Kokusai bunka kinkōkai, 1970); Roy Andrew Miller, *Origins of the Japanese Language* (Seattle: University of Washington Press, 1980); Gordon T. Bowles, "Origin of the Japanese People," in *Kodansha Encyclopedia of Japan* (Tokyo: Kodansha, 1983), vol. 4.

3. Halperin, *One Hundred Years*, p. 41f.

4. On the basis of the dissection of the brains of nineteen homosexual men, sixteen heterosexual men, and six heterosexual women, Simon LeVay has determined that some neurons in the hypothalamus (the INAH-3 nucleus), a part of the brain that "regulates instinctive behavior, including sexual behavior," are twice as large in heterosexual men as in homosexual men. Dean H. Hammer, in a study of forty-four pairs of homosexual brothers, found that thirty-three of them had identical genes on a tip of the X chromosome. He suggests that genetic influences produce the shrinkage in the hypothalamus of at least some gay men. Hammer has also found that gay men have nearly three times as many gay relatives as heterosexual men, including cousins and uncles raised in differing environments. Richard Pilard, meanwhile, finds that gay men are five times more likely than heterosexual men to have gay brothers

and that even identical twins raised separately are remarkably similar in the development of their sexual orientation. See *Boston Sunday Globe*, March 7, 1993.

5. Halperin, *One Hundred Years*, p. 40.

6. Ibid., p. 40.

7. Ibid., p. 49.

8. Among the many who have made this observation, see Ruth Benedict, *The Chrysanthemum and the Sword: Patterns of Japanese Culture* (Cleveland and New York: Meridian Books, 1967), pp. 187–188, and Takeo Doi, *The Anatomy of Dependence* (Tokyo and New York: Kodansha International, 1973), pp. 113–121

9. Ian Buruma, *Behind the Mask* (New York: Meridian, 1984), pp. 125–135.

10. "*Anata wa, otōto no nenrei no renjū kara kōi o motareru taipu da to omou kedo sō iu otoko to isshō ni neta koto wa nai no?*" Ōe Kenzaburō, *Kojinteki na taiken* (Tokyo: Shinchosha, 1966), p. 287.

11. Ōe Kenzaburō, *A Personal Matter*, trans. John Nathan (New York: Grove Press, 1964), p. 84.

12. For a recent discussion of attitudes toward homosexuality in Japan, see Neil Miller, *Out in the World: Gay and Lesbian Life from Buenos Aries to Bangkok* (New York: Random House, 1992), pp. 144–181.

13. The Gay and Lesbian Movement (OCCUR) brought suit against the Tokyo Metropolitan Government in 1991 in connection with this ban, which stemmed from a case of harassment of gay youth by soccer team members staying at the center. When the harassment victims complained to the center staff, they necessarily revealed their sexual orientation and were forbidden further use of the facility. *Mainichi Daily News* (Tokyo), February 14, 1991, p. 12.

14. Hayami Akira, "Illigitimacy in Japan," in Peter Laslett et al., eds., *Bastardy and Its Comparative History* (London: Edward Arnold, 1980), pp. 397–402; Czaja, *Gods of Myth and Stone*, p. 168.

15. Vos, "Foibles," p. 628.

16. Hayakawa Yoshisaburō, ed., *Bunmei genryū sōsho* (Tokyo: Kokusho kankōkai, 1927), vol. 1, p. 467.

17. *Eastern World* (Tokyo), May 20, 1899.

18. In fact, however, homosexual behavior as such was never criminalized. De Vos, *Socialization for Achievement*, p. 270.

19. The brilliant novelist Shiga Naoya (1883–1971) alluded, somewhat elliptically, to his own schoolday homosexual loves (*otoko dōshi no koi*) in a short autobiographical novel first published in 1912. See Shiga Naoya, "Ōtsu Junkichi," in *Wakai* (Tokyo: Kadokawa shoten, 1993), p. 97.

20. Ōtō Tokihiko, "Chigo," in *Kodansha Encyclopedia of Japan* (Tokyo: Kodansha Ltd., 1983), vol. 1, p. 274.

21. Yanagiuchi Yoshino, *Suke tōtō to gakusei* (1901), cited in Earl H. Kinmouth, The Self-Made Man in Meiji Japanese Thought (Berkeley, Ca.: University of California Press, 1981), p. 219; Mori Ogai, *Vita Sexualis*, trans. Kazuji Ninomiya and Sanford Goldstein (Rutland, Vt. and Tokyo: Tuttle, 1972), pp. 58–60.

22. Donald T. Roden, *Schooldays in Imperial Japan: A Study of the Culture of a Student Elite* (Berkeley, Ca.: University of California Press, 1980), p. 206.

23. University students in the early twentieth century sometimes published passionate statements of homosexual love, but these apparently upset both classmates and school authorities (Ibid., pp. 178–79, 214).

24. This is the term used by Mori Ogai in *Vita Sekusuarisu*.

Appendix

1. Sentence contains untranslatable pun quoting a poem in the tenth-century compilation, the *Kokinshū*.

2. As a demonstration of their sincere love; a reference to *kanniku*.

3. *Matsu* (pines) are a symbol of agelessness.

4. Literally, "to whom he can reveal 'the smoke in my breast.'" Muro no Yashima is a shrine in Tochigi Prefecture dedicated to the goddess Konohanasakuya. Having wed Ninigi, the grandson of the Sun Goddess, Konohanasakuya gave birth in a parturition hut to which she had set fire. Many popular songs used the phrase "Muro no Yashima" as a poetical epithet for smoke.

5. An allusion to a poem in the thirteenth-century compilation *Hyakunin isshu*.

6. *Shinobu-yama* refers to a mountain in Fukushima Prefecture. The name of the mountain is a homonym for a verb meaning "to endure" or "to put up with."

7. *Asuka-gawa* is another poem in the *Hyakunin isshu* which refers to disillusionment in love.

8. About 5.8 feet.

9. That is, the swordsman from the man who had ridiculed *nanshoku*.

10. Badges of samurai status.

11. A popular traditional entertainment.

12. Possible meaning; the sentence is unclear.

13. Probably a jocular reference to anal sex, as in *Tsurezuregusa*, section 90. See Keene, trans., *Essays in Idleness*, pp. 76–77.

14. The speaker contrasts the samurai tradition of *nanshoku* with the more recent phenomenon of kabuki-linked male prostitution. Boy-prostitutes, he points out, are as fickle and devious, and as destructive to one's family and finances as the courtesans disparaged by the advocate of male-male love.

15. Desire, ill will, sloth, restlessness, and doubt.

16. Buddha's favorite disciple.

17. Confucius's favorite disciple.

18. Renowned Chinese poet and painter (1036–1101).

19. For a discussion of this belief see Takemi Momoko, "'Menstruation Sutra' Belief in Japan," *Japanese Journal of Religious Studies* 10, 2–3 (1983), pp. 229–246.

20. The *Ten Kings' Sutra* (*Jūōgyō*) is an apocryphal sutra originating in China.

21. Allusion to an Indian story.

22. Source of quote has not been identified.

23. Major temple complexes.

24. This involves a woman's restriction to the home from the sixteenth day of the fourth month to the fifteenth day of the seventh month.

25. Minamoto Yoritomo (1147–1199) established the Kamakura shogunate, having overthrown the successors of Taira Kiyomori (1118–1181).

26. All these examples involve sons who avenge their fathers' murders. It is assumed that the dead soul welcomes such revenge. Men who avoid women, and who thus do not procreate, will never receive such comfort.

27. "To dwell there with my spouse, Do I build a many-fenced palace...." See Book One, Chapter 20 of the *Kojiki* (712). Philippi, trans., *Kojiki*, p. 91. Susano-o was the mischievous younger brother of the Sun Goddess.

28. These are all well-known works of the Heian period.

29. In *Genji monogatari*.

30. In the early-tenth-century work *Ise monogatari*.

31. In the late-eleventh-century work *Sagoromo monogatari*.

32. A civil war resulting from a succession dispute in 1156. It led to Taira Kiyomori's rise to power.

33. This occurred in 1441.

34. This occurred in 1185.

35. The point seems to be that a man, having committed himself to a heterosexual marriage, must witness the inevitable deterioration of his wife's beauty, whereas men fond of youths shift their affections from partner to partner as the latter age and undergo the *genpuku* ceremony.

36. A reference to Emperor Ai of the Han dynasty (r. 6 B.C.–A.D. 1) and his boy lover, Dong Xian. According to the story, the emperor was awakened to attend to some official business. Dong Xian was still asleep, lying on the sleeve of the emperor's robe. Rather than interrupt the boy's sleep, the emperor had his servant cut the robe so that he could leave without stirring him.

37. The monk Mongaku Shōnin, 1126–1205. Rokudai was a grandson of Kiyomori.

38. Names of meritorious women in ancient China.

39. Yoritomo here is in fact identified by another title, "General of the Right."

40. Hōjō Masako, 1157–1225.

41. Imperial Consort (traditional dates, 170–269).

42. The daimyo of Sendai, who died in 1636.

43. This is quite a jumble of real and fictitious model wives.

Bibliography

Japanese

Adachi Naorō. *Yūjo fūzoku sugata saiken*. Tokyo: Nasu shobō, 1962.

Asakura Haruhiko, ed. *Kanazōshi shūsei*. Vol. 5. Tokyo: Tōkyōtō, 1983.

———, ed. *Nanshoku monogatari kanazōshi*. Tokyo: Koten bunko, 1966.

Asō Isoji and Fuji Akio, eds. *Taiyaku Saikaku zenshū*. Vol. 16: *Saikaku zoku tsurezure Saikaku nagori no tomo*, by Ihara Saikaku. Tokyo: Meiji shoin, 1977.

Ayukai Fusanoshin. *Zakkai*. 5 vols. Seoul: Chikazawa shuppan, 1932.

Chikamatsu Monzaemon. *Nihon koten bungaku taikei*. 102 vols. Vols. 49–50: *Chikamatsu jōruri shū*, ed. Shigetomo Ki. Tokyo: Iwanami shoten, 1976.

Chikamatsu zenshū kankōkai, eds. *Chikamatsu zenshū*. Tokyo: Iwanami shoten, 1985.

Dentō geijitsu no kai. *Dentō to gendai*. Vol. 4: *Kabuki*. Tokyo: Gakukei shorin, 1969.

Dōmoto Masaki. "'Chigo no sōshi': Honbun shōkai," *Yasō* (Tokyo) 15 (April 1985; reprint, November 1989), special edition, *Shōnen*..

Ejima Kiseki. *Nihon meicho zenshū*. 31 vols. (Tokyo: Nihon meicho zenshū kankōkai, 1926–1929).

Ejima Tsutomu. "Ogi-uri," *Ejima Tsutomu chōsaku*, vols. 9, 11. Tokyo: Chūō kōron, 1976.

Endō Motoo, *Kinsei seikatsu shi nenpyō*. Tokyo: Yūzankaku, 1982.

Fujiwara Yorinaga. *Daiki*. 3 vols. Kyoto: Ringawa shoten, 1966.

Fukuda Kazuhiko. *Ehon ukiyoe sen*. Tokyo: Kawade shobō, 1991.

———. *Fūzoku ehon ukiyoe*. Tokyo: Kawade shobō, 1991.

———. *Mihō ukiyoe*. Tokyo: KK Bestsellers, 1988.

———. *Neya no himitsu o oshiemasu*. Tokyo: KK Bestsellers, 1991.

———. *Nikuhitsu fūzoku emaki*. Tokyo: KK Bestsellers, 1988.

———. *Sekai no ukiyoe*. Tokyo: Kawade shobō, 1987.

———. *Shikidō kinpishō*. Vols. 1–2. Tokyo: KK Bestsellers, 1991.

Gomi Fumihiko. *Inseiki shakai no kenkyū*. Tokyo: Yamakawa shuppansha, 1984.

Haga Noboru, *Edo no asobi*. Tokyo: Kashiwa shobō, 1981.

Hanasaki Kazuo, ed. *Edo no deai chaya*. Tokyo: Kinsei fūzoku kenkyūkai, 1972.

Hanayama Shōyū, ed. *Ōjōyōshū*. Tokyo: Tokuma shoten, 1972.

Hara Kōzō. "Bijitsu ni arawareta sei fūzoku." In *Sei fūzokushi*. Vol. 1: *Sōkatsu-hen*. Tokyo: Yūzankaku, 1959.

Harada Tomohiko. *Hisabetsu buraku no rekishi*. Tokyo: Asahi shinbunsha, 1975.

Harada Tomohiko et al., eds. *Zuroku kinsei josei seikatsushi nyūmon jiten*. Tokyo: Kashiwa shobō, 1991.

Hayakawa Yoshisaburō, ed. *Bunmei genryū sōsho*. Tokyo: Kokusho kankōkai, 1927.

Hayami Akira. "Tokugawa kōki jinkō hendō no chiiteki tokusei," *Mita gakkai zasshi* 64–68 (1971), pp. 67–80.

Hayashi Yoshikazu. *Edo no makura-e shi*. Tokyo: Kawade shobō, 1987.

———. *Enbon Edo bungaku shi*. Tokyo: Kawade bunko, 1991.

———. *Jidai fūzoku kōshō jiten*. Tokyo: Kawade shobō, 1977.

Higuchi Kiyoyuki. *Nihon josei no seikatsu shi*. Tokyo: Kodansha: Kōdansha, 1977.

Hiraga Gennai. *Hiraga Gennai shū*. Ed. Miura Satoshi. Tokyo: 1915.

Ihara Saikaku. *Budō denrai ki*. Ed. Asō Isoji and Fuji Akio. Tokyo: Meiji shoin, 1978.

Ihara Saikaku shū (*ISS*). 3 vols. Vol. 1, ed. Teruoka Yasuoka and Higashi Asō; Vol. 2, ed. Munemasa Isao, Matsuda Osamu, and Teruoka Yasuoka; Vol. 3, ed. Teruoka Yasuoka, Taniwaki Masashi, and Jinbō Kazuya Tokyo: Shōgakukan, 1971–1972.

Ikeda Shōichirō. *Edo jidai yōgo kōshō jiten*. Tokyo: Shinjinbutsu ōraisha, 1984.

Imaizumi Atsuo, ed. *Kyōto no rekishi*. 10 vols. Tokyo: 1968–1976.

Imoto Nōichi. *Bashō: sono jinsei to bijutsu*. Tokyo: Kōdansha, 1968.

Inoue Shōichi. "Eshi kara gaka e," part 3, *Asahi gakkan* 4, 3 (1992), pp. 188–193.

Ishii Ryōsuke, ed. *Kinsei hōsei shiryō sōsho*. Vol. 1. Tokyo: Sōbunsha, 1959.

Iwata Jun'ichi. *Honchō nanshoku kō*. Ise: Kogawa shoten, 1974.

————. *Nanshoku bunken shoshi*. Ise: Kogawa shoten, 1973.

Iwata Kōtarō, "Uchikowashi no minshū sekai." In Takahashi Yasuo and Yoshida Nobuyuki, eds., *Nihon toshi shi nyūmon*. Vol. 2: *Machi*, pp. 79–104. Tokyo: Tōkyō daigaku shuppankai, 1990.

Jinbō Kazuya, Aoyama Takeshi, Kishi Tetsuo, Taniwaki Masachika, and Hasegawa Tsuyoshi, eds. *Kanazōshishū Ukiyozōshishū*. Tokyo: Shōgakukan, 1971.

Jingū Shichō, comp. *Koji ruien*. 60 vols. Reprint edition. Tokyo: Hyōgensha, 1927–1930).

Jippensha Ikku. *Tōkaidōchū hizakurige*. Ed. Asō Isoji. 2 vols. Tokyo: Iwanami shoten, 1985.

Kaga Jushirō. *Genroku kakyū bushi no seikatsu*. Tokyo: Yūzankaku, 1970.

Kanai Madoka. *Kinsei daimyō ryō no kenkyū: Shinano Matsumoto han chūshin toshite*. Tokyo: Meicho shuppan, 1981.

Kikuchi Shunsuke, ed.. *Tokugawa kinreikō*. Tokyo: Yoshikawa kōbunkan, 1931.

Kita Sōichirō. *Edo no geisha*. Tokyo: Chūō kōronsha, 1989.

Kitajima Masamoto. "Buke no hōkōnin." In Shinjo Yoshimoto, ed., *Edo jidai bushi no seikatsu*. 2nd edition. Tokyo: Yūzankaku, 1984.

Kitamura Nobuyo. "Kiyū shoran." In *Nihon zuihitsu taisei*, vol. 2, 2nd series. Tokyo: Nihon zuihitsu taisei kankōkai, 1929.

Kobayashi Yoshimasa. *Nihon shihonshugi no seisei to sono kiban*. Tokyo: Nihon hyōronsha, 1949.

Kodama Kōta. *Genroku jidai*. Tokyo: Chūō kōronsha, 1966.

Koike Togorō. *Kōshoku monogatari*. Tokyo: Kamakura insatsu, 1963.

Krauss, Friedrich S. *Sei fūzoku no Nihonshi*. Translation of *Das Geschlechleben in Glauben, Sitte, Brauch und Gewohnheitrecht der Japaner* (1910). Tokyo: Kawade bunko, 1988.

Maeda Isamu, comp. *Edogo no jiten*. Tokyo: Kōdansha, 1979.

Matsuda Koh [Kō], editor-in-chief. *Kenkyusha's New Japanese-English Dictionary*. 4th edition. Tokyo: Kenkyusha, 1974.

Matsumura Akira, ed. *Daijirin*. Tokyo: Sanseidō, 1988.

Minakami Tsutomu. "Ikkyū," *Umi* (April 1974), pp. 22–71.

Minami Kazuo. *Edokko no sekai*. Tokyo: Kōdansha, 1980.

Minamoto Ryōen. *Giri to ninjō*. Tokyo: Chūō kōronsha, 1967.

Miura Satoshi, ed. *Hiraga Gennai shū*. Tokyo: 1915.

Miyamoto Mataji. *Edo to Ōsaka*. Tokyo: 1938.

————. *Keihan to Edo*. Tokyo: Midori gaeru dō, 1978.

————. *Ōsaka no fūzoku*. Tokyo: Mainichi hōsō, 1973.

Miyamoto Mataji and Sakamoto Heiichirō, eds. *Ōsaka Kikuyachō shūshi ninbetsuchō*. 7 vols. Tokyo: Yoshikawa kōbunkan, 1971–1977.

Miyao Shigeo. "Kobanashi ni arawareta sei fūzoku." In *Sei fūzoku shi.* Vol. 3: *Shakai hen.* Tokyo: Yūzankaku, 1959.

Miyatake Gaikotsu. *Waisetsu haigo jii waisetsu fūzokushi.* Tokyo: 1976.

Mutō Sadao, ed. *Edo kobanashi jiten.* Tokyo: Tōkyōdō, 1955.

Nakamura Yukihiko. "Hiraga Gennai ryakuden." In *Nihon koten bungaku taikei.* 102 vols. Vol. 55: *Fūrai sanjin shū,* pp. 3–26. Tokyo: Iwanami shoten, 1957–1963.

Nakano Eizō. *Kōshoku bungei hon jiten.* Tokyo: Yūzankaku, 1988.

Naramoto Tatsuya et al. *Yomeru nenpyō.* Vol. 5: *Edo hen,* vol. 1. Tokyo: Jiyūkokusha, 1982.

Negishi Kennosuke. *Kodaijin no sei seikatsu.* Tokyo: Kindai bungeisha, 1983.

Nihon daijiten kankōkai, eds. *Nihon kokugo daijiten.* 20 vols. Tokyo: Shōgakukan, 1972–1976.

Nishigori Takeo. *Yūjo to gaishō: Kyōto o chūshin toshite baishun shi.* Tokyo: Keibunkan, 1964.

Nishimiya Kazutami, ed. *Kojiki.* Tokyo: Shinchōsha, 1979.

Nishio Minoru, ed. *Hōjōki Tsurezuregusa.* Vol. 30 of Engawa Susumu, ed., *Nihon bungaku taikei.* Tokyo: Iwanami shoten, 1983.

Nishiyama Matsunosuke. "Shudō fūzoku ni tsuite." In *Sei fūzoku shi.* Vol. 3: *Shakai hen.* Tokyo: Yūzankaku, 1959.

Nishiyama Matsunosuke et al., eds. *Edo gaku jiten.* Tokyo: Kōbundō, 1984.

Noguchi Takehiko. *Edo wakamono kō.* Tokyo: Sanseidō, 1986.

Noma Kōshin, ed. *Ukiyo zōshi shū.* Tokyo: Iwanami shoten, 1988.

Odaka Toshio, ed. *Edo waraibanashi shū.* Tokyo: 1966.

Ogyū Sorai. *Seidan.* In Takimoto Seiichi, comp., *Nihon keizai taiten.* Vol. 9. Tokyo: Keimeisha, 1928.

Okada Yasushi, ed. *Nanshoku bunken tokushū.* Vol. 13: *Kinsei shomin bunka kenkyū.* Tokyo: 1952.

Ōmura Shage, ed. *Nanshoku yamaji no tsuyu.* Tokyo: Nichirinkaku, 1978.

Ōno Susumu et al., eds. *Iwanami kogo jiten.* Tokyo: Iwanami shoten, 1974.

Ono Takeo. *Edo bukka jiten.* Tokyo: Tenbōsha, 1983.

Ōsaka-shi shi hensangakari, eds. *ōsaka-shi shi.* 8 vols. Osaka: Ōsaka hensanjo, 1911–1914; Seibundō, 1978.

Saiki Kazuma. "Tokugawa shōgun seibo narabi saisho kō." In Nihon rekishi gakkai, eds., *Rekishi to jinbutsu.* Tokyo: Yoshikawa kōbunkan, 1964.

Sakamoto Tarō, ed. *Fūzoku jiten.* Tokyo: Tōkyōdō, 1960.

Sasama Yoshihiko. *Kōshoku engo jiten*. Tokyo: Yūzankaku, 1989.

Shikitei Sanba. *Ukiyoburo*. Ed. Nakamura Michio. Tokyo: Iwanami shoten, 1985.

Shinmura Izuru, ed. *Kōjien*. Tokyo: Iwanami shoten, 1969.

Sugita Kōzō. *Genroku no wakaru hon*. Tokyo: Kosaidō shuppan, 1975.

Suzuki Katsutada. *Senryū zappai kara mita Edo shomin fūzoku*. Tokyo: Yūzankaku, 1978.

Takada Mamoru. "Haishi bishōnen roku: Bakin no dōji kami shinkō," *Yasō* 15 (April 1985; reprint November 1989), special edition, *Shōnen*, pp. 66–79.

Takayanagi Shinzō and Ishii Ryōsuke, eds. *Ofuregaki kanpō shūsei*. Tokyo: Iwanami shoten, 1976.

Takeshiba Shōtarō, ed. *Tsuruya Nanboku zenshū*. Tokyo: 1971.

Takeuchi Rizō. *Kamakura ibun*. Vols. 1–. Tokyo: Tōkyōtō shuppan, 1971–.

Takimoto Seiichi, ed. *Nihon keizai taiten*. 54 vols. Tokyo: Shishi shuppansha and Keimeisha, 1928-1930).

Tamura Eitarō. *Yakuza no seikatsu*. Tokyo: Yūzankaku, 1987.

Tanaka Kōgai. *Edo jidai no danjo kankei*. Osaka: Keimeisha, 1926.

Tao Demin. "Tominaga Nakamoto no ongaku kan," *Tōhōgaku* (Tokyo) 77 (January 1989), pp. 85–100.

Teruoka Yasutaka, trans. *Gendaigo yaku Saikaku zenshū*. 12 vols. Vol. 11: *Saikaku okimiyage Saikaku zoku tsurezure Saikaku nagori no tomo*. Tokyo: Shōgakukan, 1977.

Toita Michizō. "Uguisu," *Kanze* 33, 8 (August 1968).

Tōno Haruyuki. "Nikki ni miru Fujiwara Yorinaga no nanshoku kankei," *Hisutoria* 84 (September 1979), pp. 15–29.

———. "Yorinaga to Takasue," *Izumi* (Osaka) 14 (July 1990).

Tsuda Hideo, comp. *Zusetsu Ōsaka-fu no rekishi*. Vol 27 in *Zusetsu Nihon no rekishi*. 33 vols. Tokyo: Kawade shobō, 1990.

Tsuji Mannosuke. *Nihon bukkyō shi. Chūsei hen no go*. Tokyo: Iwanami shoten, 1951.

Tsukamoto Tetsuzō, ed. *Ishikawa Masamochi shū*, by Ishikawa Masamochi. Tokyo: Yūhōdō bunko, 1918.

Ueda Akinari. *Ueda Akinari shū*. Ed. Nakamura Yukihiko. Tokyo: Iwanami shoten, 1959.

Uemura Yukiaki. *Nihon yūri shi*. Tokyo: Shunyōdo, 1929.

Wakita Haruko, ed. *Nihon joseishi*. Vol. 3: *Kinsei*. Tokyo: Tōkyō daigaku shuppankai, 1982.

Watanabe Kazuo. *Seso iromegane*. Tokyo and Osaka: Shinbun jidaisha, 1963.

Watarai Keisuke. *Kyō no hanamachi*. Tokyo: Tairiku shobō, 1977.

Yamamoto Jōchō. *Hagakure zenshū*, ed. Nakamura Toitsu. Tokyo: Gogatsu shobō, 1978.

Yasuda Yoshinari. *Yotogi no onna*. Tokyo: Futami shobō, 1990.

———. *Hatago no onna*. Tokyo: Futami shobō, 1990.

———. *Ukiyo no onna*. Tokyo: Futami shobō, 1989.

Yasukuni Ryōichi. "Kinsei Kyōto no shomin josei." In Joseishi Sōgō Kenkyūkai, eds., *Nihon josei seikatsu shi*. Vol. 3: *Kinsei* (Tokyo: Tōkyō daigaku shūppankai, 1990.

Yoshida Nobuyuki. "Edo machi kaisho kanekashitsuke ni tsuite." *Shigaku zasshi* 86, 1 (January 1977), pp. 33–59.

Western Languages

Ackroyd, Joyce. *Told Around a Brushwood Fire: The Autobiography of Arai Hakuseki*. Princeton, N.J. and Tokyo: Princeton University Press and University of Tokyo Press, 1979.

———. "Women in Feudal Japan." *Transactions of the Asiatic Society of Japan*, series 3, 30, 7 (November 1959), pp. 31–68.

Akai Tatsurō. "The Common People and Painting." In Nakane Chie and Ōishi Shinzaburō, eds., *Tokugawa Japan: The Social and Economic Antecedents of Modern Japan*, pp. 167–191. Tokyo: University of Tokyo Press, 1990.

Akutagawa Ryūnosuke. *Kappa*. Trans. Shiojiri Seiichi. Westpoint, Ct.: Greenwood, 1970.

Ariès, Philippe, and André Béjin, eds. *Western Sexuality: Practice and Precept in Past and Present Times*. Oxford and New York: Basil Blackwell, 1986.

Aston, W. G. *A History of Japanese Literature*. 1899. Reprint, Rutland, Vt. and Tokyo: Tuttle, 1972.

———, trans. *Nihongi: Chronicles of Japan from Earliest Times to* A.D. 697. Tokyo and Rutland, Vt.: Tuttle, 1972.

Banjeri, Sures Chandre. *Crime and Sex in Ancient India*. Calcutta: Naya Prokash, 1980.

Barrow, Sir John. *Travels in China*. London: T. Cadell and W. Davies, 1804.

Bender, Ross. "The Hachiman Cult and the Dōkyō Incident," *Monumenta Nipponica* 34, 2 (June 1979).

Benedict, Ruth. *The Chrysanthemum and the Sword: Patterns of Japanese Culture*. Cleveland and New York: Meridian Books, 1967.

Bergmann, Jean-Noel. *La sexualité à travers le monde: études sur la péninsule Indochinoise*. Paris: la Trèfle d'Or, 1966.

Bernstein, Gail Lee, ed. *Recreating Japanese Women, 1600–1945*. Berkeley, Ca.: University of California Press, 1991.

Beurdeley, Michel, et al. *Erotic Art of Japan: The Pillow Poem*. Hong Kong: Leon Amiel, n. d.

Blackwood, Evelyn, ed. *The Many Faces of Homosexuality: Anthropological Approaches to Homosexual Behavior*. New York: Harrington Park Press, 1985.

Bloch, Marc. *Feudal Society*. Vol. 2: *Social Classes and Political Organization*. Chicago: University of Chicago Press, 1985.

Blumenfield, Warren J., and Diane Raymond. *Looking at Gay and Lesbian Life*. New York: Philosophical Library, 1988.

Boswell, John. *Christianity, Social Tolerance, and Homosexuality: Gay People in Western Europe from the Beginning of the Christian Era to the Fourteenth Century*. Chicago and London: University of Chicago Press, 1980.

Bottomore, Tom, ed. *A Dictionary of Marxist Thought*. Cambridge, Ma.: Harvard University Press, 1973.

Bowie, Theodore. "Erotic Aspects of Japanese Art." In Theodore Bowie et al., eds., *Studies in Erotic Art*. New York and London: Basic Books, 1970.

Boxer, Charles H. *The Christian Century in Japan, 1549–1650*. Berkeley, Ca.: University of California Press, 1967.

Brandon, James R., trans. *Kabuki: Five Classic Plays*. Cambridge, Ma.: Harvard University Press, 1975.

Brandon, James R., William P. Malm, and Donald Shively, eds. *Studies in Kabuki*. Honolulu: University Press of Hawaii, 1978.

Bray, Alan. *Homosexuality in Rennaisance England*. London: Gay Men's Press, 1982.

Bremmer, Jan. "An Enigmatic Indo-European Rite: Paederasty." *Arethusa* 13, 2 (1982), pp. 279–298.

Bresler, Laurence. *The Origins of Popular Travel and Travel Literature in Japan*. Unpublished Ph.D. dissertation, Columbia University, 1975.

Bullough, Vern L. *Sexual Variance in Society and History*. New York: John Wiley and Sons, 1976.

———. *The Subordinate Sex*. Urbana: University of Illinois Press, 1973.

Burg, B. R. *Sodomy and the Pirate Tradition: English Sea Rovers in the Seventeenth-Century Caribbean*. New York: New York University Press, 1984.

Burton, Richard, and F. F. Arbuthnot, trans. *The Kama Sutra of Vatsyayana*. New York: Allen and Unwin, 1963.

Buruma, Ian. *Behind the Mask*. New York: Meridian, 1984.

Byron, John. *Portrait of a Chinese Paradise: Erotica and Sexual Customs of the Late Qing Period*. London: Quartet Books, 1987.

Cabezon, Jose Ignacio, ed. *Buddhism, Sexuality, and Gender*. New York: State University of New York Press, 1992.

Campbell, S. C. *Only Begotten Sonnets*. London: Bell and Hyman, 1978.

Caron, François, and Joost Shouten. *A True Description of the Mighty Kingdoms of Japan and Siam*, 1663. Ed. Charles R. Boxer. London: Argonaut Press, 1935.

Childs, Margaret H. "*Chigo Monogatari*: Love Stories or Buddhist Sermons?" *Monumenta Nipponica*, 35, 2 (1980), pp. 127–151.

———. "Japan's Homosexual Heritage." *Gai Saber*, 1 (Spring 1977), pp. 41–45.

———. *Rethinking Sorrow: Revelatory Tales of Late Medieval Japan*. Ann Arbor, Mi.: University of Michigan Press, 1991.

Chou, Eric. *The Dragon and the Phoenix*. New York: Bantam, 1972.

Cohen, David. "Law, Society and Homosexuality in Classical Athens," *Past and Present* 117 (November 1987), pp. 1–21.

Collcutt, Martin. *Five Mountains: The Rinzai Zen Monastic Institutions in Medieval Japan*. Cambridge, Ma.: Council on East Asian Studies, Harvard University, 1981.

Cooper, Michael S.J. *They Came to Japan: An Anthology of European Reports on Japan*, 1543–1640. Berkeley, Ca.: University of California Press, 1965.

Coward, D. A. "Attitudes to Homosexuality in Eighteenth-Century France," *Journal of European Studies* X (1980), pp. 231–255.

Czaja, Michael. *Gods of Myth and Stone: Phallicism in Japanese Folk Religion*. New York and Tokyo: Weatherhill, 1974.

Daniel, Marc. "Les amants du soleil levant," *Arcadie* 66 (June 1959), pp. 346–356.

Danielou, Alain, trans. *The Complete Kama Sutra*. Rochester, Vt.: Park Street Press, 1994.

Davis, Natalie. "Women on Top." In Davis, *Society and Culture in Early Modern France*, pp. 124–151. Stanford, Ca.: Stanford University Press, 1975.

De Bary, William Theodore, trans. *Five Women Who Loved Love*, by Ihara Saikaku. Rutland, Vt. and Tokyo: Tuttle, 1956.

Devereux, George. "Greek Pseudo-Homosexuality and the 'Greek Miracle,'" *Symbolae Osloenses* 42 (1968), pp. 69–72.

DeVos, George A. *Socialization for Achievement: Essays on the Cultural*

Psychology of the Japanese. Berkeley, Ca.: University of California Press, 1973.

Dickens, Frederick Victor, trans. *The Story of a Hida Craftsman (Hida no Takumi Monogatari)*, by Rokujiuyen [Ishikawa Masamochi]. London and Glasgow: Gowans and Gray, 1912.

Doe, Pamela. *A Warbler's Song in the Dusk: The Life and Works of Ōtomo Yakamochi (718–785)*. Berkeley, Ca.: University of California Press, 1982.

Doi Takeo. *The Anatomy of Dependence*. Trans. John Bester. Tokyo and New York: Kodansha, 1973.

Dore, Ronald. *Education in Tokugawa Japan*. Berkeley, Ca.: University of California Press, 1975.

Dover, Kenneth J. "Classical Greek Attitudes to Sexual Behaviour," *Arethusa* 6, 1 (1973), pp. 59–73.

———. *Greek Homosexuality*. Cambridge, Ma.: Harvard University Press, 1978.

Dumoulin, Heinrich. *A History of Zen Buddhism*. New York: Macmillan, 1963.

Dunn, Charles. *Everyday Life in Traditional Japan*. Tokyo and Rutland, Vt.: Tuttle, 1972.

Dunn, Charles J., and Torigoe Bunzō, trans. and ed. *The Actor's Analects: Yakusha Rongō*, Studies in Oriental Culture no. 3. New York: Columbia University Press, 1969.

Dykstra, Andrew H. *Laughing Stories of Old Japan*. Honolulu: Kanji Press, 1987.

Eberhardt, Wolfram. *Guilt and Sin in Traditional China*. Berkeley, Ca.: University of California Press, 1967.

Egerton, Clement, trans. *The Golden Lotus*. 4 vols. London: Routledge and Kegan Paul, 1939.

Elison, George. "The Cross and the Sword: Patterns in Momoyama History." In Elison and Bardwell L. Smith, *Warlords, Artists, and Commoners: Japan in the Sixteenth Century*, pp. 55–86. Honolulu: University of Hawaii Press, 1981.

———. *Deus Destroyed: The Image of Christianity in Early Modern Japan*. Cambridge, Ma.: Harvard University Press, 1973.

Encyclopedia of Homosexuality. New York and London: Garland, 1990.

Ernst, Earle. *The Kabuki Theatre*. Honolulu: University Press of Hawaii, 1974.

Evans-Pritchard, E. E. "Sexual Inversion Among the Azande," *American Anthropologist* 62 (1970), pp. 1428–1434.

Farris, William Wayne. *Heavenly Warriors: The Evolution of Japan's Military, 500–1300*. Cambridge, Ma.: Council on East Asian Studies, Harvard University, 1992.

Ferenczi, Sandor. "The Nosology of Male Homosexuality (Homo-Erotism)." In idem., *First Contributions to Pyschoanalysis*. London: Hogarth Press, 1952.

Fisher, Saul H. "A Note on Male Homosexuality and the Role of Women in Ancient Greece." In Judd Marmor, ed., *Sexual Inversion: the Multiple Roots of Homosexuality*, pp. 165–172. New York: Basic Books, 1956.

Foucault, Michel. *The Use of Pleasure: Volume Two of the History of Sexuality*. New York: Vintage, 1985.

———. *The Care of the Self: Volume Three of the History of Sexuality*. New York: Pantheon, 1986.

Freud, Sigmund. *Collected Papers*. New York: Basic Books, 1959.

———. *Three Contributions to the Theory of Sex*. New York: E. P. Dutton, 1962.

Friday, Karl F. *Hired Swords: The Rise of Private Warrior Power in Early Japan*. Stanford, Ca.: Stanford University Press, 1992.

Gernet, Jacques. *Daily Life in China on the Eve of the Mongol Invasions, 1250–1276*. Stanford, Ca.: Stanford University Press, 1962.

———. *La civilisation chinoise*. Paris: Librairie Armand Colin, 1928.

Gichner, Lawrence E. *Erotic Aspects of Chinese Culture*. Washington, D.C.: n.p., 1967.

———. *Erotic Aspects of Japanese Culture*. New York: n.p., 1953.

Gilbert, Arthur N. "Buggery and the British Navy, 1700–1861," *Journal of Social History* 10 (1976), pp. 72–98.

———. "Conceptions of Homosexuality and Sodomy in Western History." In S. J. Licata and R. B. Petersen, eds., *Historical Perspectives on Homosexuality*, pp. 57–68. New York: Haworth Press, 1981.

Godelier, Maurice. "The Origins of Male Domination," *New Left Review* 127 (1981), pp. 3–27.

Golovnin, V. *Memoirs of a Captivity in Japan, During the Years 1811, 1812, and 1813, with Observations on the Country and the People*. 2nd edition. 3 vols. London: H. Colburn and Co., 1824.

Goodich, Michael. *The Unmentionable Vice: Homosexuality in the Later Medieval Period*. Santa Barbara, Ca.: ABC-Clio, 1979.

Gray, J. Patrick. "Growing Yams and Men." In Evelyn Blackwood, ed., *The Many Faces of Homosexuality: Anthropological Approaches to Homosexual Behavior*, pp. 55–68. New York: Harrington Park Press, 1985.

Greenberg, David F. *The Construction of Homosexuality*. Chicago: University of Chicago Press, 1988.

Griffis, W. E. *The Mikado's Empire*. 2 vols. New York: Harper and Brothers, 1987.

Grilli, Peter. *Furo: The Japanese Bath*. Tokyo: Kodansha International, 1985.

Groner, Paul. "The *Lotus Sutra* and Saichō's Interpretation of the Realization of Buddhahood with This Very Body." In George J. Tanabe and Willa Jane Tanabe, eds., *The Lotus Sutra in Japanese Culture*, pp. 53–74. Honolulu: University of Hawaii Press, 1989.

Grosbois, Charles. *Shunga: Images du printemps*. Geneva: Nagel, 1964.

Gunji Masakatsu. *Kabuki*. Trans. John Bester. Tokyo: Kodansha International, 1969.

———. "Kabuki and Its Social Background." In Nakane Chie and Ōishi Shinzaburō, eds., *Tokugawa Japan: The Social and Economic Antecedents of Modern Japan*, pp. 192–212. Tokyo: University of Tokyo Press, 1990.

Hall, John Whitney. "The Castle Town and Japan's Modern Urbanization." In Hall and Marius Jansen, eds., *Studies in the Institutional History of Early Modern Japan*, pp. 15–51. Princeton, N.J.: Princeton University Press, 1968.

———. "Feudalism in Japan—A Reassessment." In Hall and Marius B. Jansen, eds., *Studies in the Institutional History of Early Modern Japan*, pp. 15–54. Princeton, N.J.: Princeton University Press, 1968.

———. "Forerunner of the Modern Statesman: Tanuma Okitsugu." In Murakami Hyoe and Thomas J. Harper, eds., *Great Historical Figures of Japan*, pp. 208–218. Tokyo: Japan Culture Institute, 1978.

———. *Japan from Prehistory to Modern Times*. New York: Dell, 1971.

Halperin, David M. *One Hundred Years of Homosexuality and Other Essays on Greek Love*. New York: Routledge, 1990.

Halperin, David M., John J. Winkler, and Froma I. Zeitlin, eds. *Before Sexuality: The Construction of Erotic Experience in the Ancient Greek World*. Princeton, N.J.: Princeton University Press, 1990.

Hamada Kengi, trans. *Tales of Moonlight and Rain: Japanese Gothic Tales*. Tokyo: University of Tokyo Press, 1971.

Hamill, Sam, trans. *Narrow Road to the Interior*, by Matsuo Bashō. Boston and London: Shambala, 1991.

Hare, Thomas Blenman. *Zeami's Style: The Noh Plays of Zeami Motokiyo*. Stanford, Ca.: Stanford University Press, 1986.

Harootunian, H. D. *Things Seen and Unseen: Discourse and Ideology in Tokugawa Nativism*. Chicago: University of Chicago Press, 1988.

Harris, Mervyn. *The Dilly Boys: The Game of Male Prostitution in Picca-dilly*. London: New Perspectives, 1973.

Hayami Akira. "Illegitimacy in Japan." In Peter Laslett et al., eds., *Bastardy and Its Comparative History*. London: Edward Arnold, 1980.

Henderson, Hamish. "The Women of the Glen: Some Thoughts on Highland History." In Robert O'Driscoll, *The Celtic Consciousness*, pp. 255–264. New York: Braziller, 1981.

Henthorn, William E. *A History of Korea*. New York: Free Press, 1971.

Herdt, Gilbert H. *Guardians of the Flutes: Idioms of Masculinity*. New York: Columbia University Press, 1981.

———, ed. *Ritualized Homosexuality in Melanesia*. Berkeley, Ca.: University of California Press, 1984.

Hibbett, Howard. *Ejima Kiseki and the Hajimonjaya: A Study in Eighteenth-Century Japanese Fiction*. Unpublished Ph.D. dissertation, Harvard University, 1950.

———. *The Floating World in Japanese Fiction*. Tokyo and Rutland, Vt.: Tuttle, 1975.

Hillier, Jack Ronald. *Utamaro: Colour Prints and Paintings*. New York: Dutton, 1979.

Hinsch, Bret. *Passions of the Cut Sleeve: the Male Homosexual Tradition of China*. Berkeley, Ca.: University of California Press, 1990.

Hinton, William. *Fanshen: A Documentary of Revolution in a Chinese Village*. New York: Vintage Books, 1966.

Hitomi Tonomura. "Women and Inheritance in Japan's Early Warrior Society," *Comparative Studies in Society and History* 32, 3 (July 1990), pp. 592–623.

Hocquenghem, Guy. *Homosexual Desire*. Durham, N.C. and London: Duke University Press, 1993.

Huusen, Arend H., Jr. "Sodomy in the Dutch Republic During the Eighteenth Century." In Robert Purks Maccubbin, ed., *'Tis Nature's Fault: Unauthorized Sexuality During the Enlightenment*, pp. 169–178. New York: Cambridge University Press, 1987.

Ihara Saikaku. *The Great Mirror of Male Love*. Trans. Paul Schalow. Stanford: Stanford University Press, 1990.

———. *The Great Mirror of Male Love*. Trans. Paul Schalow. Harvard University Ph.D. dissertation, 1985.

———. *The Life of an Amorous Man*. Trans. by Hamada Kengi. Tokyo and Rutland, Vt.: Tuttle, 1963.

———. *The Life of an Amorous Woman and Other Writings*. Trans. by Ivan Morris. New York: New Directions, 1963.

————. *Tales of Samurai Honor*. Trans. Caryl Ann Callahan. Tokyo: Monumenta Nipponica, 1981.

Jackson, Earl Jr. "Kabuki Narratives of Male Homoerotic Desire in Saikaku and Mishima," *Theatre Journal* 41, 4 (1989), pp. 459–477.

Jansen, Marius B. *China in the Tokugawa World*. Cambridge, Ma: Harvard University Press, 1992.

Jenkins, Donald. *Ukiyoe Prints and Paintings: The Primitive Period, 1680–1745: An Exhibition in the Memory of Margaret O. Gentles, November 6–December 26, 1971*. Chicago: Art Institute of Chicago, 1971.

Jinnai Hidenobu. "The Spatial Structure of Edo." Trans. Conrad Totman. In Nakane Chie and Ōishi Shinzaburō, eds., *Tokugawa Japan: The Social and Economic Antecedents of Modern Japan*. Tokyo: University of Tokyo Press, 1990, pp. 124–146.

Jowett, B., trans. *Plato: Five Great Dialogues*. Roselyn, NY: Walter J. Black, 1942.

Kaempfer, Engelbert. *The History of Japan Together with a Description of the Kingdom of Siam, 1690–92*. Trans. J. G. Scheuchzer. 3 vols. Glasgow: James MacLehose and Sons, 1906.

Karlen, Arlo. *Sexuality and Homosexuality: A New View*. New York: W. W. Norton, 1971.

Katō Shūichi. *A History of Japanese Literature: The First Thousand Years*. Tokyo: Kōdansha, 1979.

Keene, Donald, comp. *An Anthology of Japanese Literature*. New York: Grove, 1955.

————, trans. *Chūshingura: The Treasury of Loyal Retainers*. New York: Columbia University Press, 1971.

————. "The Comic Tradition in Renga." In John Whitney Hall and Toyoda Takeshi, eds., *Japan in the Muromachi Age*, pp. 241–277. Berkeley, Ca.: University of California Press, 1977.

————, trans. *Death in Midsummer and Other Stories*. New York: New Directions, 1966.

————, trans., *Essays in Idleness: The Tsurezuregusa of Kenkō*. New York: Columbia University Press, 1967.

————. "Jōha, a Sixteenth-Century Poet of Linked Verse." In George Elison and Bardwell L. Smith. *Warlords, Artists and Commoners: Japan in the Sixteenth Century*. Honolulu: University Press of Hawaii, 1981.

————, trans. *Major Plays of Chikamatsu*. New York: Columbia University Press, 1961.

————. *Nō: The Classical Theatre of Japan*. Tokyo: Kodansha International, 1966.

————. *Travelers of a Hundred Ages*. New York: Henry Holt and Co., 1989.

————. *World Within Walls*. New York: Grove Press, 1976.

Kenny, Don. *A Guide to Kyogen*. Tokyo: Hinoki Shoten, 1968.

Keuls, Eva. *The Reign of the Phallus: Sexual Politics in Ancient Athens*. New York: Harper and Row, 1985.

Keyes, Roger S., and Keiko Mizushima. *The Theatrical World of the Osaka Prints*. Boston: Philadelphia Museum of Art, 1973.

Kinmouth, Earl H. *The Self-Made Man in Meiji Japanese Thought*. Berkeley, Ca.: University of California Press, 1981.

Kirkwood, Kenneth P. *Renaissance in Japan: A Cultural Survey of the Seventeenth Century*. Rutland, Vt. and Tokyo: Tuttle, 1970.

Kitagawa Hiroshi and Bruce T. Tsuchida, trans. *The Tale of the Heike*. 2 vols. Tokyo: University of Tokyo, 1975.

Kiyooka Eiichi, trans. *Fukuzawa Yukichi on Japanese Women: Selected Works*. Tokyo: University of Tokyo Press, 1988.

Kobayashi Takashi. *Ukiyoe*. Tokyo: Kodansha International, 1982.

Kodansha Encyclopedia of Japan. 8 vols. Tokyo: Kodansha, 1983.

Kodera, Takashi James. *Dōgen's Formative Years in China: An Historical Study and Annotation of the Hōkyō-ki*. Boulder, Colo.: Prajna Press, 1980.

Kronhausen, Phyllis and Eberhard. *The Complete Book of Erotic Art*. 2 vols. New York: Bell, 1987.

Kuno, Yoshi Saburo. *Japanese Expansion on the Asiatic Continent: A Study in the History of Japan*. Berkeley, Ca.: University of California Press, 1937; New York: 1967.

Kyoko Motomochi Nakamura, trans. *Miraculous Stories of the Japanese Buddhist Tradition: The Nihon ryōiki of the Monk Kyōkai*. Cambridge, Ma.: Harvard University Press, 1973.

La Barre, Weston. "Some Observations on Character Structure in the Orient." *Psychiatry: Journal of Biology and the Pathology of Interpersonal Relations* 8, 3 (August 1945), pp. 319–342.

LaDerriere, Matte. "Yoshizawa Ayame (1673–1729) and the Art of Female Impersonation in Genroku Japan." In Gordon Daniels, ed., *Europe Interprets Japan*, pp. 233–237. London: Oxford University Press, 1984.

LaFleur, William R. "Hungry Ghosts and Hungry People: Somaticity and Rationality in Medieval Japan." In Michel Feher, ed., *Fragments for a History of the Human Body*, pp. 270–303. Part 1. New York: Urzone, 1989.

Laqueur, Thomas. *Making Sex: Body and Gender from the Greeks to Freud*. Cambridge, Ma.: Harvard University Press, 1990.

Lee, Peter, trans. *Lives of Eminent Korean Monks*. Cambridge, Ma.: Harvard University Press, 1969.

Lesoualc'h, Theo. *Érotique du Japon*. Barcelona: Editions Henri Veyrier, 1987.

Leupp, Gary P. "Population Registers and Household Records as Sources for the Study of Urban Women in Tokugawa Japan," *Gest Library Journal* (Princeton University) 5, 2 (Winter 1992), pp. 49–86.

———. *Servants, Shophands, and Laborers in the Cities of Tokugawa Japan*. Princeton, N.J.: Princeton University Press, 1992.

———. "Tsuneo Watanabe and Iwata Jun'ichi, *The Love of the Samurai*: A Thousand Years of Japanese Homosexuality" (review), *Society of Lesbian and Gay Anthropologists Newsletter* 12, 3 (October 1990), pp. 51–54.

Leutner, Robert. *Shikitei Sanba and the Comic Tradition in Edo Fiction*. Cambridge, Ma.: Council on East Asian Studies, Harvard University, 1985.

Levy, Howard Seymour. *Chinese Sex Jokes in Traditional Times*. Taipei: Orient Cultural Service, 1974.

———. *Japanese Sex Jokes in Traditional Times*. Washington, D.C.: The Warm-Soft Village Press, 1973.

———. *Korean Sex Jokes in Traditional Times: How the Mouse Got Trapped in the Widow's Vagina and Other Stories*. Washington, D.C: The Warm-Soft Village Press, 1972.

Levy, Ian Hideo, trans. *The Ten Thousand Leaves*. Princeton, N.J.: Princeton University Press, 1981.

Licata, S. J., and R. B. Petersen, eds., *Historical Perspectives on Homosexuality*. New York: Haworth Press, 1984.

Link, Howard A., et al. *Primitive Ukiyoe from the James A. Michener Collection in the Honolulu Academy of Art*. Honolulu: University Press of Hawaii, 1980.

Longstreet, Stephen and Ethel. *Yoshiwara: The Pleasure Quarter of Old Tokyo*. Tokyo and Rutland, Vt.: Tuttle, 1970.

Maccubbin, Robert Purks, ed. *'Tis Nature's Fault: Unauthorized Sexuality During the Enlightenment*. New York: Cambridge University Press, 1987.

MacFarland, H. Neill, *Daruma: the Founder of Zen in Japanese Art and Popular Culture*. Tokyo and New York: Kodansha, 1987.

Mackerras, Colin P. *The Rise of the Peking Opera, 1770–1870: Social Aspects of the Theatre in Manchu China*. London: Oxford University Press, 1972.

Maes, Hubert. *Hiraga Gennai et son temps*. Paris: École françois d'ext-rême-Orient, 1970.

Manniche, Lise. *Sexual Life in Ancient Egypt*. New York: Routledge and Kegan Paul, 1987.

Marcuse, Herbert. *One-Dimensional Man*. Boston: Beacon Press, 1964.

Marks, Alfred H., trans. *Forbidden Colours*, by Mishima Yukio. London: Penguin Books, 1971.

Marotta, Toby. *Adolescent Male Prostitution, Pornography, and Other Forms of Sexual Exploitation*. San Francisco: Urban and Rural Systems Associates, 1982.

Marrou, Henri I. "Pederasty in Classical Education." In *A History of Education in Antiquity*, pp. 26–35. Trans. George Lamb. New York: Sheed and Ward, 1956.

Marx, Karl, and Friedrich Engels. *The German Ideology: Parts I and II*. New York: International Publishers, 1967.

Massarella, Derek. *A World Elsewhere: Europe's Encounter with Japan in the Sixteenth and Seventeenth Centuries*. New Haven, Ct.: Yale University Press, 1990.

Matignon, Jean-Jacques. "Deux mots sur la pederastie en Chine," *Archives d'anthropologie criminelle* XIV, 38 (1899), pp. 38–53. Also in Matignon, *Superstition Crime et Misère en Chine* (Paris: A. Maloine, 1902.

Matsudaira Susumu. "Hiiki Renchū (Theatre Fan Clubs) in Osaka in the Early Nineteenth Century," *Modern Asian Studies* 18, 4 (October 1984), pp. 699–709.

Matsumoto Shigeru. *Motoori Norinaga, 1730–1801*. Cambridge, Ma.: Harvard University Press, 1970.

Matsunaga, Daigan and Alicia. *The Buddhist Concept of Hell*. New York: Philosophical Library, 1972.

McClain, James L. *Kanazawa: A Seventeenth-Century Japanese Castle Town*. New Haven: Yale University Press, 1981.

McCullough, Helen Craig, trans. *The Tales of Ise: Lyrical Episodes from Tenth-Century Japan*. Stanford, Ca.: Stanford University Press, 1968.

———, trans. *Yoshitsune: A Fifteenth-Century Japanese Chronicle*. Stanford, Ca.: Stanford University Press, 1966.

McCullough, William. "Japanese Marriage Institutions in the Heian Period," *Harvard Journal of Asiatic Studies* 27 (1967), pp. 103–167.

McEwan, J. R., trans. *The Political Writings of Ogyū Sorai*. Cambridge: Cambridge University Press, 1962.

McMahon, Keith. *Causality and Containment in Seventeenth-Century Chinese Fiction*. Leiden: E. J. Brill, 1988.

Meijer, M. J. "Homosexual Offenses in Ch'ing Law," *T'oung Pao* 71 (1985), pp. 109–133.

Michener, James. *Japanese Prints: From the Early Masters to the Modern*. Rutland, Vt. and Tokyo: Tuttle, 1959.

Miller, Neil. *Out in the World: Gay and Lesbian Life from Buenos Aires to Bangkok*. New York: Random House, 1992.

Mills, D. E. *A Collection of Tales from Uji: A Study and Translation of Uji Shui Monogatari*. Cambridge: Cambridge University Press, 1970.

Miner, Earl, Odagiri Hiroko, and Robert E. Morrell. *The Princeton Companion to Classical Japanese Literature*. Princeton, N.J.: Princeton University Press, 1985.

Mitamura Taisuke. *Chinese Eunuchs: the Structure of Intimate Politics*. Tokyo and Rutland, Vt.: Tuttle, 1970.

Monter, William. "Sodomy and Heresy in Early Modern Switzerland." In S. J. Licata and R. B. Petersen, eds., *Historical Perspectives on Homosexuality*. New York: Haworth Press, 1984.

Mori Ogai. *Vita Sexualis*. Trans. Kazuji Ninomiya and Sanford Goldstein. Rutland, Vt., and Tokyo: Tuttle, 1972.

Morris, Ivan. "The Hierarchy of Lust in Seventeenth-Century Japan." In Maurice Schneps and Alvin D. Coox, eds., *The Japanese Image*. Tokyo and Philadelphia: Orient/West, 1965.

———. *The World of the Shining Prince: Court Life in Ancient Japan*. Oxford and New York: Oxford University Press, 1964.

Mukoh Takao. *The Hagakure: A Code to the Way of the Samurai*. Tokyo: Hokuseido Press, 1980.

Murakami Hyoe and Thomas J. Harper, eds. *Great Historical Figures of Japan*. Tokyo: Japan Culture Institute, 1978.

Murdoch, James. *A History of Japan*. 3 vols. Kobe and London: K. Paul, Trench, Trubner and Co., 1923–1926.

Nagai Kafu. *Geisha in Rivalry*. Trans. Kurt Meissner with Ralph Friedrich. Tokyo and Rutland, Vt.: Charles E. Tuttle, 1963.

Nakai, Kate Wildman. *Shogunal Politics: Arai Hakuseki and the Premises of Tokugawa Rule*. Cambridge, Ma. and London: Council on East Asian Studies, Harvard University, 1988.

Nakane Chie. *Japanese Society*. Berkeley, Ca.: University of California Press, 1970.

Nakane Chie and Ōishi Shinzaburō, eds. *Tokugawa Japan: The Social and Economic Antecedents of Modern Japan*. Tokyo: University of Tokyo Press, 1990.

Nanda, Serena. "The Hijras of India: Cultural and Individual Dimensions of an Institutionalized Third Gender Role." In Evelyn Blackwood, ed., *The Many Faces of Homosexuality: Anthropological Approaches to Homosexual Behavior*. New York: Harrington Park Press, 1986.

Nelson, Andrew Nathaniel. *The Modern Reader's Japanese-English Character Dictionary*. 2nd revised edition. Tokyo and Rutland, Vt.: Tuttle, 1974.

Nery, Lamberto C. "The Covert Subculture of Male Homosexual Prostitutes in Metro Manila," *Philippine Journal of Psychology* 12 (1979).

Ng, Vivian. "Ideology and Sexuality: Rape Laws in Qing China," *Journal of Asian Studies* 46, 1 (February 1987), pp. 57–70.

Nitobe Inazō. *Bushido, the Soul of Japan*. Tokyo and Rutland, Vt.: Charles E. Tuttle, 1969.

Noguchi Takenori and Paul Schalow. "Homosexuality." In *Kodansha Encyclopedia of Japan*, vol. 3. Tokyo and New York: Kodansha, 1983.

Noordam, Dirk Jaap. "Sodomy in the Dutch Republic, 1600–1725." In Kent Gerard and Gert Hekma, *The Pursuit of Sodomy: Male Homosexuality in Renaissance and Enlightenment Europe*. New York and London: Harrington Park Press, 1989.

Nosco, Peter. "Masuho Zankō, a Shinto Popularizer." In idem., ed., *Confucianism and Tokugawa Culture*. Princeton, N.J.: Princeton University Press, 1984.

Nye, Robert A. *Masculinity and Male Codes of Honor in Modern France*. New York: Oxford University Press, 1993.

O'Driscoll, Robert, ed. *The Celtic Consciousness*. New York: Braziller, 1981.

Ortolani, Benito. *The Japanese Theatre: From Shamanistic Ritual to Contemporary Pluralism*. Leiden: E. J. Brill, 1990.

Ōtō Tokihiko. "Chigo." In *Kodansha Encyclopedia of Japan*, vol. 1, p. 274. Tokyo: Kodansha Ltd., 1983.

Paul, Diana Y. *Women in Buddhism: Images of the Feminine in the Mahayana Tradition*. 2nd edition Berkeley, Ca.: University of California Press, 1985.

Pelzel, John C. "Human Nature in the Japanese Myths." In Albert M. Craig and Donald H. Shively, eds., *Personality in Japanese History*, pp. 29–56. Berkeley: University of California Press, 1970.

Perry, Mary Elizabeth. "The 'Nefarious Sin' in Early Modern Seville." In Kent Gerard and Gert Hekma, *The Pursuit of Sodomy: Male Homosexuality in Renaissance and Enlightenment Europe*, pp. 67–90. New York and London: Harrington Park Press, 1989.

Pflugfelder, Gregory M. "Male-Male Sexual Behavior in Tokugawa Legal Discourse." Unpublished manuscript, 1990.

Philippi, Donald L., trans. *Kojiki*. Princeton, N.J. and Tokyo: Princeton University Press and University of Tokyo Press, 1969.

———. *Norito: A Translation of the Ancient Japanese Ritual Prayers*. Princeton: Princeton University Press, 1990.

Pollak, Michael. "Male Homosexuality or Happiness in the Ghetto." In Philippe Ariès and André Béjin, eds., *Western Sexuality: Practice and Precept in Past and Present Times*, pp. 98–113. Oxford and New York: Blackwell, 1986.

Putzgar, Edward. "Inu Makura: The Dog Pillow," *Harvard Journal of Asiatic Studies* 28 (1968), pp. 98–113.

Ratti, Rakesh, ed. *A Lotus of Another Color: An Unfolding of South Asian Gay and Lesbian Experience*. Boston: Alyson Publications, 1993.

Rawson, Philip. *Erotic Art of the East: The Sexual Theme in Oriental Painting and Sculpture*. London: Weidenfeld and Nicolson, 1973.

Raz, Jacob. *Audience and Actors: A Study of Their Interaction in the Japanese Traditional Theater*. Leiden: E. J. Brill, 1983.

Reich, Wilhelm. *Sex-Pol: Essays* 1929–1934. Ed. Lee Baxandall. New York: Vintage Books, 1972.

Reischauer, A. K., trans. "Genshin's Ojo Yoshu: Collected Essays on Rebirth into Paradise," *Transactions of the Asiatic Society of Japan*, 2nd series, 7 (1930), pp. 16–97.

Reischauer, Edwin O., trans. *Ennin's Diary: The Record of a Pilgrimage to China in Search of the Law*. New York: Ronald, 1955.

Renaudot, Abbe, trans. "An Account of the Travels of Two Mohammedans through India and China in the Ninth Century." In John Pinkerton, ed., *A Collection of the Best and Most Interesting Voyages and Travels in All Parts of the World*. Vol. 7. London: Kimber and Conrad, 1811.

Rey, Michel. "Parisian Homosexuals Create a Lifestyle, 1700–1750: The Police Archives." In Robert Purks Maccubbin, ed., *'Tis Nature's Fault: Unauthorized Sexuality During the Enlightenment*, pp. 179–191. New York: Cambridge University Press, 1987.

———. "Police et sodomie à Paris au XVIIe siècle," *Revue d'histoire moderne et contemporaine* 29 (1982), pp. 113–124.

Rhys, T. W.. and Hermann Oldenberg, eds. *Vinaya Texts*. Vol. 4 of F. Max Fuller, ed., *The Sacred Books of the East*. Oxford: Clarendon Press, 1881.

Roden, Donald T. *Schooldays in Imperial Japan: A Study of the Culture of a Student Elite*. Berkeley, Ca.: University of California Press, 1980.

Rousseau, G. S. "The Pursuit of Homosexuality in the Eighteenth Century: 'Utterly Confused Category' and/or Rich Repository?" In Robert Purks Maccubbin, ed., *'Tis Nature's Fault: Unauthorized Sexuality During the Enlightenment*. New York: Cambridge University Press, 1987.

Rozman, Gilbert. *Urban Networks in Ch'ing China and Tokugawa Japan*. Princeton, N.J.: Princeton University Press, 1973.

Rubin, Jay. *Injurious to Public Morals: Writers and the Meiji State*. Seattle: University of Washington Press, 1984.

Ruggiero, Guido. *The Boundaries of Eros: Sex Crime and Sexuality in Renaissance Venice*. New York: Oxford University Press, 1985.

Rutt, Richard. "The Flower Boys of Silla (Hwarang): Notes on the Sources," *Transactions of the Korean Branch of the Asiatic Society of Japan* 38 (1961).

Ryavec, Carole A. "Daimyo in an Age of Strife: Takeda Shingen." In Murakami Hyoe and Thomas J. Harper, eds., *Great Historical Figures of Japan*, pp. 141–153. Tokyo: Japan Culture Institute, 1978.

Sanford, James H. *Zen-Man Ikkyū*. Chico, Ca.: Scholars Press, 1981.

Sansom, George B. *A History of Japan, 1615–1867*. Stanford, Ca.: Stanford University Press, 1963.

Sargent, G. W. *The Japanese Family Storehouse, or the Millionaire's Gospel Modernized*. Cambridge: Cambridge University Press, 1959.

Saslow, James M. *Ganymede in the Renaissance: Homosexuality in Art and Society*. New Haven, Ct.: Yale University Press, 1986.

Satchell, Thomas, trans. *Hizakurige or Shank's Mare: Japan's Great Comic Novel of Travel and Ribaldry by Ikku Jippensha*. Tokyo and Rutland, Vt.: Tuttle, 1960.

Saunders, E. Dale. *Buddhism in Japan, With an Outline of Its Origins in India*. Philadelphia: University of Pennsylvania Press, 1964.

Schalow, Paul Gordon. "The Invention of a Literary Tradition of Male Love: Kitamura Kigin's *Iwatsutsuji*," *Monumenta Nipponica* 48, 1 (Spring 1993), pp. 231–261.

———. *"The Great Mirror of Male Love" by Ihara Saikaku*. Unpublished dissertation, Harvard University, 1985.

———, trans., *The Great Mirror of Male Love*, by Ihara Saikaku. Stanford: Stanford University Press, 1990.

————. "Kūkai and the Tradition of Male Love in Japanese Buddhism." In Jose Ignacio Cabezon, ed., *Buddhism, Sexuality, and Gender*, pp. 215–230. New York: State University of New York Press, 1992.

————. "Male Love in Early Modern Japan: A Literary Description of the 'Youth.'" In Martin Duberman, Martha Vicinus, and George Chauncey, Jr., *Hidden From History: Reclaiming the Gay and Lesbian Past*, pp. 118–128. New York: Meridian, 1989.

————. "Saikaku on 'Manly Love,'" *Stone Lion Review* (Harvard University) 7 (Spring 1981), pp. 3–7.

Seidensticker, Edward C., trans. *The Gossamer Years: A Diary of a Noblewoman of Heian Japan*. Tokyo and Rutland, Vt.: Tuttle, 1964.

————, trans. *The Makioka Sisters*. New York: Perigee, 1957.

————, trans. *The Tale of Genji*. New York: Alfred A. Knopf, 1976.

Seigle, Celia Segawa. *Yoshiwara: The Glittering World of the Japanese Courtesan*. Honolulu: University of Hawaii Press, 1993.

Sergent, Bernard. *La homosexualite dans la mythologie grecque*. Paris: Payot, 1984.

————. *L'homosexualite initiatique dans l'Europe ancienne*. Paris: Payot, 1986.

Shively, Donald. "Bakufu versus Kabuki." In John W. Hall and Marius B. Jansen, eds., *Studies in the Institutional History of Early Modern Japan*, pp. 231–261. Princeton, N.J.: Princeton University Press, 1968.

————. *The Love Suicide at Amijima*. Cambridge, Ma.: Harvard University Press, 1953.

————. "The Social Environment of Tokugawa Kabuki." In *Studies in Kabuki*, ed. James R. Brandon, William P. Malm, and Donald Shively. Honolulu: University Press of Hawaii, 1978.

————. "Tokugawa Tsunayoshi, the Genroku Shogun." In Albert Craig and Donald Shively, eds., *Personality in Japanese History*. Berkeley, Ca.: University of California Press, 1970.

Sitkin, David Asher. *An Edo Satire: Hiraga Gennai's Nenashigusa*. Unpublished master's thesis, University of Hawaii, 1977.

Smith, Henry D. "Consorts and Courtesans: The Women of Shogun." In idem., ed., *Learning from Shogun: Japanese History and Western Fantasy*. Santa Barbara, Ca.: Program in Asian Studies, University of California, Santa Barbara, 1980.

Smith, Robert J., and Ella Lury Wiswell. *The Women of Suye Mura*. Chicago: University of Chicago Press, 1982.

Sparling, Kathryn, trans. *Yukio Mishima on Hagakure: The Samurai Ethic and Modern Japan*. Tokyo and Rutland, Vt.: Tuttle, 1976.

Spence, Jonathan D. *Emperor of China: Self-Portrait of K'ang-hsi.* New York: Knopf, 1974.

————. *The Memory Palace of Matteo Ricci.* New York: Viking, 1984.

Sprio, Melford E. *Buddhism and Society: A Great Tradition and Its Burmese Vicissitudes.* Berkeley, Ca.: University of California Press, 1982.

Statler, Oliver. *Japanese Inn.* New York: Arena Books, 1961.

Stevens, John. *Lust for Enlightenment: Buddhism and Sex.* Boston: Shambala Publications, 1990.

Stone, Lawrence. *The Family, Sex and Marriage in England, 1500–1800.* Abridged version. London: Peregrine, 1979.

Straub, Kristina. *Sexual Suspects: Eighteenth-Century Players and Sexual Ideology.* Princeton, N.J.: Princeton University Press, 1992.

Takahatake Takamichi. *Young Man Shinran: A Reappraisal of Shinran's Life.* Ontario: Wilfrid Laurier University Press, 1987.

Takekoshi Yosaburō. *The Economic Aspects of the History of the Civilization of Japan.* 3 vols. London: Allen and Unwin, 1930.

Takemi Momoko, "'Menstruation Sutra' Belief in Japan," *Japanese Journal of Religious Studies* 10, 2–3 (June–September, 1983), pp. 229–246.

Tannahill, Reay. *Sex in History.* New York: Stein and Day, 1980.

Trumbach, Randolph. "London's Sodomites: Homosexual Behavior and Western Culture in the Eighteenth Century," *Journal of Social History* 11 (Fall 1977), pp. 1–33.

Tsukahira, Toshio G. *Feudal Control in Tokugawa Japan: The Sankin-Kotai System.* Cambridge, Ma.: Harvard University Press, 1966.

Tsunoda Ryūsaku et al., eds. *Sources of Japanese Tradition.* 2 vols. New York: Columbia University Press, 1958.

Tsurumi, E. Patricia. "The Male Present versus the Female Past: Historians and Japan's Ancient Female Emperors," *Bulletin of Concerned Asian Scholars,* 14, 4 (1983), pp. 71–75.

Turnbull, Stephen. *Samurai Warlords: The Book of the Daimyo.* London: Blandford Press, 1989.

Uraki Zirō [Jirō], trans. *The Tale of the Cavern.* Tokyo: Shinozaki Shorin, 1984.

Van der Meer, Theo. "The Persecutions of Sodomites in Eighteenth-Century Amsterdam: Changing Perceptions of Sodomy." In Kent Gerard and Gert Hekma, *The Pursuit of Sodomy: Male Homosexuality in Renaissance and Enlightenment Europe,* pp. 263–307. New York and London: Harrington Park Press, 1989.

Vanggaard, Thorkil. *Phallos: A Symbol and Its History in the Male World.* New York: International Universities Press, 1973.

Van Gulik, Robert H. *Sexual Life in Ancient China*. Leiden: E. J. Brill, 1974.

Varner, Richard. "The Organized Peasant: The *Wakamonoyado* in the Edo Period," *Monumenta Nipponica* 32 (1977), pp. 459–484.

Veyne, Paul, ed. *A History of Private Life: From Pagan Rome to Byzantium*. 3 vols. Cambridge, Ma.: Harvard University Press, 1987–1989.

Von Siebold, Philipp Franz, et al. *Manners and Customs of the Japanese in the Nineteenth Century*. Tokyo and Rutland, Vt.: Tuttle, 1973.

Vos, Frits. "Forgotten Foibles—Love and the Dutch at Dejima (1641–1854)." In Lydia Brüll and Ulrich Kemper, eds., *Asien Tradition und Fortschritt: Festschrift für Horst Hammitzsch zu seinem 60. Geburtstag*, pp. 614–643. Wiesbaden: Otto Harrassowitz, 1971.

Wakeman, Frederic, Jr. *The Great Enterprise: The Manchu Reconstruction of Imperial Order in Seventeenth-Century China*. 2 vols. Berkeley, Ca.: University of California Press, 1975.

Wakita Haruko. "Marriage and the Family in Premodern Japan from the Perspective of Women's History," *Journal of Japanese Studies* 10, 1 (1984), pp. 73–99.

Waley, Arthur, trans. *The Tale of Genji*. New York: Anchor, 1955.

———. *Yuan Mei, Eighteenth Century Chinese Poet*. Stanford, Ca.: Stanford University Press, 1956.

Walker, Benjamin. *The Hindu World: An Encyclopedic Survey of Hinduism*. New York: Praeger, 1968.

Watanabe Tsuneo and Iwata Jun'ichi. *The Love of the Samurai: A Thousand Years of Japanese Homosexuality*. London: Gay Men's Press, 1989.

Watson, Burton, trans. *Han Fei Tzu: Basic Writings*. New York: Columbia University Press, 1964.

———, trans. *Records of the Grand Historian of China*. 2 vols. New York: Columbia University Press, 1964).

Weaver, Mary Jo. "Pornography and the Religious Imagination." In Susan Gobar and Joan Huff, eds. *For Adult Users Only: The Dilemma of Violent Pornography*. Bloomington and Indianapolis: Indiana University Press, 1989.

Wile, Douglas. *Art of the Bedchamber: The Chinese Sexual Yoga Classics, Including Women's Solo Meditation Texts*. New York: State University of New York Press, 1992.

Williams, Walter L. *The Spirit and the Flesh: Sexual Diversity in American Indian Culture*. Boston: Beacon, 1986.

Willig, Rosette F., trans. *The Changelings: A Classical Japanese Court Tale*. Stanford, Ca.: Stanford University Press, 1983.

Wilson, William Scott, trans. *Hagakure: The Book of the Samurai*. Tokyo: Kodansha, 1979.

Yamamura, Kozo. "The Decline of the Ritsu-Ryō System: Hypotheses on Economic and Institutional Change," *Journal of Japanese Studies* 1, 1 (1974).

Yamane Yūzō. "Ogata Kōrin and the Art of the Genroku Era." *Acta Asiatica* 15 (1968), pp. 69–86.

Yang Hsien-yi and Gladys Yang, trans. *The Scholars*, by Wu Jingzi. Peking: Foreign Languages Press, 1957; New York: Grosset and Dunlap, 1972.

Yazaki Takeo. *Social Change and the City in Japan: From the Earliest Times Through the Industrial Revolution*. Tokyo: Japan Publications, 1978.

Yoshida Kenkō. *Essays in Idleness: The Tsurezuregusa of Kenko*. New York: Columbia University Press, 1967.

Young, Blake Morgan. *Ueda Akinari*. Vancouver: University of British Columbia, 1982.

Zolbrod, Leon, trans. *Ugestsu Monogatari: Tales of Moonlight and Rain*, by Ueda Akinari. Tokyo and Rutland, Vt.: Tuttle, 1977.

Index

Numbers in italics refer to figures

Compositor: Asco Trade Typesetting Ltd.
Text: Caledonia
Display: Caledonia
Printer: Malloy Lithographing, Inc.
Binder: John H. Dekker & Sons